Retelling, Relating, Reflecting

BEYOND THE 3 R'S

SUSAN SCHWARTZ • MAXINE BONE

IRWIN PUBLISHING

TORONTO, ONTARIO

Copyright © 1995 by Irwin Publishing

Canadian Cataloguing in Publication Data

Schwartz, Susan, 1951 —
Retelling, relating, reflecting

Includes bibliographical references.
ISBN 0-7725-2098-4

1. Teaching. 2. Language Arts. I. Bone, Maxine,1943 —
II. Title.

LB1025.3.S35 1995   371.3   C94-932173-7

Design: ArtPlus Limited/Sylvia Vander Schee – Brant Cowie
Illustrations: Sylvia Vander Schee
Cover Photo: José L. Pelacz/Masterfile
Photographs on pages 5, 25, 101, and 185: Ken Johns
Photographs on pages 145, 163 and 183 by Stephen Isleifson
Editor: Norma Pettit

Printed and bound in Canada by Tri-Graphic Printing (Ottawa) Ltd.

1 2 3 4 5 T-G 98 97 96 95 94

Published by
Irwin Publishing
1800 Steeles Avenue West
Concord, ON
L4K 2P3

Contents

3. Assessing and Evaluating   101

Draft Planning Sheets

Reference

Sample Letters

Learner Record Sheets

CREDITS

The authors and publisher would like to thank the following organizations for permission to reproduce bags with their logos in our "Bookful of Bags" illustrations on page 135:

Cultures Restaurants Inc.

Loblaws Supermarkets Limited

Toys 'R' Us

ACKNOWLEDGEMENTS

SUSAN AND MAXINE

We are most appreciative and thankful for the opportunities we have both had, over the past ten years, to work as course directors for the Faculties of Education, In-Service programs at York, Nipissing, Queen's and Ottawa universities. It was these opportunities, during evening and summer courses, that encouraged our ideas to germinate and formulate, and allowed us to interact with many teachers. It is these types of professional development opportunities that invite and encourage lasting change.

For their ideas and for written contributions to *Retelling, Relating, Reflecting: Beyond the 3 R's*, a very special thanks to:

- Patricia Adams, Principal, Northumberland-Clarington Board of Education
- Joan Brake, Vice-Principal, Peterborough Victoria Northumberland-Clarington Separate School Board of Education
- Eva Carter, Teacher/Consultant, York Region Board of Education
- Nadia Clark, Student, North York Board of Education
- Patricia Hildebrand, Teacher, North York Board of Education
- Cheryl Jones, Teacher, Simcoe County Board of Education
- Jane Murphy, Teacher, York Region Board of Education
- Dr. Deborah Nieding, Assistant Professor of Teacher Education, Gonzaga University, Spokane, Washington
- Ellen Palmer, Teacher, York Region Board of Education
- Marilyn Peavoy, Teacher, Peterborough Country Board of Education
- Chris Roberts, Teacher, York Region Board of Education
- Kerry Russ, Teacher, North York Board of Education
- Linda L. Smith, Teacher, Northumberland-Clarington Board of Education
- Tammy Waxman, Teacher/Consultant, Durham Board of Education
- Students, families and teachers at Shoreham Public School and at Harrison Public School, North York Board of Education

An extra special thanks to Mary Cox, Manager, National Book Service, Ottawa Showroom, for her assistance in the completion of our literature bibliography.

SUSAN

I give my love and special thanks to my husband Saul, to my children Marnie, Rena and Michael, and to my family and friends — who were very supportive during the writing of this book. They always encouraged and supported me, even when they missed me on my frequent book-writing weekends away from home.

With sincere gratitude for her friendship and support, I cannot say enough about my friend Mindy Pollishuke. She continues to be my confidant, colleague and friend, sharing with me in every aspect of my personal and professional life.

I would also like to give sincere thanks to the administrative staff in North York, who gave me their support and confidence throughout the writing of this book.

To the many children, teachers and families who became true partners and learned along with me in this journey of learning and teaching, I thank you for your risk taking, your openness, and your endless enthusiasm and questions.

And to Maxine, who shared with me her passion for literature, teaching and learning, who introduced me to nature, art and travel, I owe many thanks and words of appreciation. I value our many hours talking on the phone, shopping, travelling, writing and sharing together. Thank you, Maxine!

MAXINE

In the summer of 1984, at a summer writing course for teachers, I was inspired by three people: Nancie Atwell, Mary Ellen Giacobbe, and Don Graves. From that time on, I have continued to think about writing and learning differently. For them, warm hugs of thanks, always!

Throughout my life, I have been fortunate to have special friends who believed in me and cared. They share my passion for children, teaching, learning, and wondering. I give special appreciation and thanks to my lifelong and closest friends.

I owe a different and unique gratitude to Susan for working beside me every step of the way. We have written this book together, but we have talked many others and on a wide variety of topics. Thank you, Susan!

I have a tremendous shower of thanks for the hundreds of children, teachers, and families who watched, listened, tried things, questioned, and learned together with me about learning, teaching, caring and sharing. We were all true learning and teaching partners.

In the three school boards I have worked in — Essex County Separate, York Region Public, and Lanark County Public — I have been fortunate to have had support and encouragement from many educators who encouraged me to grow and develop professionally. I appreciate these unique opportunities and extend thanks to the many people I have worked with over the past thirty years. A special thanks to my present board, Lanark, for continuing to value my talents and abilities and for providing me with opportunities to work with and beside the administrative staff, teachers, families, and children in all the schools.

I wish to thank my husband Ken Johns for inviting me to travel into his worlds of music and art. Together we are able to look at and experience the world of nature differently through the lens of the camera. He believes in me and is always there. Susan and I especially thank him for his photographic contributions to *Retelling, Relating, Reflecting: Beyond the 3 R's*.

I wish to dedicate this book to:
• My father who continues to model a passion for reading and questioning
• My mother who passes on her love of storytelling, reciting verse, singing ditties, telling jokes, and always saying, "I'll get your dad!" whenever I call on the telephone

- My country grandmother who taught me life is both beautiful and painful by telling me her life stories
- My town grandmother who demonstrated how to be financially independent and bake great apple pies
- My sons Tony and Shannon who helped me to learn about the real worlds of learning and teaching — parenting. They nudged me on from the time they were born, filling my life with love and wonderings. They are my best listeners and my lifelong friends.

Introduction

We sat in our hotel room in Phoenix, Arizona, and talked and talked. We read and wrote and talked some more. Conversations, memories, ideas flowed back and forth. All around us, we could see the culture of the city — road maps, travel brochures, hotel information, newspapers, advertising pamphlets, post cards, bags, rocks, photographs, environmental print, souvenirs... Surrounding us also were samples from the many cultures and voices of the conference we were attending — registration information, program, brochures, new professional books, articles, author pamphlets, posters, displays, buttons, bookmarks, bags, and beautiful children's books.

We were immersed in the magic of a new place and new people, and in the excitement of a large international conference where teachers, administrators, researchers, authors, storytellers, poets, and families had all come together to share common goals. We were involved in stimulating conversations in which people from around the world shared experiences and ideas. Through these conversations, we made connections to our personal and professional lives, and we were gently nudged into reflecting on our experiences, beliefs and ideas.

In this atmosphere of learning, our talking and thinking over the past three years — our reading and internalizing, demonstrating, approximating and examining, working with children, with families, with teachers in classrooms and as instructors in our in-service courses at York University — came together. We had pondered over the order and form of *Retelling, Relating, Reflecting: Beyond the 3 R's* many times before. But now, the shape of each chapter flowed, and we could envision the parts and the whole simultaneously.

We started writing this book where it all began — with our **"3 R's" framework of "retelling, relating and reflecting."** This framework, originally developed by Maxine, provides the underpinning for each chapter. The visual models throughout illustrate our words and understandings as we create meaning in diagram form. These models went through many changes, as we talked and sketched, conferenced with others, revised again and again, and clarified our thinking. We hope you will find them useful as "carry-about" references.

Chapter 1, "Understanding How Learners Learn," provides the theoretical underpinning for our 3 R's framework. It is a description of learning, and highlights and builds on the ideas and theories of such renowned educators and researchers as Brian Cambourne, Mary Ellen Giacobbe, Nancie Atwell, Ken and Yetta Goodman, and others.

The second chapter, "Using a Framework: The 3 R's," is the most important chapter for all our readers to read. It explains our 3 R's framework of retelling, relating and reflecting and illustrates its application. The 3 R's framework is easy to implement and provides an invaluable tool for ensuring effective learning by learners of all ages — for ensuring successful reading, writing, thinking and talking, both inside and outside the classroom.

Assessment and evaluation practices are continuous and essential parts of the teaching/learning process. In Chapter 3, "Assessing and Evaluating," we talk about getting to know learners, and establishing a base of information about each of them — what each learner knows and can do, what the learner wants to know about, and where the learner needs help. We discuss how using the 3 R's framework can help to establish this **baseline knowledge**, which is a clear example of diagnostic assessment and evaluation. We share our ideas about assessment and evaluation — what we value and evaluate. Valuing and evaluating what we value become what we do each day when we learn and teach.

Chapter 4, "Negotiating Curriculum," discusses the planning process and negotiating curriculum with learners. We provide a real-life illustration as well as a theory-based understanding of the main requirements and conditions that we, as lifelong learners and teachers, need in order to continue to understand and reflect upon the learning/teaching process. We provide practical examples for you to use and modify when planning and implementing curriculum with your learners.

In Chapter 5, "Family-Teacher Partnerships," we outline two sample workshops that can be used with families. We stress involving families as a necessary and important part of the teaching/learning process. These workshops illustrate and clarify, in concrete and hands-on ways, many of the ideas in *Retelling, Relating, Reflecting: Beyond the 3 R's*. In the first workshop, we show how the 3 R's framework can be used to help families talk and listen with their children. In the second workshop, we show how learners of all ages can use manipulatives and active/interactive learning experiences to explore the world around them. In these workshops, we value and invite learners to talk — to have many conversations and make personal and professional connections.

In many of the chapters in *Retelling, Relating, Reflecting: Beyond the 3 R's*, we include sections entitled "Practising." These are practical strategies that clearly outline how you can apply the understandings presented in the chapter in your classroom. They are strategies we have used successfully ourselves or that others have shared with us. We invite you to select and experiment with any of these strategies.

We have included a "Literature Bibliography" in which we list the titles of the children's literature we have referred to in *Retelling, Relating, Reflecting: Beyond the 3 R's*. In our bibliography "Keeping in Touch Professionally," we offer some professional reading suggestions for you — and for interested families — to help you continue to grow professionally. We organized this list into two sections, "Getting Started" and "Moving Forward." We hope this organization will make it easy for you to choose the reading materials that will match your needs and comfort levels.

At the end of *Retelling, Relating, Reflecting: Beyond the 3 R's*, we offer "Draft Planning Sheets" in blackline master form that we hope you will photocopy, use, adapt, and share. We have divided the Draft Planning Sheets into four sections: "Reference" (Draft Planning Sheets that can be enlarged and posted as reference, can be made into overhead transparencies to be used with a large group in a workshop or teaching situation, or can be used as handouts), "Sample Letters," "Student Record Sheets," and "Teacher Record Sheets." We invite you to adapt and revise these draft formats to meet your particular needs and interests.

We believe that all educators will find *Retelling, Relating, Reflecting: Beyond the 3 R's* useful and practical — useful in the sense that it will provide further understandings of the learning/teaching process, and practical in that it will provide concrete ways to approach the challenges of teaching, learning and living. We hope our book will encourage you, our readers, to scratch beneath the surface of active/interactive and natural language learning, to probe further and deeper to better understand yourselves, what you are doing and thinking, and where you are going. We hope it will encourage you to discover exciting ways to continue your personal learning and teaching journeys.

Understanding How Learners Learn

"Learning experiences take place in many settings — a supermarket, an art gallery, a fire station, a zoo, a puppet show, a theatre, a wooded area, a stream or a puddle."
(page 7)

"When learners reflect upon what they know, ask questions and explore ideas, they are learning more than information. *They are learning **how** to learn.*"
(page 9)

In this chapter, we present a theoretical and visual description of learning based on the most up-to-date research on how learners learn. We highlight and build on the ideas of several renowned educators and researchers, such as Brian Cambourne, Mary Ellen Giacobbe, Nancie Atwell, Ken and Yetta Goodman, and others. This chapter provides the theoretical underpinning for our 3 R's framework.

ACTIVE/INTERACTIVE LEARNING

Active/interactive learning is learner centred. It takes place when people, both adults and children, are involved in and have ownership of and responsibility for their own learning. Current knowledge of developmental patterns typical of learners clearly demonstrates that effective, long-term learning is initiated by the learner rather than handed down or transmitted by the teacher. For these natural learning situations to occur, the following components are important:

- experiencing
- interacting
- communicating
- internalizing

Active/interactive learning takes place when learners are involved in one, some, or all of these components. (See Draft Planning Sheet 1, "How We Learn.") As we discuss each component, you will see how the components are connected to one another. Figure 1.1 illustrates four components of active/interactive learning with the learner at the centre.

Figure 1.1   Components of Active/Interactive Learning

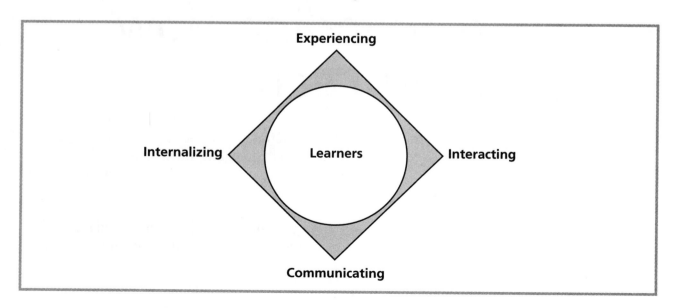

Experiencing

Learning is an active process where everyone learns by doing. **Experiencing** is "doing." In order to learn, people need many and varied opportunities to **experience** by examining, exploring and working with people, places and things in the learning environment and in the world around them. They need to be involved in identifying, reciting, comparing, taking apart, estimating, illustrating, predicting, creating, interviewing, constructing, solving, and deciding. A balance of opportunities is necessary to promote thinking at divergent and varied levels.

People actively and interactively experience the world by using their senses to examine and study everything around them. When they use their senses, they really look at the world. They notice, for example, the environmental print that is evident everywhere. The term "environmental print" means any form of print used to communicate. This includes logos, symbols, pictures, shapes, colours, sizes, rebuses, acronymns... Environmental print is found on boxes, billboards, signs, cars, cards, clothes, bags... The world is saturated with environmental print.

> Children need to feel and touch language as well as see and hear and speak it.
>
> — Margaret Mooney, *Reading to, with and by Children*

We believe that learners naturally use all of their senses when experiencing, examining and exploring. We invite learners to use technology when we as teachers add a variety of tools to the learning environment. For example, when examining a real apple, learners can look critically, feel, taste, smell and hear (by shaking to hear the seeds rattle if the apple is completely ripe). When peelers, corers, graters, measuring tapes, weigh scales, a cooking pot, stove or other tools are provided, learners can go beyond gaining knowledge through their senses, and can experiment and discover using technology. When print materials (a variety of books and pictures) on the topic of apples are included, learners are able to research further, seeking answers to their questions or discovering new nuggets of knowledge. When learners visit a supermarket, they can examine many different kinds of apples and apple products, interview the salespeople as to the names and origins of different kinds of apples, and gain more knowledge.

As teachers, we encourage such holistic learning experiences and connections across the curriculum, touching social studies, health, the arts, math, science, technology, and language in a natural way.

When people visit places, they usually find particular things to spark their interest. They become fascinated with objects, materials, literature and artifacts, and these experiences add to their knowledge base. Learning experiences take place in many settings — a supermarket, an art gallery, a fire station, a zoo, a puppet show, a theatre, a wooded area, a stream or a puddle... Places near and far are visited and revisited. Repeated visits to the same places at different times during the year are valuable. New things can be learned when people return and visit familiar places. Opportunities to experience learning — to use all one's senses to become visually perceptive, aware and knowledgeable — are limitless.

Interacting

Interacting involves active **interaction** with people and with things in the environment. When people interact with real objects or materials, they are naturally curious and have questions. They use all their senses when they manipulate, explore and examine these things.

In the scientific sense, we teachers invite our learners to interact with, manipulate and handle objects in order to observe and study the objects' reactions. When learners experience, examine, explore and experiment with a wide variety of objects, they acquire knowledge. Piaget identifies this kind of learning as "physical knowledge."

> Physical knowledge is acquired when children handle objects and observe how they react. This is why manipulation is essential for children — and adults — to acquire physical knowledge.
>
> — Connie K. Williams and Constance Kammi, *How Do Children Learn by Handling Objects?*, page 23

In the mathematical sense, we invite learners to put objects together in a variety of ways to discover different relationships. For example, when learners sort and classify, they learn about these relationships. The manipulation of objects is particularly important for young children because, as Piaget writes, "Young children think better when they physically act on objects."

We believe it is essential that opportunities be provided for learners to interact with a wide variety of materials in order to become problem solvers. Encouraging children to become hands-on problem solvers is much more effective than our telling them how to solve a problem. When we assess and evaluate learners, we need to value *how* the learners interact with objects in the world around them.

Interacting with people is also an essential part of active/interactive learning. It is here that we as teachers encourage learners to experience and understand the life skills of cooperation. It is here that we foster the development of social skills. To encourage thinking and internalizing, we provide opportunities for learners to create situations that are personally meaningful. Learners make decisions and exchange viewpoints with others.

Communicating

Communicating means actively and interactively listening, speaking, viewing, writing, reading, creating, experimenting, problem solving — in meaningful and purposeful situations.

Communicating begins with experiences. People communicate when they are experiencing and interacting with the people, places and things around them. They are communicating when they manipulate things, explore and go places, when they use their senses, and value these opportunities and experiences. They are communicating when they retell, describe, remember, make connections and relate their experiences. They are communicating when they read, write, think, question, and share ideas and wonderings.

As teachers, we must provide opportunities for learners to gain communication skills through personal and social experiences, through manipulative investigations, and through interacting with people, places and things. By providing opportunities for learners to play with and explore materials, and to interact with people, places, and things, we encourage learners to talk and to demonstrate their understandings and learning. The language of questions, explanations, discussions, guesses and hypotheses emerge from the learners' observations, manipulative and creative experiences, and experimentation.

As teachers, we need to value the talk and questions of the learners as an integral part of each and every learning experience. We show this valuing by waiting longer for learners to respond and by allowing the talk to develop from learner to learner rather than from teacher to learner. We invite and encourage spontaneous responses during read-alouds, demonstrations, sharing times... We develop reference charts showing and describing what a good listener, reader, writer, viewer and speaker looks like, and we provide time and opportunities for learners to talk about the people, places and things in their lives.

Internalizing

Internalizing means knowing something so well that it becomes a part of us. When we internalize knowledge and skills, we use them naturally and spontaneously in thinking, observing, communicating, and doing. They become a natural part of us and we use them automatically in all teaching and learning situations.

Internalizing happens when the people, places and things important to learning and teaching are reviewed and revisited. Each time learners read selected books, they learn new and different things and revisit and review some known things. Over time and with repetition, they internalize these books. This same experience happens when learners examine and reexamine things and when they explore and re-explore places. These continual emerging questions keep taking them back into spending time with a variety of people, places and things. They seek answers and information — they experience, they interact and they communicate — over and over again in different ways until they internalize. Even then, after a span of time, they look back and revisit those experiences in their minds as they reflect. Thus begins the journey of learning once again.

We believe it is critical to invite learners to take risks, use their knowledge and understandings, internalize and become lifelong learners.

FOUNDATIONS OF LEARNING

When learners reflect upon what they know, ask questions and explore ideas, they are learning more than information. *They are learning **how** to learn.*

Our reading and our own experience as educators and learners have convinced us that for learning to take place, four essential components are required:

- time
- ownership
- response
- celebration

These components make up the foundations of learning (see Figure 1.2). When we make sure that these components are inherent in the learning environment and in the learning experiences we provide for our learners, we greatly facilitate the teaching/learning process.

Figure 1.2   Foundations of Learning

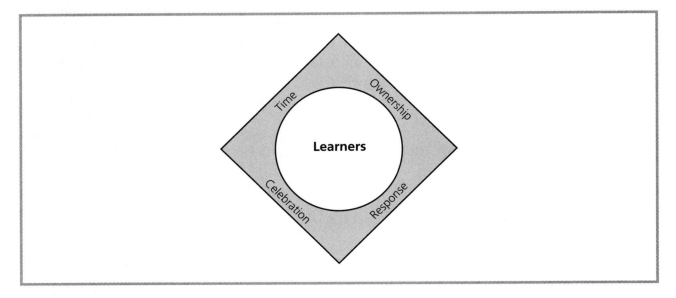

Mary Ellen Giacobbe, Donald Graves and Nancie Atwell talk about the elements of time, ownership, and response. Nancie Atwell used **time, ownership**, and **response** as a guideline when teaching her Grade 8 students. She writes:

> Like writers in the writing workshop, all readers — all learners — need Mary Ellen Giacobbe's three basics of time, ownership and response.

> — Nancie Atwell, *In the Middle*, page 275

We believe **celebration** is another vital element in the learning process. Celebration helps to make changes in learning and teaching long-lasting and durable. When people share with others, especially with families and other learners, what they have learned, they are celebrating. We think celebration is one way of making the learning explicit.

 # Time

Time is an essential element in the learning and teaching process. We need to schedule large blocks of time to provide opportunities for us to watch, listen, take field-notes, and teach. By providing these blocks of time, we also give learners opportunities to practise processes and to create products.

We realize there can be many factors affecting how time is used in the day-to-day environment. We encourage the use of daily planning strategies. Ideally, everyone benefits from large blocks of time for teaching and learning. Integration, timetabling for one day extended over two days, or large blocks weekly are some approaches teachers have found helpful when designing time schedules.

Also effective is when **we schedule our own time** as opposed to scheduling the learners' time. In a timetable posted for all the learners to see, we list our own activities, our demonstration lessons, and the names of the learners with whom we will meet at particular times. In this way, the learning process is continuous and ongoing with many different ending points, but the teaching and assessing process is firmly in place for each day and for each learner.

We need to provide time daily for:

- whole-class and small-group teaching sessions
- mini-lessons
- demonstrating and modelling
- conferencing with individual learners or small groups
- observing and record keeping
- self-evaluation
- celebrating successes
- independent research
-

Learners are expected to be involved in learning continuously, and at different times for different reasons. They might work in interest groups and ability groups. They have opportunities to be part of large groups and small groups, and to take part in individual activities. In between these scheduled times, they continue to work independently.

Thinking about using time this way keeps the learners at the centre of learning and makes the connections between what we know about the learners' needs, interests and questions and how we spend our time to meet those needs, facilitate their learning, and monitor their progress and process. We can strive to use time purposefully to facilitate authentic learning, teaching and evaluating, and to teach the learners the next small part they need to know as they continue to become lifelong learners. We constantly make connections about teaching, learning and evaluating.

Ownership

Ownership means that learners are involved in choosing topics, materials, tools, and/or a particular learning activity. We encourage our learners to choose what they need in order to help them seek answers to their questions and to share this knowledge with others. We invite them to take risks, make decisions, practise, rehearse, create, share, and present. Together we make decisions about performing or publishing...going public.

Ownership promotes caring, interest and enthusiasm for *what* is learned and *how*. We provide opportunities for our learners to choose from resources including people, places or things. They may choose from one, two or a combination of all three. They may choose with whom they want to work (people), where they would like to work (places), and what they will need (things). The richer the selection of materials and resources and the more divergent the learning environment, the greater the choice. The more time we provide for our learners to practise choosing, taking risks and making decisions, the more competent and confident the learners will become.

Donald Graves writes:

> We teachers must become totally aware of our awful daily temptation to take control away from them, whether by too much prescription or correction or even advice....Freedom to choose what they wanted to write about, especially when it involved their own feelings, interests, ideas and opinions, was what "turned students on" to writing most.
>
> — Donald Graves, *Don Graves in Australia*, page 9

In the same way, we believe that learners need to have a high degree of ownership for *all* their learning in order to "turn them on" to learning.

Figure 1.3 illustrates a learner with high ownership.

Figure 1.3   A Learning Situation Involving High Learner Ownership

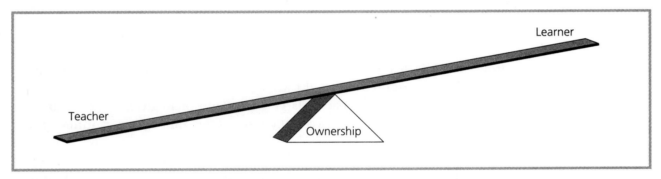

The teacher in Figure 1.3 has given the learner a great deal of ownership, yet the teacher still has an important role and does not disappear from the learning picture. Teachers need to actively facilitate the process of learner ownership. This process means that we teach or actively instruct at the appropriate time to meet the needs and interests of the learners. We need to have ongoing conversations with our learners. We need to observe, monitor and keep records of the learning process and the learners' progress so that we know what our learners know and can do, what they want to do, and where they may need help. This process is an integral part of assessing, evaluating, planning and programming.

Figure 1.4 illustrates a learner with a low degree of ownership.

Figure 1.4   A Learning Situation Involving Low Learner Ownership

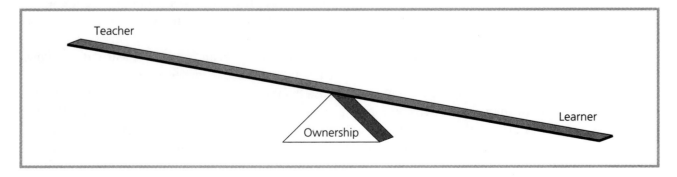

Here, the teacher made the decisions for the program and gave little consideration to what the learner already knew and wanted to know. There was minimal interaction between the teacher and learner in negotiating the curriculum.

We believe that as teachers we need to reflect continuously by asking ourselves:

- What are the purposes of this teaching?
- How does it help the learners?
- Why am I doing what I am doing?
- How can I plan programs and create learning environments that will facilitate the highest possible degree of ownership in order to engage the learners?

We believe these questions will help us as teachers to keep teaching, learning and evaluating from becoming fragmented.

 ## Response

As lifelong learners, we generally respond to experiences we have with people, places or things. In our minds, we naturally respond by thinking or saying, *"I know..."*, *"I remember..."*, *"I wonder..."*, *"I want to..."* These responses happen before an experience when we predict or decide. Frequently, they happen in the form of conversations. We need to invite our learners to make connections and share their responses. It is important that we as teachers provide learners with a mirror that reflects and values their responses. An effective teacher response might be, "Oh, that's an interesting solution. Tell me more about it," instead of "No, do it this way." It is saying **"Oh,"** instead of **"No."** It is asking the questions, **"Why?" "What if...?" "How did you find out about that. . .?"**

We call this thinking and talk **learner-centred response.** Together with our learners, we have conversations and make connections about the learning process. We see where the learners are and where they want to go next.

We listen, watch and respond by accepting and valuing what the learners know and have found out. We accept and value the diversity of the products and the individuality of the processes. We respond to a piece of writing with the same value and respect as we do to a block structure. Response *from* learners and how we respond *to* learners are essential parts of the teaching, learning, assessing and evaluating processes. The flavour of how we respond represents what we value. What we value is what we ultimately evaluate.

You will notice throughout this book how applying our 3 R's framework of retelling, relating and reflecting to any of the features of learning we discuss in this chapter heightens and clarifies the teaching/learning experience and encourages lifelong learning patterns. It is in the area of response, however, that the 3 R's proves particularly effective. When we respond to our learners by retelling what they have said, by relating their talk/response to something in our own lives, and by reflecting on meanings, insights and/or questions their talk/responses have evoked, we are able to assist and support them in what they choose and want to do or learn about next.

 # Celebration

Celebration is sharing the excitement and wonders of learning. It is sharing the enthusiasm of new discoveries. It brings closure to one aspect of learning and unfolds new areas to discover.

Learners assess, evaluate, and celebrate learning when they:

- have a conversation
- present a play
- share a work of art
- read a story
- put together a scrapbook
- publish a piece of writing
- photograph or sketch the design of a block structure
- design an overhead presentation
- explain how gears work
- use audio and video to demonstrate their learning
-

Celebration is closely connected to responses to learning. As teachers, we celebrate learning when we value sharing. We celebrate learning by providing spontaneous as well as scheduled times and places for learners to present and/or perform. We celebrate learning by inviting learners to choose selectively what they will share and how they will present their work to others. We assess, evaluate and celebrate learning by encouraging and supporting:

- conversations
- author's chair
- student authors/illustrators
- the selection of art pieces for framing
- daily announcements highlighting contributions
- classroom responsibilities for everyone
- visual displays
- slide shows
- videos
- book fairs
- demonstrations of experiments
- descriptions, diagrams, webs of how something works
- carnivals
- festivals
- family curriculum evenings
- musicals
-

We celebrate learning when we consistently value what learners know, what the learners have learned, and how and what the learners can do. We are continuously assessing, evaluating and celebrating learning.

*The components of **time**, **ownership**, **response**, and **celebration** comple-ment our understandings of **how** we learn. We, as lifelong learners, take time and make decisions about how we will respond and how we will celebrate what and how we learn from the world around us. We are in charge of choosing, planning and directing our own learning. Our goal is for all learners to be in charge of their own learning.*

CONDITIONS OF LEARNING

Dr. Brian Cambourne, head of the Centre for Studies in Literacy at Wollongong University in Australia and author of numerous professional books and articles, believes that there are several basic conditions required for successful learning. In his book *The Whole Story*, Cambourne uses these conditions to discuss literacy and language development. *We use these same conditions as a way to examine effective teaching and learning experiences.* These conditions provide a natural checklist we can use as teachers to assess and evaluate the learning environment, learning experiences and our teaching.

Cambourne calls these conditions:

- immersion
- demonstrations
- expectations
- responsibility
- approximations
- practice
- feedback
- engagement

In Figure 1.5 we illustrate how these conditions fit together with teaching and learning. (See also Draft Planning Sheet 2, "A Way of Looking at Learning.")

Figure 1.5 Conditions of Learning

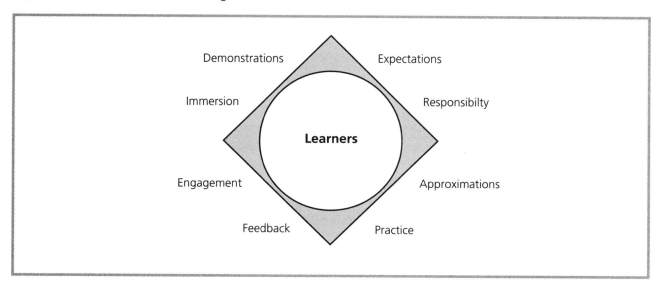

Cambourne emphasizes that these conditions are not necessarily linear nor are they necessarily sequential. However, for the purposes of this chapter, we will discuss them one at a time.

Immersion

From the time we are born, most of us are immersed in spoken language. We hear it from the people all around us. Research has shown that the best and easiest way to learn a new language is to be in a place where that language is constantly being spoken, so that we are continually immersed in the language and culture of the place.

When we want to learn something new, we immerse ourselves in that something new. We do this by:

- talking to **people**
- seeking out **things** to study
- going **places** to learn

As teachers, we provide environments that immerse learners in all aspects of the curriculum. When we work together with our learners to collect baseline data, we discover areas of interests and needs. We invite learners to immerse themselves in the learning environment in order to answer their questions in pursuit of their learning.

There are different levels of quality with respect to immersion. High quality immersion requires time. It is more than a quick sampling from the buffet of learning. It is more than one activity or strategy. It is an encompassing part of teaching and learning. When we are planning, we need to consider first and foremost the aspect of **immersion.**

When we involve learners in an in-depth study over a longer period of time, their learning tends to be more long-lasting. Providing opportunities each month of a school year for learners to study a variety of authors and illustrators — e.g., one author or illustrator per month — is more effective than providing such opportunities once a year or once a term. We invite you to examine your yearly plans and think about how you can select, plan and choose learning experiences that will immerse your learners for longer periods of time.

Demonstrations

People continually learn from **demonstrations** and models. Models provide concrete and natural examples. Teachers and family members set examples for learners when they practise behaviours that they would like to see copied. For example, when family members read personally — the newspaper, novels, picture books — or when teachers read in front of learners, they are **modelling** that reading is a valued activity. On the other hand, when we teachers think aloud and explain to learners how we learned to read and what reading strategies we are using, we are **demonstrating** *how to read*. Modelling is a natural demonstration and may be ongoing and regular. Demonstrations are planned or spontaneous and involve an explicit action.

Learners continually observe and/or seek out people to model and demonstrate for them what they are interested in and want to know about. They look for a variety of things to explore, examine and study, and when possible, they travel to new places to expand their background of experience and knowledge. They watch, listen and use their senses in order to learn from the world around them. Brian Cambourne states:

> The world is filled with demonstrations and if we engage with one of them, we internalize some aspect or portion of that particular demonstration. If we engage with repeated demonstrations of the same action and/or artifact, we begin to select other aspects of it to internalize and, as a consequence, we begin to interpret, organize and reorganize our developing knowledge until we can perform and/or produce that demonstration or a variation of it. This is another way of saying we learn.
>
> — Brian Cambourne, *The Whole Story*, page 47

As teachers, we incorporate demonstrations by:

- modelling and setting examples
- presenting mini-lessons at the point of need
- demonstrating lessons with large groups, small groups or individuals
- inviting purposeful repetition
- teaching in a variety of ways
- making resources (artifacts, books...) readily available
- explaining and encouraging self-evaluation
- designing assessment and evaluation strategies as an integral part of the learning and teaching process
-

When we talk out loud and explain what we are learning, how we are thinking and why, we are providing natural and effective demonstrations for our learners. We need to provide a wide variety of relevant and divergent demonstrations, and invite learners to choose from these demonstrations and to become engaged in the learning and evaluation processes. We teach by continually inviting learners to practise and try out our demonstrations. Demonstrations are not "one-shot deals." They happen in a series over time and are revisited and re-presented using a wide variety of strategies and materials.

Expectations

Having **expectations** means expecting that all learners will learn, each in different ways. Expectations are very closely related to building high self-esteem in learners and developing self-confidence. Through our expectations, we as teachers and the learners' families send the message to learners that they are valued and that what they do will be accepted. We communicate our trust and confidence in sincere and overt ways.

It is critical that we teachers state clear expectations and find ways of making these expectations explicit to everyone involved in the learning/teaching process. Some ways to make expectations explicit are

- posted goals
- posted schedules
- pamphlets
- flyers
- brochures
- newsletters
- yearly calendars
- handbooks
- framed photos and quotations
-

We need to know our learners and have appropriate expectations that match their strengths, needs and knowledge. These expectations need to be realistic, clear and explicit. We need to find a variety of ways to show learners what our expectations look and sound like. Some methods we can use to do this are by working together with our learners to create cooperative charts, diagrams, webs, etc., to highlight:

- what an effective reader looks like
- what an effective listener looks like/sounds like
- what an effective writer looks like
- what an effective illustrator looks like/acts like
- what an effective problem solver says/does/uses
-

We can ensure that our learners have clear expectations by working together with them to set goals at the beginning of the year. Together with our learners, we review and revise these goals two or three times throughout the year, or more, based on the needs and strengths of the learners. These goals should be shared, recorded, posted and be visible. The goals we establish should be connected to and form an important part of the assessment and evaluation process.

We may choose to work with the whole group, small groups or individuals, setting goals at different times of the year for different learning experiences or subjects. With younger learners, we might invite each child to state one goal and record the goal on a chart with the child's name in brackets. With older groups, we might hold a group discussion about goal setting and expectations, and then invite the learners to write their own sets of personal goals.

Responsibility

Natural learning occurs when opportunities for **choice** are provided, and when learners are invited to take **responsibility** for their own learning. When learners are encouraged to choose different ways to use and respond to a variety of materials, they make decisions and take responsibility for their own learning. We need to immerse our learners in a rich environment where they have demonstrations, are expected to make choices, and practise being responsible for their own learning.

In a learner-centred environment, many things remain constant. Within this predictable environment, we continuously change the materials, the expectations and the demonstrations depending upon the age, stage of development, interests and needs of the learners. As learners make decisions about their own learning, they take responsibility, and choose different ways to use and respond to the variety of materials.

We invite you to think about the different purposes for your demonstrations based on what you know about your learners, and to make explicit what your expectations are for that particular age or grade. We encourage you to connect these appropriate expectations with assessment and evaluation practices. The responsibility learners take will look and sound different depending on their age or grade. We invite you to think about your own responsibilities in order to encourage learner **"response...ability."**

Approximations

Approximations, or making guesses, are what learners do naturally. When young children are learning to talk, approximations naturally occur and are valued. Families accept, encourage and support this natural learning process.

Approximations are learners "thinking in draft." Drafts can be messy and are not final copy form. Approximations are part of all learning and assessment and evaluation, and should be valued. They reflect teachers and learners saying *"Have a go,"* instead of *"No."* When learners are encouraged to approximate, they realize that all people make mistakes and that they learn from and through their mistakes. In the home and in the classroom, an atmosphere of risk taking should be encouraged.

Ken and Yetta Goodman call approximations in reading "miscues." As teachers, we use the information from such miscues to understand how learners read and learn. We can then use this information and these understandings to plan appropriately for the learners in our classrooms.

> Errors in language and in conceptual development reflect much more than a mistake that can be eradicated with a red pencil or a verb admonition. What an adult perceives as wrong may in actuality reflect development in the child. Errors, miscues or misconceptions usually indicate ways in which a child is organizing the world at that moment...

and

> "Errors" also indicate interpretations....The kidwatcher who understands the role of unexpected responses will use children's errors and miscues to chart their growth and development and to understand the personal and cultural history of the child.
>
> — Ken and Yetta Goodman, *Kidwatching*, page 13

In play situations, learners are free to take risks and the valuing of approximations happens naturally. "Play is probably the most obvious real world situation which coerces learners into using language" (Brian Cambourne, *The Whole Story*, page 71). Play can be by oneself, beside another, with one other, or with several others. It is age-less, grade-less, and lifelong. We all learn and problem-solve when we play.

Play provides windows into the learning and development of children. By observing play and recognizing significant points of growth and development, play becomes a natural vehicle for assessment and evaluation. Play provides a context for "learner-watching" and "learner-listening." It provides opportunities for us to assess and evaluate the learners' stages of development and to plan teaching/learning experiences that will extend and enrich their growth. Play, with the approximations inherent in it, is an essential part of learning.

 ## Practice

Learners need many opportunities to practise and use their skills, attitudes, and knowledge in authentic ways. We need to provide time for learners to practise in large and small groups and by themselves. Cambourne refers to practice as "playing around." This particular condition of learning requires time — to experience, choose, use new innovations, experiment, read, write, problem-solve and become self-directed learners.

Learners use repetition as one strategy of practising until they are satisfied with their understandings. This repetition can be self-initiated and/or teacher-initiated. Usually, practising over and over and over is enjoyable and fun — like playing a game. An example might be teachers showing learners how to make a pop-up book and for several days, the learners create a number of different pop-up books for a variety of purposes. Once the learners feel the practising is complete for that time, they become engaged in new learning experiences. They may use these skills and concepts at a later time for different purposes.

Everyone needs opportunities and time to practise. We believe practice is an integral part of lifelong learning.

Feedback

Feedback happens continuously. It is how we respond to learners. We include **celebration** as an integral part of feedback. Feedback is based on watching, listening and making connections by **retelling**, **relating** and **reflecting**.

When we provide feedback, we need to be sure that it supports the learner and values what the learner can do, while still keeping in mind what the learner needs to know for that age and grade level. Feedback demonstrates to learners what it is that they are trying to learn and how they are going about their learning.

Teachers and others provide feedback throughout all learning experiences — when learners appear to need or ask for help, when learners finish a learning experience, and when learners embark on a new learning experience. Offering authentic feedback regularly is an important part of instruction, assessment and evaluation. Responses include accepting, celebrating, evaluating, and demonstrating during real learning experiences.

As teachers, we respond explicitly and implicitly. By *explicit*, we mean direct comments clearly describing the learning. For example, "I see you made the dough, peeled and sliced the apples, added the ingredients and baked an apple pie... Congratulations!" By *implicit*, we mean more subtle or less obvious response. For example, "Oh, by the way, I enjoyed the piece of pie. Thanks!" Learners benefit most when we respond *explicitly* to their learnings. We need to be sure we are continuously providing *explicit* feedback. Such feedback helps learners continue to acquire a deeper understanding of the learning process.

As Figure 1.6 illustrates, responding to learners is a cyclical process that takes learning and teaching back to demonstrations.

Figure 1.6 Responding to the Learner

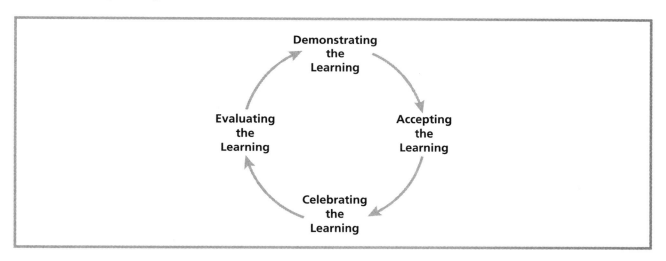

Such demonstrations emerge naturally when learners are immersed in learning experiences and they receive feedback. When we take time to know our learners well, our feedback becomes spontaneous, genuine, natural and purposeful.

Engagement

Even when all the conditions of learning discussed above are present, it is not an assurance that every learner will engage in the learning process. Frank Smith says in his article "Demonstrations, engagement, and sensitivity: A revised approach to language learning" (*Language Arts*, 1981) that when learning does not seem to be taking place, there is something missing from the learning equation called **"engagement."**

We intentionally invite learners to become engaged in the learning process when through our demonstrations, we show that we learn by doing. By integrating active/interactive involvement in learning experiences, we demonstrate that learners practise *doing*. When we provide time for learners to practise, they come to understand that this engagement is an essential part of lifelong learning. We as teachers and learners need to value approximations as part of practising demonstrations, and through appropriate feedback, offer continuous opportunities for learners to experience success and confidence.

Both Cambourne and Smith invite us continuously to reexamine and re-question the learner-teacher relationship in order to gain further insights and reasons for learners engaging or not engaging in the learning process. We need to remember that the more successfully the first seven conditions of learning are met, the higher the probability that learners will engage in the learning process.

Our personal understandings of learning and teaching integrate all of the components and connections we have discussed throughout this chapter. Assessment and evaluation practices are connected to, are part of, and are embedded in these components and connections. Figure 1.7 illustrates the many learning/teaching connections we see.

Figure 1.7 Learning Connections

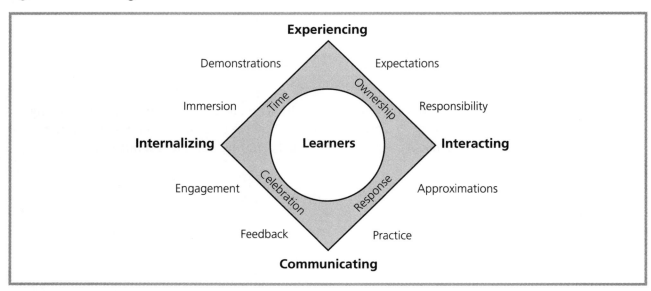

*It is out of our understandings of how learning happens that we construct-ed our 3 R's framework of **retelling, relating and reflecting**. And it is using our 3 R's framework that has enabled us more effectively to ensure that these components and connections are available in the learning environment that we provide for our learners.*

Using a Framework:
The 3 R's

"With the 3 R's framework, we see more clearly into the windows of learning
and teaching from birth to old age."
(page 34)

"When the 3 R's framework of retelling, relating and reflecting becomes automatic
and natural, it gives us a tool to use in reading, responding, discussions, writing,
and for creating."
(page 88)

In this chapter, we outline our 3 R's framework of retelling, relating and reflecting. This easy-to-implement framework provides an invaluable tool for ensuring effective, long-lasting learning — for ensuring successful reading, writing, talking and thinking for learners of all ages, in the classroom and outside the classroom. We describe the 3 R's framework and how it works. We present our personal stories of how the framework evolved, and we include a "PRACTISING" section in which we suggest practical classroom applications for the framework.

BEYOND THE 3 R'S

When we hear the term "the 3 R's," many of us think of "Reading, Writing and Arithmetic" — the 3 R's of education. Our 3 R's goes beyond this traditional view of learning. Our 3 R's framework of **retelling, relating and reflecting** is a natural way of responding to any experience and, is, we believe, central to all learning throughout life.

In the same way that learners naturally use all of their senses when they learn, the 3 R's framework reflects what happens naturally in conversations and thinking. We **retell** when we talk about our experiences or what we have done, read about or seen. We **relate** when we make connections to past experiences or feelings, and we **reflect** when we wonder and question. Our 3 R's represent a process of learning, teaching and making meaning. (See Draft Planning Sheets 3 and 7, "The 3 R's Framework: Retelling, Relating and Reflecting" and "The 3 R's Framework in an 8-Page Book Format.")

As Gordon Wells writes in his book *The Meaning Makers*:

> Learning is first and foremost a process — a continuous making and remaking of meanings in the lifelong enterprise of constructing a progressively more and more effective mental model of the world in which one lives. Learning is never complete.

> — Gordon Wells, *The Meaning Makers*, page 124

Our years of teaching and learning and our professional reading have convinced us that watching and listening are at the heart of teaching and learning, and that they are central to assessment and evaluation. It was as we watched and listened that we discovered our natural framework of the 3 R's.

Our 3 R's framework of retelling, relating and reflecting is an ongoing learning process based on *watching, listening, speaking* and *thinking*. It accepts and values natural talk and encourages personal response and the making of *connections*. Once practised and internalized, the 3 R's framework enables teachers and learners alike to express themselves effectively and confidently, both orally and in writing. As teachers, we invite learners to share their knowings by **retelling**. We encourage learners to respond from their own experiences and perspectives by **relating**, and we nudge them to **reflect** — to think, question and wonder at different and divergent levels.

In the learner-centred classroom, it is important that we be extremely perceptive when watching, listening, and responding to learners. We need to become reflective "people-watchers" and "people-listeners." An important part of our role is knowing what to observe or watch for, what to listen for, how to interpret this information, and what and how to teach. We need to know how to respond naturally and effectively, nudging learners into thinking and reflecting, helping them to take the next step.

Many components need to be in place before we can realistically turn our attention to this important part of our role. For example, the physical set-up of the classroom needs to be planned and well organized so that learners have visual stimulation, organization, space, and a feeling of warmth and security. Materials and resources need to be readily available and easily accessible in order to invite learners to become responsible for choosing appropriate tools.

Flexible timetables need to be created, designed, and adapted to meet the learner's ever-changing needs and to allow for adjusting to changes in planning and programming throughout the year. We need to schedule and plan for blocks of time to allow for longer sustained attention to tasks, and to accommodate intensive, extensive and active investigations. We need to provide opportunities for learners to pursue their own areas of interest and to plan collaboratively with us.

The timetabling process involves scheduling what we do with our learners. It is actually more a timetable for us, than for the learners. (Learners develop and use their own intrinsic natural timetables when the learning environment and experiences value their personal knowledge and questions.) We need to schedule times to rove and walk about, interacting with, observing and monitoring learners. We need to schedule "stand-back, watch and listen times" in order to learn and teach more effectively. It will be these mini-observation times that will enable us to know what we need to teach in order to take our learners that next small step.

We also need to schedule time to collaborate with our learners in order to develop a **baseline of knowledge** for each learner. We need to find out what the learners already know, what they remember or relate to, what they understand, and what they want to or need to know.

With careful thought and planning, we can collaborate with our learners to create a warm, caring and comfortable classroom atmosphere. We can establish a learning environment in which risk taking, peer teaching, decision making, problem solving, cooperation, and collaboration are promoted and valued (see Draft Planning Sheet 2, "A Way of Looking at Learning"). It is a good idea to develop together, outline, and post the expectations for teaching and learning in the classroom. It is in this kind of atmosphere that routines and positive attitudes for learning are established.

When we have the above aspects of the learning/teaching process in place, we can turn our attention to our professional responsibility of effectively **watching and listening.** We notice and critically analyze how learners **respond** to experiences and conversations. We consciously think about our role as models and demonstrators for the learners in our classrooms.

We become "facilitators of learning" as we circulate, observe, analyze, evaluate, assist and instruct individuals, small groups and the large group. In our role as instructors, we continue to model, demonstrate and teach attitudes, skills, and knowledge in this carefully orchestrated learning environment. By internalizing the retelling, relating and reflecting framework, our observed learnings become more meaningful, and learning and teaching continuously evolve and emerge into authentic and purposeful opportunities and experiences. The 3 R's framework is useful in any learning environment with any age and any grade level. It is equally valid in and out of the school setting.

To show clearly how the 3 R's framework works, we will first outline each of the 3 R's separately, compare our framework to Bloom's Taxonomy, and talk about the necessity of balancing the 3 R's. We will then outline our own hands-on experiences as we developed and refined the framework, and, finally, we will provide practical suggestions for how the framework can be applied in the classroom.

Retell

Retelling is an important component of oral language development. Early experiences with talking are some of our first retellings. **Retelling becomes a sharing of our knowledge, or what we know, have heard, read, understood or experienced — our "knowings."** Everyone has experiences and shares these experiences with others. **This sharing is *conversation* or *talk* — what we call *retelling*.** The talk might be about the most significant part of an experience. It might describe the part remembered, valued or enjoyed the most. It can be retold in different ways — in sketchy, detailed, humorous or serious ways.

As teachers, we frequently encourage our learners to remember and recount the events they hear or experience. Retelling is a familiar way of finding out what learners know. It is an integral part of the classroom and of daily life. Retelling is naturally, automatically and continuously used in the learning environment. Learners tell back what they have heard, experienced or know. For example, when learners are involved in retelling, they might say or think:

- This is about...
- It happened...
- I noticed that...
- I like the part when...
- I especially like it when...
- In this piece...
- You mean to say that...
-

(You may wish to create a poster by enlarging Draft Planning Sheet 4, "Retell," and post it as a reference chart for your learners to refer to as necessary, or you can make it into an overhead transparency for a large-group lesson, or you may want to hand out copies to the learners.)

It is important for us to invite and encourage our learners to retell after a read-aloud, storytelling, or any personal or class experience. Learners retell directions, how they discovered something, what their picture, construction, or experiment is about — their learnings and knowings. We hear our learners' descriptions and feel their excitement.

In response to a story, we can invite our learners to practise by encouraging them to:

- turn to the closest person and retell
- retell what happens in their heads as they listen — their feelings, understandings, meanings
- sketch and use the drawings to retell
- make jot notes and retell
- retell the story in a large group, one person starting and others continuing
- retell the story in small groups of two to four, each person taking a turn and adding one or two sentences (if the story changes, it is accepted and a new story develops)
- retell in a variety of ways, using art, story, drama, construction, dance...
-

As teachers, we accept and value all our learners' retellings. They bring their own meaning to these learning experiences and use a variety of ways to demonstrate personal meanings and interpretations.

Relate

Relating happens naturally and spontaneously when people, places and things spark connections and memories. When we share experiences and feelings, thoughts and images naturally appear in our minds. These thoughts and images often create connections to previous knowledge and experiences. *We call these connections **relating**.* These connections help everyone to comprehend, understand and create meaning. In relating, everyone actively listens, thinks, remembers and connects. They make connections to prior knowledge, past experiences, stories, pictures, music, art... These connections are related in different ways.

Many of us naturally and spontaneously relate what we already know to what we are learning. In our minds, we think "This reminds me of...," or "I remember when...". Our remembering helps us to connect experiences outside the classroom with those inside the classroom. Relating makes teaching learner-centred, authentic and purposeful.

Relating is an important component of learning, growth and development. Our early experiences with talking and listening are some of our first retellings and relatings. Oral language and listening develop when people retell and relate. It is a natural way of *responding*. **Our relatings are our understandings and feelings as well as our connections to our lives. Relating is the making of our own meaning.**

Relating in the read-aloud situation is a natural way to encourage and invite learners to talk about their own lives in connection with what they are hearing in literature. When we involve our learners in relating, we model and demonstrate relating. We might say, for example:

- This reminds me of...
- I remember when...
- It makes me think of...
- It makes me feel that...
- That happened to me, too, when...

- When I was young...
- That situation is just like...
- This is different from...
- This compares to...
- It sounds like...
-

(You may wish to create a poster by enlarging Draft Planning Sheet 5, "Relate," and post it as a reference chart for your learners to refer to as necessary, or you can make it into an overhead transparency for a large-group lesson, or you may want to hand out copies to the learners.)

We can encourage relating in the classroom by inviting learners to:

- talk about what the story (the events, characters, style, illustrations...), music, art, experiment, etc., reminds them of
- display related books, stories, poetry, pictures, films for reading, viewing, comparing, contrasting...
- use a related object or artifact from a story to tell personal stories
- seek out and share related literature, music, artifacts...
-

By knowing our learners, we are able carefully to select areas of study and plan a learning environment or experience. Daily relating can be modelled, demonstrated, encouraged and integrated into the program. Personal understandings are valued and all connections are accepted in order to deepen and enrich everyone's learning experience.

 # Reflect

We may think or wonder about a concept, an experience, or a reading. *We call these "wonderings" and "thinkings" reflecting.* In reflecting, we wonder, question, suppose, or predict, and we are nudged into different and divergent levels of thinking and learning. We might:

- wonder about the cause and effect of any experience
- think of another way to deal with an experience
- question in order to search out more information
- make predictions about what might happen next
- make inferences and draw conclusions
- explore and share our insights and our "aha's"
- want to investigate further and/or explore other related topics
-

Reflecting, too, is an important component of learning, growth, and development. Reflecting involves talking, listening, viewing, inquiring and discovering. Our experiences with inquiry are some of our first reflections. Oral language, listening and thinking develop naturally and automatically when people retell, relate and reflect. The process becomes internalized. It is a natural way of responding to our experiences.

Our reflections are the making of deeper meaning and richer understandings. Our reflections are our dreams, our ideas, our questions, our initiatives, our visions — our journeys of lifelong learning and teaching.

We have found it very effective to invite learners, through modelling, demonstrating and questioning, to respond, think and reflect. For example, in a read-aloud situation, when we are involved in reflecting, we might say or think:

- I wonder how...
- I wonder if...
- I wonder why...
- I wonder when...
- The part about _____ really interests me. I think I will...
- This gives me an idea to...
- Why do you think...
- What do you think about...
- I think that...
- Now I understand that...
- I want to...
-

(You may wish to create a poster by enlarging Draft Planning Sheet 6, "Reflect," and post it as a reference chart for your learners to refer to as necessary, or you can make it into an overhead transparency for a large-group lesson, or you may want to hand out copies to the learners.)

Only inviting learners to retell keeps them tied to what they have been told, have experienced or have read without moving them beyond the basic information and comprehension level. When we invite learners to relate and reflect, we expect them to elaborate, explain and expand their knowledge and understandings. By fostering and valuing higher order thinking, and developing deeper understandings, we nudge learners beyond the basic levels of thinking.

There is no one way to model, demonstrate or share retellings, relatings and reflections. Many strategies and techniques need to be explored to enable learners to demonstrate their relatings and reflectings.

We have found that when we share our 3 R's framework with our learners, it helps them to make their thinking and learning explicit and clear. Figure 2.1 (next page) provides a visual model as a tool that will help you and your learners begin to use and internalize the 3 R's framework. (Figure 2.1 also appears as Draft Planning Sheet 3, "The 3 R's Framework: Retelling, Relating and Reflecting." You may want to blow this Planning Sheet up and post it as a reference chart for your learners to refer to as necessary, or you can make it into an overhead transparency for a large group lesson, or you may want to hand out copies to the learners.)

Just as conversations and connections are interactive and circular, as Figure 2.1 shows, our 3 R's framework, too, is interactive and circular. Retelling, relating and reflecting do not necessarily occur in any specific order when we listen, speak and learn. Sometimes we begin our conversations by sharing our memories **(relate)**. Other times, we share anecdotes or artifacts **(retell)** and begin speaking by questioning or wondering **(reflect)**. Often, the most natural place we begin a conversation is

Figure 2.1 The 3 R's Framework: Retelling, Relating, Reflecting

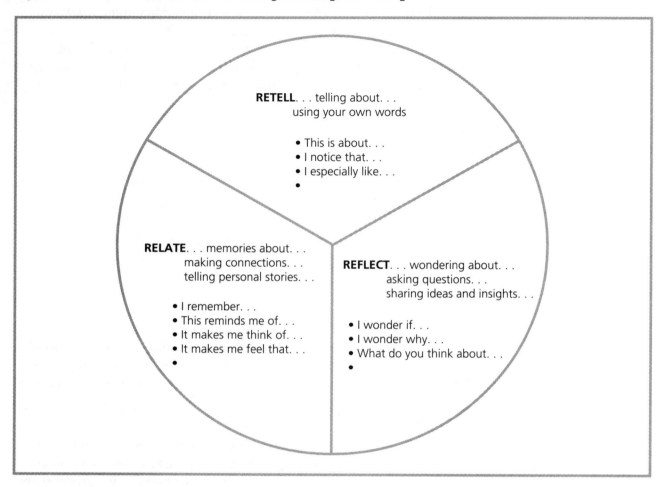

RETELL. . . telling about. . .
using your own words

- This is about. . .
- I notice that. . .
- I especially like. . .
-

RELATE. . . memories about. . .
making connections. . .
telling personal stories. . .

- I remember. . .
- This reminds me of. . .
- It makes me think of. . .
- It makes me feel that. . .
-

REFLECT. . . wondering about. . .
asking questions. . .
sharing ideas and insights. . .

- I wonder if. . .
- I wonder why. . .
- What do you think about. . .
-

when we tell about an experience **(retell)**. As we listen to and examine conversations, we learn that conversations begin anywhere.

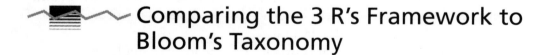

Comparing the 3 R's Framework to Bloom's Taxonomy

In developing the 3 R's framework, we built upon our knowledge and experiences as educators and learners, upon the professional reading we had done, and on the thinking and learning models that we had internalized over the years. One thinking and learning model we revisited was **Bloom's Taxonomy.** Bloom's Taxonomy is a framework developed by Benjamin Bloom to illustrate the hierarchical levels of thinking. It is useful as a tool for us as teachers to use to encourage learners to move beyond the basic level of knowledge to higher and more divergent levels of thinking. When we compare and contrast Bloom's Taxonomy to our 3 R's framework, we realize that they are complementary and somewhat similar. Both outline higher levels of thinking involved in teaching and learning. Both describe similar processes. Both provide a guide for teachers to help them develop higher level thinking skills.

Bloom's Taxonomy shows teachers and learners **why** it is necessary to move beyond the *knowledge* and *comprehension* levels of thinking to the higher levels of *application, analysis, synthesis* and *evaluation*. Our 3 R's framework shows teachers and learners **how** to move beyond the *retell* level to higher levels of *relating* and *reflecting*. When we *retell*, it is similar to the knowledge and comprehension levels of Bloom's Taxonomy. When we *relate*, it is similar to the application and analysis levels of Bloom, and when we *reflect*, it is similar to the two highest levels of Blooms' Taxonomy, synthesis and evaluation. Figure 2.2 highlights these comparisons and connections.

Figure 2.2   The 3 R's Framework and Bloom's Taxonomy

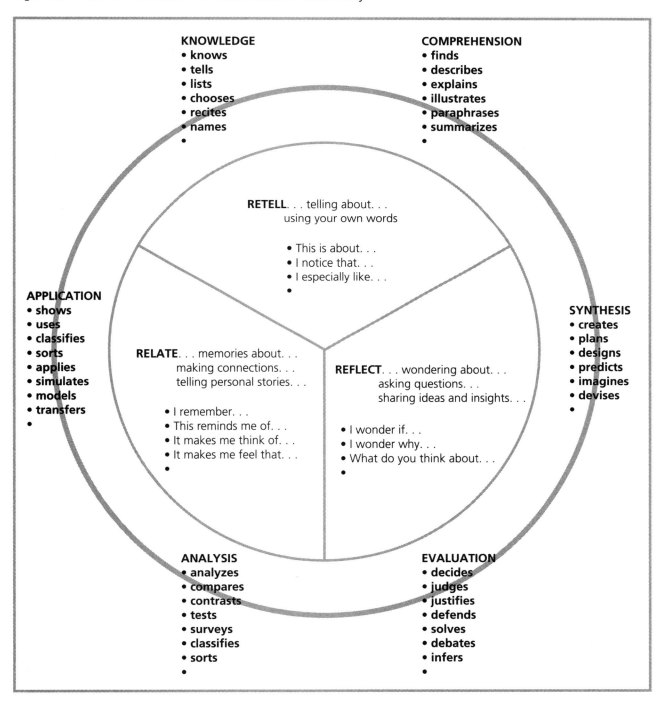

Balancing the 3 R's

There needs to be a **balance** of retelling, relating and reflecting opportunities and experiences in order to provide learning experiences at all the levels of thinking. This balance is not always easy to see or achieve.

As teachers, we are all comfortable in using **retelling** as a familiar way of encouraging learners to show what they know. Learners retell naturally, automatically and continuously in the learning environment. We regularly require learners to tell back what they have been told, have experienced or know. We use this strategy as a major component to assess and evaluate learning.

Relating happens naturally and spontaneously when people, places or things spark personal connections and memories. We as teachers *model* and *demonstrate* relating by sharing our personal stories with our learners. When we do this, we become "real" for our learners. When we model and demonstrate risk taking, our learners feel more comfortable sharing their stories with us. When we invite learners to practise relating, they experience another level of thinking.

When we take the time to know our learners, we are better able to select meaningful areas of study and plan a learning environment or experience where daily relating is fostered, encouraged and integrated into the program. With practice, we will come to feel just as secure in inviting learners to relate as we do inviting them to retell. Relating is equally important when assessing and evaluating what learners know and have learned.

Reflecting is more difficult to encourage and value. Reflecting usually happens by invitation and takes place less consistently throughout the learning/teaching process. We need to provide time for learners to practise reflecting and allow for ample wait-time in order to encourage, value and support their reflecting. When we listen carefully to learners, we hear their wonderings, questions, ideas and reflections. By incorporating reflecting as an integral component of our program, we integrate the assessment, evaluation and programming aspects of teaching. This integration helps to provide a road map for learning and teaching. By intentionally providing our learners with opportunities to reflect, we invite them to experience and practise higher order thinking.

All three parts of our 3 R's framework are important and interrelated. When we consciously practise retelling, relating and reflecting, we develop for ourselves a framework for listening and really hearing, for watching and really seeing, and for recording and really understanding. We become more mindful and consciously see and hear the world around us. The 3 R's framework can help us know when and how to provide appropriate learning materials, opportunities and teaching times. It can help create more effective teachers, families and individuals. And by giving our learners the 3 R's as a personal framework for their learning, we provide them with a framework that ensures long-lasting learning, a framework they can use for the rest of their lives.

With the 3 R's framework, we see more clearly into the windows of learning and teaching from birth to old age. Through the different panes, we continue to see and gain new understandings of how and what learning looks like for people of all ages, in all walks of life and work, in the home, in situations outside the home, and in classrooms spanning all grade levels — elementary, intermediate and secondary, as well as in in-service courses and research studies.

We have our own three-paned window of "retelling, relating and reflecting." We continue to listen, watch, and re-present our learnings and understandings about the world — both inside and outside the walls of classrooms. Our thinking and conversations continue to be our connections to lifelong learning and teaching. We invite you to join us on this journey and to take more time to stop, look, listen and talk together with everyone along the way.

THE 3 R'S IN REAL-LIFE SITUATIONS INSIDE AND OUTSIDE THE CLASSROOM: PERSONAL STORIES

To provide a perspective about the history of the 3 R's framework, in the next section we tell our own stories — our personal experiences with the 3 R's framework. We have been fascinated with the 3 R's framework since the summer of 1988 when we began working with the participants in our university in-service courses for teachers. We share our stories and insights — concrete snapshots illustrating the 3 R's framework, from its discovery and development to its practical uses in many classroom and out-of-classroom settings.

Experiences With Response Journals: *Maxine*

The 3 R's framework began as an idea that grew out of my work as course director at York University working with teachers, and as consultant helping teachers with programming. I was experimenting with a framework for response with the adults in a faculty of education course I was teaching. At the same time, I was helping a Grade 1 classroom teacher and her children begin to use response journals, and I was reviewing the work of Nancie Atwell and her use of journals with her Grade 8 students. In her book, In the Middle, Nancie writes:

> In other words, what I say in my half of the dialogue journal comes from my knowledge of how a student reads and thinks, of what the student knows. My responses grow from what I've learned about a reader and how I hope to move the reader's thinking. In general my comments do three things, to affirm, challenge, or extend the reader's thinking. These comments take various forms: gossip, questions, recommendations, jokes, restatements, arguments, suggestions, anecdotes, instruction, and "nudges."
>
> — Nancie Atwell, *In the Middle*, page 275

Using Nancie Atwell's advice to "affirm, challenge and extend the reader's thinking" as a base, I developed sentence prompts or guidelines to use as models to help the children in the Grade 1 class respond, and to help the teacher respond effectively and purposefully to the children's journal entries:

- Write one sentence telling what the story or learning experience is about.
- Write a second sentence making a connection — what the story or learning experience reminds you of.
- Write a third sentence as a question beginning with, "I wonder..."

We began by using read-aloud situations, and both the teacher and I demonstrated by retelling, relating and reflecting. For example, for the read-aloud Roxaboxen *by Alice McLerran, I said:*

*"This is a story about children playing together and creating an imaginary place **(retell)**. I remember when my friends and I raked leaves in the fall and used the leaves to make a leaf-house, adding objects and toys to create our imaginary floor plan where we each had rooms and particular roles **(relate)**. I wonder what other books this author has written **(reflect)**?"*

With the children, we created a chart to use as a reference poster.

RESPONSE JOURNALS	
Retell:	"This is about..."
Relate:	"I remember..."
Reflect:	"I wonder..."

We invited the children to practise retelling, relating and reflecting by turning to the person closest to them and telling each other three things — one a retelling, one a relating, and one a reflecting. We practised this format several times after different read-alouds. To begin written response, we invited a small group of children to practise responding in their journals after their personal reading time, and we wrote back to them in these journals.

By modelling and demonstrating with the whole class and with individuals, we were providing mini-lessons and demonstrations that we invited our learners to imitate and continue to practise. Later, we further developed the linear chart by adding other sentence starters. (See Figure 2.3.)

Figure 2.3   A 3 R's Framework Reference Chart: Linear Model

RETELL	RELATE	REFLECT
• I especially like. . . • I notice that. . . • I feel that. . . • This _____ is about. . . •	• I remember. . . • This reminds me of. . . • It makes me think of. . . • It's hard to believe. . . •	• Now I want to know. . . • I wonder if. . . • Now I understand. . . • What do you think about. . . •

Each time I had the opportunity to work with learners and teachers, I practised the framework. I practised when I responded to children's paintings, stories, constructions, and experiments. The following is an example of a conversation in the block centre:

Child: "Look, we made a castle. It has a bridge and towers."

Teacher: "You've made a castle with a bridge and towers **(retell).** It makes me think of the castles in some fairy tale picture books **(relate).** How does this bridge work **(reflect)**?"

I shared the 3 R's model, practised it, and continued to "people-watch" and "people-listen," make connections, learn and teach. It was when I took the time to stand back and watch and listen that I observed natural teaching and learning. During that fall on Thanksgiving weekend, my parents came for a visit. We spent one evening in the kitchen making pies. All the time my mom and dad were peeling the apples, they talked and talked. As I watched and listened, my mind automatically heard them retelling, relating and reflecting. I was intrigued by the natural flow of talk. Their conversations sounded like this:

Remember when... Do you know that... When I was young... Did you see... Did you hear... I know about that... I wonder who...where...what happens now... If you do this, will it work better...

Most of the talk was about topics of conversations unrelated to the making of pies. Some, when necessary, related directly to the task at hand. My parents were retelling, relating and reflecting continuously, not in any particular order, about a number of topics — people, places and things. As I reflected, I suddenly realized that the 3 R's framework was not linear, but circular. That morning, I designed and sketched the 3 R's circular framework. It was my first attempt to create a visual diagram. (See Figure 2.4, next page.)

During our time together, the teacher I was working with wrote in her professional journal:

I'm reading *In the Middle* by Nancie Atwell and I can't put it down. It contains a concept that I'm so excited about and my "kids" and I are loving it daily — reading journals. Maxine thought the kids might really respond to writing about their reading, so she suggested we begin with 2 children each day. The closeness, give and take, back and forth sharing of ideas shows the wonder of kids and the deepness there. Nancie says in her book, "I've become an evolutionist and the curriculum unfolds now as my kids and I learn together." She talks about "listening, waiting, and nudging" — I love that term. My kids are writing comments, answering my questions and asking questions too, following the model. They call me E.P. [the teacher's initials, similar to the character the students knew from the movie *E.T.*] and just wait for my response. Believe you me, I can't wait to read the remarks and their little theories about literature. Seeing their journals is worth at least a thousand words. I felt really ill last week but was so eager to launch this new idea that I just couldn't be away. It was just so fascinating.

— Personal journal entry by Ellen Palmer, teacher, January, 1989

Figure 2.4 The 3 R's Framework: The Circular Model

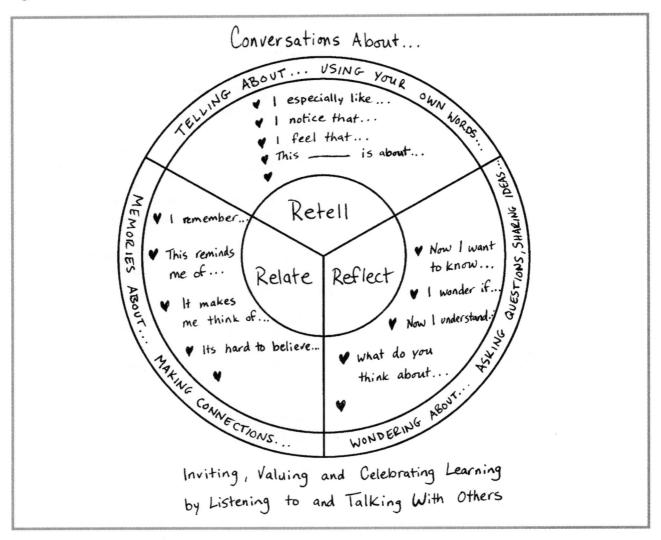

The teacher and I both continued to be fascinated by this teaching and learning experience. We felt it necessary to keep the reference chart close by as we continued to practise the 3 R's. We realized that using a reference or framework gave us a prop for comfort as we practised risk taking, learned along with the children, and became more confident in our teaching.

Experiences With Reading Response and "Teacher as Researcher": *Susan*

After my experience working with Maxine at York University teaching teachers and experimenting with the 3 R's as response, I decided in my role as vice-principal to undertake a study to encourage children to respond naturally to literature. For several weeks, every day and at the same time each day, I met with four nine-year-old children of varying ability levels and backgrounds for a thirty-minute period. During our time together, I read aloud to the children (a

book of my own choosing with a powerful impact, issue or message). We had conversations about the book, we all wrote for five minutes, and then we shared what we had written. Throughout the study, I modelled and demonstrated the 3 R's framework in my talk and in my writing, and after several sessions together, I shared the 3 R's circular model (Figure 2.1) for them to use as reference.

The following are samples of one child's draft writing collected during this study. Nadia easily learned to use all parts of the framework to express herself in writing.

On the first day of the study, I read the book <u>Once There Were Giants</u> by Martin Waddell and Penny Dale. In response, Nadia wrote:

> I liked the girl in nersery school when she was getting yelled at by the teacher.
>
> I liked when she was in a rase with her brother.
>
> I like when she was a baby and she said that there were giants in her house.
>
> I like when she says that she is the one that is puffing.
>
> I like the pa tern and the pictures in the book.
>
> I like the title of the book.

In this sample, Nadia retold by telling what she liked about the story.

On the second day of the study, I read <u>Wilfrid Gordon McDonald Partridge</u> by Mem Fox and I introduced the idea of relating and memories. I modelled the 3 R's framework in my conversation:

This story is about a little boy who brings back this old woman's memory by bringing her some objects. With each object, she remembers **(retell)**. This story reminds me of my father-in-law who is quite old and sometimes has trouble remembering. The shell reminds me of my Florida vacation because I bought a shell there just like the one in the story **(relate)**. I wonder what this story reminds you of **(reflect)**?

Nadia related in her writing:

The egg that the boy picked up reminds me of the time I went to an apple farm.

The boy in the story reminds me of my little sister that makes so much trouble.

The old woman named Miss Nancy reminds me of my grandma.

And the old man that talks like a giant reminds me of a book called the giant's house.

On the fifth day of the study, I shared the 3 R's framework and then the group and I looked at our previous writing, identifying the "retell, relate and reflect" statements we had written.

After listening to the poem "Kidnapped" by Shel Silverstein, Nadia wrote:

Today we read a poem. It was funny because the girl was making up this big story that sounded so true but at the end we found out that she was just making up a story because at the end she said and that's why I'm late for school. I wonder what she was really doing that let her come to school late. This poem makes me think that about people in my class at school because thir just like the girl in the pome because when their late they make up long storys just like the girl in the poem.

I included non-fiction books as part of the study. The first non-fiction book I read was a book called Gravity Is a Mystery by F. M. Branley.

In response, Nadia wrote:

> Today we read a mistery story. it was called the gravity mistery. In the book it told you that if you dig a hole in the center of the earth you would end up on the Indian Ocean. It shows that gravity pulls everything down. in other words, it says that gravity is almost like the weight of the thing. I wonder if gravity is just like a magnet in the center of the earth? I wonder if what makes gravity and how does gravity pull everything down to the center? I wonder how you could find out exclly where the center of the earth is. The part of the book I like is when it shows how much you would weigh on the different planets. The book that we read today was called the gravity mistery. It was a non-fiction book. I like non-fiction books because they give you a lot of questions.

Nadia's last line was significant. Non-fiction provides information, yet along with this information comes wondering and questioning. Reflecting becomes a natural experience as learners read, make meaning and wonder.

By the last day of the study, Nadia was easily and naturally using the 3 R's framework. In fact, all the children's talk was enthusiastic, interesting and relevant to the reading heard, and they were all using parts of the 3 R's naturally. They related — talking about their own experiences and what the stories reminded them of, although the relating did not always appear in their writing. They were able to retell competently and they enjoyed talking about their favourite parts. They listened to one another, and the listening deepened when they began to piggyback onto one another's talk.

Throughout this study, it seemed clear that the more these learners were invited to use the framework in conversations, the more often they used it in their writing. For the most part, the content of the writing usually resembled, in some way, the talk. The talk served as the rehearsal for their writing.

The writing samples I collected showed that using the 3 R's framework has great potential for helping children in their learning. Retelling came naturally to the children, and was most often used. They began the study only retelling — in talk and writing, "I like the part when..." They continued to retell and needed encouragement as well as modelling and demonstrating to do anything else. Relating made the talk and writing very personal. It presented a fuller picture of the child — the child outside the school setting, the child's *feelings and memories. I noticed that the more I related in my own talk and in my writing, the more the children did. They seemed to really enjoy finding out about me, and they often piggybacked onto my talk. "Oh. That reminds me of..." Reflecting was there in the talk, but it was much more difficult to see in the children's writing. I realized that unless we are listening carefully, we can sometimes miss the learners' questions and wonderings. Knowing the learners' questions gives us clear insights into what they are thinking and what they want to learn about. Where reflecting was present in the talk and writing, it was evident that the children were predicting and inferring, thinking further about issues and events, spurred on by the read-aloud experience.*

From this study, it was clear that the content and fluency of the four children's writing had improved. Upon reflection, I realized that even though we had talked together and we had written and shared our writing in conversation, at no time had the children seen my writing in print. I wonder if I had written back to them and had demonstrated specific skills, concepts or interesting spellings of words, what effect this would have had on their writing?

From my study, I was struck by the fact that new and continuing questions were naturally arising that needed answering. I had the starting point for other interesting studies based on my actions, connections and reflections.

*With any action research, we are usually left with different questions to pursue. As we **retell** our classroom stories, **relate** them to our personal experiences, and **reflect** upon our classroom learning opportunities, we wonder and continue to search for answers. This use of the 3 R's becomes personal inquiry and lifelong learning.*

Experiences With Professional Reading and Writing: *Susan and Maxine*

As university course directors for summer in-service courses for teachers, we invited the teachers in our classes to use the 3 R's framework to respond to personal experiences, course meetings, speakers and professional readings. They wrote to the same partner every other day in a dialogue response journal. Here is one letter sent to the course participants inviting them to begin a response journal.

Dear Friends,

During the following weeks together, everyone will be keeping a journal or a notebook in which to write, doodle, sketch...and to share with another. Your notebook is mostly a place for you and your partner to talk day-by-day for four weeks about books, reading, writing, authors, illustrators, ideas, experiences, and course activities.

The purpose of this journal is to invite the writers and readers to **retell**, **relate** and **reflect**, by recording understandings and knowledge (*retell*), connections to related events or experiences (*relate*), questions, positions, ideas, or just wonderings (*reflect*) — a kind of "Draft Thinking" book of writings. You will be chatting in letter form to me and to your partner. The pattern will be to write one day and read and write back (*respond*) the next. I will be the reader on the side. All the letters will stay together chronologically as a record of the thinking, learning, writing and reading we do together.

I am looking forward to your journal of letters.

Maxine

After writing and responding regularly for about three weeks, several participants wrote:

The notion of Retell, Relate and Reflect — known as the 3 R's — is now an internal chant! Retelling helps me to remember. Relating adds a personal touch to the learning as well as a reason to think and internalize the retelling. It is the reflection aspect that is the hardest but the most important aspect to include.

— Linda Smith

A subtle change has crept into our learning. Yes, we are still retelling what we have heard, read and done, but we have begun to do more relating and reflecting. The information which we have taken in has assumed more meaning for us as we relate it to our own experiences, and reflection is a natural outgrowth of the relating as we take a step back and attempt to gain perspective on our experiences.

— Marilyn Peavoy

I think the focus of this course is reflection. I think that you have taken on the task of teaching teachers to reflect — to think.

I thought I was prepared for this course. I was prepared to write 50-page essays if need be. I was prepared to sit and soak. I was prepared to read book after book. I was prepared to do a gigantic display on environmental studies or some other topic of interest. I was NOT prepared to think.

It has not been painless. My husband keeps asking me what is wrong. The workload does not SEEM heavy. I am not typing for hours. I answer, "Leave me alone please. I have to think. Thinking hurts." He worries that I am not well.

By writing in our journals, we were forced to think — to retell, to relate, to reflect — to think about the endless stream of good ideas in this course.

This course is about growth — growth as a person, growth as a teacher, growth as a writer, growth as a professional, and growth as an intellectual, as a thinker. This course is also about risk taking, because we have been encouraged to take risks and make mistakes in a non-threatening, relaxed and comfortable atmosphere.

— Joan Brake

These three people consciously practised the framework of retelling, relating and reflecting in their talking and writing, and through this practice, they realized its potential for thinking. We are convinced that the more one uses the framework, the more the talking and thinking flow. The "internal chant" continues to grow spontaneously and naturally in all areas of life. It encompasses all learning and teaching.

Experiences With Personal Response at the Secondary School Level: *Susan*

As a parent of sixteen-year-old twin daughters, I often found myself being asked by them to help revise and edit their assignments. Of course I shared the 3 R's framework with them, and as I worked with them, I noticed that their writing abilities improved dramatically when they began to use the 3 R's framework in their work. In fact, their teachers now think they are excellent writers because they are able to capture the essence of their topics (retell), they connect their own personal experiences and feelings (relate), and their reflections are usually intriguing and thought-provoking (reflect).

In Marnie's English course, part of each student's responsibilities was to tutor a younger student who needed help. After the students in Marnie's English class read the book <u>Dead Poets Society</u> by N. H. Kleinbaum, they were asked to write a response. Marnie wrote:

> Todd Andersen, one of the main characters in this book *Dead Poets Society*, went through many changes as a student and as a person. I felt the struggle between Todd Andersen and himself was a central theme in the book. Throughout the book, he was struggling with himself to overcome his loneliness, his low academic and social skills and his low self-esteem. He wanted to be in control with confidence, but at the start, he was unsociable and distant. He could not talk in public or in the classroom. He was uncomfortable when in a crowd of people and enjoyed his own company only. Throughout the book, with the support of his teacher Mr. Keating, he began to work and change and make a difference in himself. He tried new techniques with his studies, and he experienced new things with his friends. Towards the end of the story, he protests his teacher's dismissal and becomes a leader, standing up in the class on his desk, speaking his mind, speaking out for his friend. At the end of the book, he had won the struggle for confidence and security, and he was stronger, had a high self-esteem and had overall succeeded.
>
> Todd's success represents what we have the potential to do with our students in this course. They are struggling with themselves to try new ways of reading and writing. I wonder how these students feel when they have to read silently in class yet do not understand what they are reading, when they are asked to read out loud in the class and they stumble over every word, when they feel that they are stupid because they are confused and frustrated? These students with literacy problems, like Todd Andersen at the beginning of the book, must feel very low and sad. I'm glad that in this course, we are doing something to help shape these students with problems into better scholars. We are attempting to change their work habits, improve their skills, encourage them to want to learn and stay in school, just like the teacher, Mr. Keating, did in the book. We are working to help them to improve their level of knowledge and literacy. Hopefully, by the end of our course, they will develop and improve as much as Todd has in this story, and hopefully, they will succeed in school in the long run.

In Marnie's first paragraph, she retells the main ideas in the story, and reflects when she includes her own ideas, interpretations and insights — e.g., "...he had won the struggle for confidence and security..." In her second paragraph, she relates by making connections between the relationships in the book and her role as tutor. Her statements beginning with "I wonder..." add to the impact and appeal of the paragraph and encourage the reader to reflect with her. She ends with a hopeful prediction for the future (reflect).

It is interesting to analyze the writing of secondary school learners to see how often they retell, relate and reflect in their written responses or essays. I believe the quality of their writing will improve when they are introduced to the 3 R's framework.

Experiences Using the 3 R's When Assessing and Evaluating: *Susan and Maxine*

Using the 3 R's framework for assessing and evaluating is another practical use for the framework. As course directors, we used the 3 R's framework as a tool to watch, listen and provide feedback to participants making presentations. Pairs or triads of teachers presented to a small group on a topic or issue of their choice. We visited each session and recorded our observations on a circular framework, one for each pair or triad of presenters (see Figure 2.5; Figure

Figure 2.5   Using the 3 R's Framework for Assessment and Evaluation

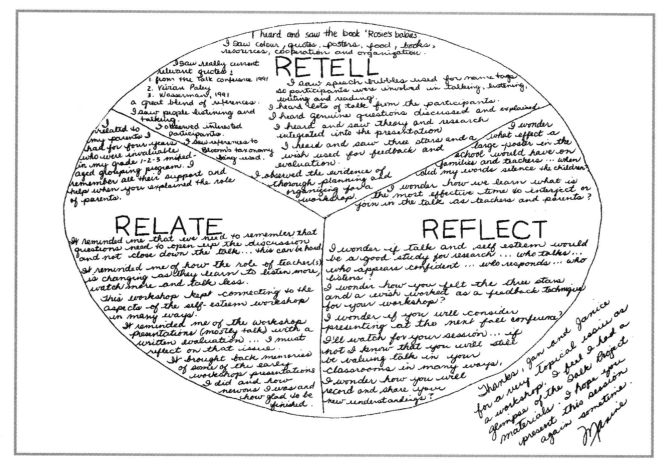

2.5 is reproduced — not filled in! — as Draft Planning Sheet 8, "Using the 3 R's Framework To Assess and Evaluate").

This assessment and evaluation tool helped us keep our observations and recordings focussed and non-judgemental. This technique is particularly useful when working with learners in classrooms as a tool for recording what we see and hear when learners participate in various presentations.

Experiences With Literature Circles: *Maxine*

In my role as course director, I was working with a small group of teachers who were taking their Reading Specialist Course. In this group, there were teachers from all grades and divisions, including teachers working in special education positions. We were all familiar with the 3 R's framework. Each teacher had a copy of the circular model for reference and was practising in a shared response journal.

We decided to spend one of our sessions practising and experiencing "literature circles." I had read and talked about the topic of literature circles, and had worked with children with this teaching strategy, but I had not yet worked with other adults.

I chose the novel <u>Hare's Choice</u> by Dennis Hamley and illustrated by Meg Rutherford. This is a powerful novel about two children who discover the dead body of a beautiful hare on their way to school one morning. They gently wrap it in a sweater and carry it to school. Their teacher receives it positively and encourages the wondering, and the entire class becomes involved in a cooperative writing session creating and telling the story of the "Queen of the Hares." Later in this novel, the dead hare has a choice to make in the afterlife — whether to join with the large masses of dead animals, or to enter into the world of storybook characters. This choice encourages much reflection and debate.

We began this literature circle experience by agreeing to prepare for the next session by independently reading the novel. That was our shared homework! This was the only instruction, direction and expectation.

The next session, I came with my rereading done, an open mind, and my professional journal. I had decided that I would act as listener, not as talker or questioner. I arrived with book in hand having acquired new feelings, ideas, interpretations, and wonderings about this story.

To begin, I invited each participant to say something about the book. I had no prearranged set of questions, yet no one had difficulty responding. It was fascinating! We sat together around a big rectangular table and the talk continued for the entire morning. I became one of the group, yet as group leader, I was conscious of my role and was careful not to control the talk. Each person shared individual responses unique to his or her experiences and knowledge.

Some piggybacked onto another's talk, making connections, asking questions, providing insights, extending the thinking. We were all able to retell, relate and reflect, each in our own way. It was indeed a special experience for me, and I believe, for the group. Creating and exploring literature together as we did provided us with an understanding of literature circles that we will always remember because we actually did it — we were engaged and took responsibility for our own learning.

Before we decided to spend a session experiencing a literature circle, we had read professional books and articles to gain the theory and knowledge. I had presented how literature circles might be organized, what they might look and sound like, and how one might begin. The hands-on experience of a literature circle provided each one of us with the opportunity to practise and apply what we knew and understood about this strategy. We gave one another feedback that day, and further along in the course. Following our course, everyone practised and applied this strategy with different groups — teachers and children.

Later that year, I worked with a larger group of people using the same text. There were three groups with about seven members in each group. This time, I provided some points as backup items to discuss and I moved from group to group. What was fascinating to me was that no group began the same way or even with similar points. One group used chart paper to diagram their shared understandings.

The experience for the people in this larger group was similar to the other group I had worked with, but it was very different for me because I was moving in and out of the groups.

Literature circles is a powerful strategy that can be used with one small group, with several small groups or with the whole class. It provides a purposeful and natural opportunity for everyone to retell, relate and reflect. It frees the teacher and the learners, allowing them to talk together about the selection, story structures, unique facts and techniques that can be learned from books. The questions emerge from the readers, and the teacher and learners act as listeners and/or questioners.

Based on my own experiences, I am personally most comfortable working with one group at a time. However, I did learn that literature circles can be done with the whole class and there is still an indescribable excitement — certainly memorable experiences for everyone.

I wonder how it would be for children to have these ongoing opportunities in all areas of the curriculum. If we were to provide our learners with literature circles in all areas of the curriculum, we could give them many opportunities to practise, accept responsibility, value responding, and experience the joy of learning. Perhaps they would learn to talk about books and all kinds of experiences, and this experience would become a skill for life-long learning.

Experiences With Book Talks: *Maxine*

One day, in my role as coordinator, I visited some primary classes to read aloud. Before beginning, I asked the children to think of their favourite book. I described a favourite book as the book that they would most like to have read to them, that they would like to read again and again and again, or the one that is nearly falling apart from being used so much.

I gave them a few minutes to think. I asked them if they would share with me their titles. I heard the title Black Beauty *and before that* The Secret Garden*. I heard someone say, "My mom and dad are both reading to me* James and The Giant Peach*." I heard many titles mentioned, such as:*

- *Go, Dog, Go by Gail Gibbons*
- *Me Too by Mercer Mayer*
- *Dr. Seuss's ABC by Dr. Seuss*
- *One Fish, Two Fish, Red Fish, Blue Fish by Dr. Seuss*
- *The Littlest Mermaid by John T. Stapleton*
- *Sleeping Beauty*

The children's favourite books ranged from books about fairy tales, grocery stores, book clubs, to novels owned or borrowed.

I responded after each learner shared his or her favourite by retelling, relating and reflecting:

- *"I know that author..."*
- *"That book is similar to..."*
- *"I read a version of that book to my children."*
- *"I wonder who read the story to you?"*
- *"I wonder where you got that book?"*

Nearly every learner told about a book, a poem, a song or a story from home, or pointed to one in the classroom. These were what they remembered and could read or listen to. Their talk provided me and their classroom teacher with many insights into their language, literacy, story development and experience. Their talk became more data for the teacher's collection of baseline knowledge about each learner. We were able in this situation to observe and record what the learners were sharing about their personal story experiences.

That day I was filled with wonder! I wonder what would happen if we invited the children to bring their books into the classroom for awhile? I wonder what would happen if we began the year with sharings of favourite titles? I wonder if we invited the children to draw or paint or write or tell about a particular part or person or place from their favourite books, what the classroom bulletin boards would look like? I wonder what I would hear if there were small reading (literature or poetry) circles, and learners were invited to talk and ask questions about these favourite books? I wonder...

Experiences Using the 3 R's in the Role of "Administrator as Coach": *Susan*

During the summer of 1990, a teacher-consultant participated in our in-service course for teachers. The following year, she was promoted to the role of vice-principal. After one year in this new role, she talked about her experiences and learnings using our 3 R's framework. As a result of her summer experience practising retelling, relating and reflecting, she had internalized the framework and she used it often and naturally in talk and in writing. She shared how she used it in her role as administrator for evaluation and professional discussion with teachers.

She said:

When I go into a teacher's classroom to observe and evaluate, I take a pen and lots of paper with me. I sit myself off to the side of the room and I write everything I see and hear. Before my visit, I tell the teacher what I am going to do so that he or she will not be nervous when I write. I tell the teacher that I will share everything I write — there are no secrets. I draw a line down the middle of the page and I write everything I see in the first column. Here, I am retelling. I relate in my mind, and in the second column, I write questions that come to me as I watch and listen. Here I am reflecting.

Afterwards, I go to the photocopy machine and make a copy for the teacher. I meet with the teacher as soon after as possible, hand him or her the copy of my writing, and we discuss my observations and reflections, and the teacher's perceptions. We have a copy of my visit in writing and a place to begin our dialogue. The 3 R's framework helps me to structure my thinking.

— Patricia Adams, Principal

It was because of this teacher's experience that when I became principal, I began to use the 3 R's framework to help structure my observations and thinking when I evaluate a teacher's performance. I find that teachers welcome the objective retell because it acts as a mirror of my visit. They appreciate the constructive feedback I give in the form of suggestions when I reflect. We both relate orally when we talk together afterwards. Figure 2.6 provides a sample of one of my visits.

Figure 2.6   Jill: Observations and Reflections

When I walked into the classroom, many children were seated on the floor, some were at their desks, and you were seated in the rocking chair at the side of the room. The room is organized, bright and colourful with many displays of children's work. There is a warm comfortable atmosphere in the room.

You were having a discussion with the whole group about their recent winter holiday. You invited everyone who wanted to contribute to speak. You stopped the group a number of times and reminded everyone to listen. The children responded to the signal of putting your hand up and attended immediately. Some specific ways you used to remind children to attend were making eye contact, putting your hand gently on their shoulders and whispering quietly to individuals. These strategies ensured that everyone listened without you singling out individuals. This is another part of the warm, comfortable atmosphere in the room.

You listened to the children's stories with interest. They enjoy watching you talk because your facial expressions and body language show your enthusiasm and interest. The questions you asked were genuine questions that are often part of informal conversations. The children's stories were informative and I learned a great deal about what they do during vacations. I was very impressed by the interest, participation and listening ability of all the children.

This whole class group experience ended at recess time. Since a few children still needed to tell their stories, you promised them there would be time later. It was recess and the class left the room quickly.

This large group discussion time reminded me of some of my meetings and how it seemed to be a long time to concentrate and attend before a break.

I wonder if you could have achieved your outcomes in a more interactive way? For at least 60 minutes, the children were sitting listening to one another talk and to you asking questions. Although it was an enjoyable, relaxed discussion with many children offering input or asking questions, it created a situation where you needed to remind them several times to listen to others, remember to be polite, stay on task... I wonder if the children had been asked to work in pairs or small groups, as well as a whole group, if this would have provided a different level of participation and involvement? For example, the lesson might be structured in the following way:

With the large group:

. choose only three or four learners to tell their stories to the whole group (e.g., pick a name out of a hat, or choose a child who went on a trip, a child who stayed in the city, one who had company, one who did something very unusual, etc.).

In partners (and/or small groups of 3 or 4 learners):

. take turns telling their story while others listen and ask questions
. discuss what features of the holiday they experienced
. use chart paper to record, e.g.:

   - features in common
   - trips they went on
   - number of people who went somewhere (can lead to graphing)
   - where they went (can lead to mapping)
   - highlights of each person's holiday
   - number of people they encountered during the holiday from the class
   - number of new people they met
   - TV shows, videos, movies they watched...
   -

. choose a favourite story to tell the whole group

Figure 2.6   continued

Jill, I continue to enjoy working and talking with you. You listen to suggestions and make effective modifications. Your knowledge and understanding of the personalities and abilities of every child shines through whenever you talk about them. I enjoy your sense of humour, and your willingness to listen and respond with understanding and caring to everyone. I look forward to working together again and talking about the changes and modifications you incorporate into your teaching practices as you continue to strive to use learning and teaching strategies in order to promote and develop interactive experiences for everyone.

PRACTISING THE 3 R'S IN CLASSROOM SITUATIONS

In the following section, we outline practical strategies for the classroom, highlighting clearly what the 3 R's framework looks like and what it sounds like in many different teaching and learning situations.

Our experiences have taught us that after we model and demonstrate the 3 R's framework several times in a variety of ways in whole-class sessions, our learners learn effectively in small groups and individually when we give each learner a copy of or post a chart of the framework for reference. We invite you to reproduce Draft Planning Sheets 3, 4, 5, and 6, "The 3 R's Framework: Retelling, Relating and Reflecting," "Retell," "Relate," and "Reflect," for your learners' use.

Any time we directly teach the use of the 3 R's framework and when we give out or post the framework and the starter phrases, we remind our learners that the 3 R's framework is **circular**. We point out and demonstrate that they can retell, relate, and reflect in any order when they respond to their learning — they may reflect first, then retell, etc.

NOTE: If you teach in a school with a large English-as-a-second-language population, you need to have available books, newspapers, or magazines in the children's native languages. Before you encourage these children to respond in English, you may wish to encourage them to speak in their native language, especially when they are first learning how to apply the 3 R's framework. You may need to translate any notes you send home. In this way, families will understand what is happening in their children's classrooms. They will be encouraged to read and talk together about shared experiences in the languages used in their homes.

# Practising the 3 R's in Read-Aloud

Read-aloud is an essential teaching/learning strategy that brings the world of story, poetry, information, and a wide variety of quality literature to learners of all ages. It allows learners to be immersed in and appreciate many genres. Learners benefit by hearing the sound and structure of language. Read-aloud is teacher modelling and demonstrating, and it encourages learner response, thinking, discussing and questioning.

Read-aloud is when teachers do some of our best teaching. We practise read-aloud when we want to share information, issues or ideas, when we want to share something we love and appreciate, or when read-aloud offers opportunities for integration across the curriculum. We practise read-aloud when it initiates, extends and enriches curriculum, or when we use it to teach skills and techniques of reading. Read-aloud should be practised at every opportunity — preferably several times daily.

We can discover a great deal about our learners when we practise read-aloud. We use the read-aloud to learner-watch and learner-listen. We continue to collect and interpret information about individual learners in order to program appropriately. We record significant observations as part of valuing and evaluating the teaching and learning experiences.

One way to value read-aloud experiences is to keep a log of the read-aloud titles used by month, term and year. Such a log provides us with a written record we can use to self-evaluate as we look back over the year and reflect on the balance of literature in our program. **Balance** means many things. It means a balanced study of the works of male and female authors and illustrators. It means a balance between the literature from a learner's own country and literature from around the world. It means intentionally considering a balance and variety of the different genres of literature (fiction, poetry, wordless, rhyme, folklore, concept, alphabet, fantasy, non-fiction, chapters, how-to's...), and a balance of focus in the different curriculum areas.

Figure 2.7 provides one teacher's planning sheet showing a literature-balanced program at-a-glance.

This format can be used as a flexible planning sheet that lists possible read-alouds for the upcoming year, or it can be used as a continuous record sheet for read-aloud experiences throughout the year. It becomes a record of the year's literature experiences and can be used as a communication pamphlet for families.

We invite you to use Figure 2.7 (Draft Planning Sheet 50, "Literature: A Year-at-a-Glance") to record your journey towards a literature-balanced program. An alternative format is suggested in Figure 2.8 on page 54 (Draft Planning Sheet 51, "Balancing a Literature-Based Program"). We also invite you to use Figure 2.9 on page 55 (Draft Planning Sheet 54, "Guide for Investigating Literature") which lists things to think and talk about when reading, examining and exploring all aspects of a book, during read-aloud experiences and throughout the day.

In the classroom, the read-aloud situation is an extremely effective way to model and demonstrate the 3 R's framework. When we teachers practise retelling, relating and reflecting about the literature we share with large groups, small groups or individuals, we invite and encourage thinking, talking, writing, creating and questioning. We encourage our learners to respond naturally, automatically and uniquely.

Figure 2.7   Literature-Based Program: A Year-at-a-Glance

19 _90_ to 19 _91_

Category headings:

- **SOCIAL/EMOTIONAL**
  - **P.I.E.S.** • Feeling • Sharing • Thinking • Reflecting • Succeeding • Celebrating
  - **Self and Society**
- **INTELLECTUAL**
  - **Math, Science and Technology** • Exploring • Investigating • Patterning • Predicting • Constructing • Problem Solving
  - **Language** • Listening • Speaking • Reading • Writing • Dramatizing • Viewing
- **PHYSICAL**
  - **The Arts** • Music • Drama • Movement • Visual Arts • Viewing • Creating

First Term

Month	Self and Society	P.I.E.S.	Math, Science and Technology	Language	The Arts (Physical)
September	Swimmy, Leo Lionni	Where the Sidewalk Ends, Shel Silverstein	Salmon for Simon, Betty Waterton; House for Hermit Crab, Eric Carle	By the Sea, Mary Hoffman; Sea Swan, Kathryn Lasky; Zoom at Sea, Tim Wynne-Jones	My Very First / Last Time; Reflections, Ann Jonas; Do Not Open; Playing With Plasticine / By the Sea, Barbara Reid
October	Away, Arlette Lavie	Jelly Belly, Dennis Lee; Half a World Away	One Watermelon Seed; The Amazing Apple Book, Paulette Bourgeois	Heckedy Peg, Audrey Wood; Tailypo, Joanna and Paul Galdone; The Witches, Roald Dahl; Hallowe'en ABC, Eve Merriam	Scary Scary Halloween, Eve Bunting; The Colour Dance, Ann Jonas; Where the Forest Meets the Sea, Jeannie Baker
November	Here I Am!, Jean Little	Miss Rumphius, Barbara Cooney	The Last of the Dinosaurs, Jim Murphy; Hey! Get Off Our Train, John Burningham	Farewell to Shady Glade, Bill Peet; How I Captured a Dinosaur, Henry Schwartz	Dinosaur Dream, Robin M. Koontz; The Little Drummer Boy, Ezra Jack Keats
December	Love You Forever, Robert Munsch	William's Doll, Charlotte Zolotow	The Cobweb Curtain, Jenny Koralek and Pauline Baynes; The Empty Pot, Demi	Christmas Alphabet, Carolyn Wells; The Night Before Christmas, Clement C. Moore; The Best Christmas Pageant Ever, Barbara Robinson; Snow White in New York, Fiona French	Christmas and Each Peach Pear Plum, Janet and Allan Ahlberg; Jingle Bells, Maryann Kovalski

Second Term

Month	Self and Society	P.I.E.S.	Math, Science and Technology	Language	The Arts (Physical)
January	Tales of a Fourth Grade Nothing, Judy Blume	Jumanji, Chris Van Allsburg	Five Secrets in a Box, Catherine Brighton; Dr. Zed's Surprise Science, Gordon Penrose	Sylvester and the Magic Pebble, William Steig; The True Story of the Three Pigs, Jon Scieszka	The Jolly Postman, Janet and Allan Ahlberg; King Bidgood's in the Bathtub, Audrey Wood; Pop-Ups
February	George's Marvelous Medicine, Roald Dahl	Light in the Attic, Shel Silverstein	Simon and the Snowflakes, Gilles Tibo; Sadie and the Snowman, Allen Morgan; Mike Mulligan and His Steam Shovel, Virginia Lee Burton	Puddleman, Ted Staunton; The Pancake Boy, Lorinda Bryan Cauley	The Snowman, Raymond Briggs; How to Make Pop-Ups, Joan Irvine
March	Ralph and the Motorcycle, Beverly Cleary	Block City, Robert Louis Stevenson	Katy and the Big Snow, Virginia Lee Burton; Machines as Tall as Giants, Carolyn Paul Strickland	Angela's Airplane, Robert Munsch; The Biggest Truck, David Lyon	Wheels on the Bus, Maryann Kovalski; Matthew and the Midnight Tow Truck, Allen Morgan

Third Term

Month	Self and Society	P.I.E.S.	Math, Science and Technology	Language	The Arts (Physical)
April	What's That Noise?, Michèle Lemieux	Velveteen Rabbit, Margery Williams	Wolf Island, Celia Godkin; The Great Northern Diver, B. Esbensen; The Goodnight Circle, Carolyn Lesser	Owl Moon, Jane Yolen; Sparrow's Song, Ian Wallace; Wildlife ABC, Jan Thornhill	Catching the Wind, Joanne Ryder; All I See, Cynthia Rylant
May	The Important Book, Margaret Wise Brown	Don't Eat Spiders, Robert Heidbreder	Ant Cities, Arthur Dorros; Have Fun With Magnets: An Ontario Science Centre Book; Nancy Winslow Parker and Joan Richards	Two Bad Arts; Doodlebug Series, Stephen Cosgrove	Went A-Courting, Wendy Watson; A Kettle of Hawks, Jim Arnosky
June	(Margaret Wise Brown)	Once There Were Giants, Martin Waddell; Rosie's Babies, Martin Waddell	Spiders, Margaret Wise Brown	Elbert's Bad Word; The Important Book, Karen Patkau / Penny Dale	The Napping House, Audrey Wood; There Was an Old Lady, Pam Adams

Figure 2.8 Balancing a Literature-Based Program

Balancing a Literature-Based Program

Teacher's Name: _C. Jones_

Grade: _4_

Term: _Spring_

TITLE OF SELECTION	TYPE OF LITERATURE (fiction, non-fiction, poetry, rhyme, folklore, concept, alphabet fantasy, chapter book, picture book, wordless book, how-to...)	AREAS OF CURRICULUM FOCUS (Language, Math, Science and Technology, Self and Society, the Arts)	AUTHOR/ ILLUSTRATOR (Canadian, American, or International? Male or Female?)
All I See	picture book fiction	Visual Art	Cynthia Rylant (American female)
Wolf Island	picture book fiction	Science and the Environment — Balance in Nature	Celia Godkin (Canadian female)

Figure 2.9 Guide for Investigating Literature

Guide for Investigating Literature

Title of Book: _____

Author(s): _____

Illustrator: _____

Explore, think and talk about:

- **the book jacket/cover**
  - the title
  - the author
  - the illustrator
  - the publisher
- **the title**
  - a statement, a question or a list of words
  - the number of words
  - the type of print
  - the punctuation used
  -
- **the title page**
  - the title
  - the author
  - the illustrator
  - the publisher
  -
- **the copyright page**
  - date of publication
  - how many reprints
  - copyright holder
  - original publisher
  - country (city) where published
  -
- **the end pages**
  - the dedication
  - how it is worded
  - pictures...
  -
- **information about the author and/or illustrator**
- **the illustrations**
  - initial impressions
  - colour
  - size
  - style
  - technique
  - background
  -
- **the format**
  - large and/or mini illustrations
  - where print is on the page
  -

- **the text**
  - size of print
  - type of print
  - amount on a page
  -
- **the language**
  - adverbs
  - adjectives
  - verbs
  - metaphors
  - unique words
  -
- **the language structures**
  - contractions
  - possessives
  - quotation marks
  -
- **the print**
  - style of print used
  - colour
  - size
  - shape
  -
- **the structure**
  - plot
  - sequence of events, key events
  - tension, conflict
  -
- **the characters**
  - how they emerge and develop
  - flat or full (highly developed)
  - what they say and do and when
  - interaction among characters
  -
- **the setting** — place(s), period, time, predictions...
- **the time**
  - chronological
  - sequential, flashbacks, jumps forward, how is it noted

- **the point of view** — author's position, first person, third person, how author's point of view is revealed...
- **the mood** — emotions, feelings, dialogue, attitude revealed by text and illustrations....
- **the symbols** — meaning through symbols...
- **the figures of speech** — metaphors, similes...
- **the style** — first impressions, the sound of the piece, how language, illustrations, characterization are used...
- **the beginning and the ending**
  - how does it begin, how does it end
  - what text, illustrations, print... are used, similarities and differences, connections...
- **the genre** — fairy tale, poetry, historical fiction, non-fiction...
- **the unique elements** — an unusual dedication, a book of letters...
- **the kind of book/format**
  - wordless
  - novel
  - picture book
  - paperback
  - how-to
  - pop-up
  - accordion
  -
- **curriculum connections**
- **other**

It is our important responsibility to select the read-aloud carefully. We need to be very familiar with the selection before we read aloud. We look for the potentials and possibilities in each piece and make connections to curriculum and instructional goals. We use what we know about our learners (their strengths, interests and needs) to select appropriate read-alouds. We connect this knowledge about our learners with our knowledge of the curriculum and learning expectations to make purposeful selections. We also remember that listening levels for learners are usually three to four years beyond the learners' grade and age, and we consider this fact when we select read-alouds.

Questions emerge naturally from read-aloud experiences. We invite learners to talk about the text, and we give them time to talk. By inviting learners to retell, and encouraging them to tell one another what the text reminds them of, we are providing the learners with a process to foster, support and value their conversations. When we model and demonstrate by sharing our own wonderings, unanswered questions and ideas, learners begin to share in return. Together, everyone learns and practises questioning and thinking. By joining in the process through retelling, relating and reflecting, we discover a framework for talking about any text or experience naturally and automatically. Shared learnings begin to blend and merge together in a sea of understandings, wonderings, seekings, solutions and discoveries.

The following is one way to structure a read-aloud situation.

Beginning

- Organize the classroom to provide a comfortable place to gather together for read-aloud time.
- Carefully select the read-aloud.
- Practise the read-aloud in advance to enhance your oral reading skills, to model ways of reading expressively and dramatically, and to plan appropriate instruction or discussion points.
- Have conversations with learners, and invite predictions and questions by looking at the cover, title, pictures, author, illustrator, diagrams, table of contents, index...
- Examine the illustrations.
- Share related experiences.

During the read-aloud

- Begin to read.
- Accept spontaneous talk.
- Be sensitive to and value the listeners' comments and questions.
- Watch and listen.
- Pause when appropriate. (Practising the read-aloud in advance helps to identify natural pauses.)

After the read-aloud

- Share personal responses.
- Model the framework of retell, relate, reflect — "This is about...", "It reminds me of...", "I wonder why..."

- Invite the learners to turn to the person closest to them and talk about the text and/or illustrations.
- Watch and listen carefully to their conversations.
- Consider recording some of the responses on chart paper for later reference.

Assessing and Evaluating

- Decide on a system of record-keeping and evaluation. (You may want to use Draft Planning Sheet 8, "Using the 3 R's Framework To Assess and Evaluate," to record your observations. See also Draft Planning Sheets 52 and 53, "Shared Reading Record" and "Guided Reading Record.")
- Continue to watch and listen, asking yourself:

Are the learners **retelling** by:
  - talking about their favourite parts
  - recalling what happened
  - retelling the facts or events in sequence
  - sharing the text structure — characters, setting, plot...
  -

Are the learners **relating** by:
  - making connections to their own lives
  - relating events to their own experiences
  - making comparisons to other stories, television programs, films, or things they have heard about
  - comparing characters to relatives, friends or people they know, or to characters from other sources — books, film, television, theatre...
  -

Are the learners **reflecting** by:
  - wondering about something in particular or asking questions
  - making statements based on new understandings
  - suggesting a variety of ideas
  - saying "I want to's," reading the story again, drawing pictures, finding similar texts, rewriting the text, constructing the setting...
  -

Continuing

- Choose another text to read.
- Continue to model/demonstrate the 3 R's framework.
- Continue to watch and listen carefully to learners' responses.
- Share the importance of read-alouds and the "year-at-a-glance" record sheet with learners, families, and other educators.

Some titles you might begin with are

- *Everybody Needs a Rock* by Byrd Baylor
- *The Great Northern Diver: The Loon* by Barbara Juster Esbensen
- *Owl Moon* by Jane Yolen
- *Island Boy* by Barbara Cooney
- *Dawn* by Molly Bang

- *Sea Swan* by Kathryn Lasky
- *All I See* by Cynthia Rylant
- *Wolf Island* by Celia Godkin
- *Joyful Noise: Poems for Two Voices* by Paul Fleischman

For additional titles to use in the read-aloud learning experience, check with a teacher-librarian for John Newbury and Caldecott Award winning titles, or write to the Canadian Children's Book Centre (CCBC) for a list of award-winning titles, or consult Jim Trelease's *Read-Aloud Handbook*.

 ## Practising the 3 R's in Shared Reading and Paired Reading

Shared Reading can be practised with a large group, small group or with a partner. It is a collaborative reading strategy where everyone in a group reads aloud together, from a big book, chart, overhead or board, or from multiple copies of the same text or page. It is based on the bedtime story experience in which the reader shares in the reading and rereading of stories, rhymes, poems, songs and information.

The strategies of *chanting*, *choral reading* and *dramatic reading* are examples of shared reading. *Chanting* is a form of supportive reading aloud together and is often accompanied by some body movement, such as clapping, snapping or tapping. *Choral reading* is usually a large group activity in which different groups or individuals read aloud specific parts of the selection. Often, the participants decide how to vary their voices in speed, volume, pitch, tone and rhythm. Choral reading is usually rehearsed several times before a presentation. *Dramatic reading* is a group reading of a play or script, which includes different characters speaking. It is sometimes material created by teachers and learners when they rewrite stories and legends. A narrator might read the parts of the story that cannot be expressed in dialogue.

When shared reading is experienced in groups of two, it is referred to as **paired reading**. Paired reading may also be called *buddy reading* or *partner reading*. The groups of two in paired reading may be peers, older students partnered with younger students, or students paired with adults (parent/guardian volunteers, university students, seniors, grandparents...) from the school and community. When two individuals read together, the more fluent readers often take leadership roles, while the beginning and developing readers gain valuable exposure to higher levels of reading material. Paired reading is an ideal way to promote the reading of novels or "chapter" books, or informational texts.

Partners involved in paired reading might read a shared copy of one title, two copies of the same title, two related titles, or two unrelated titles. The two readers might read in unison or each reader might read individually while the other one listens and reads along. In this latter case, the two readers decide who reads first and they take turns reading, listening, talking and questioning.

When the material is read by first one reader, and then the same line or passage is repeated by the second reader, the process is called *echo reading*. This technique is effective in helping to build confidence in the reader who is doing the repeating.

During these paired reading situations, the framework of retelling, relating and reflecting can be used to encourage and value talking, thinking and learning about the material. Modelling, demonstrating and practising reading encourage learners to respond to literature naturally. Paired reading techniques invite and value personal stories. All age groups enjoy reading and talking together. Young learners buddied with older learners, or fluent readers buddied with beginning readers, help to encourage leadership and cooperative skills. The older fluent readers can be responsible for a larger amount of the reading, but both partners take turns responding. In this way, everyone becomes involved in reading, listening, talking, viewing and thinking.

The following outlines one way to structure a paired reading session. We call this particular format *"Paired Read and Respond."*

Beginning

- Organize the learners in groups of two.
- Organize a collection of books.
- Include a variety of poetry, fiction and non-fiction titles.
- Collect two copies of the same titles.
- Demonstrate by role playing what the experience will look and sound like.
- Outline expectations on a chart or the blackboard.
- Invite the pairs of learners to choose two copies of the same book from the collection.
- Encourage the pairs of learners to choose a place in the room to read together.

During the experience

- Clearly give instructions to the learning-partners:
  - Decide who reads first.
  - The first reader reads a "chunk."
  - The listener retells, makes a personal connection (relates) and shares any wonderings or questions (reflects).
  - The listener now reads aloud another chunk.
  - The partner listens and retells, relates, and reflects.
  - Readers and listeners take turns, continuing to read and talk together until the material is finished.

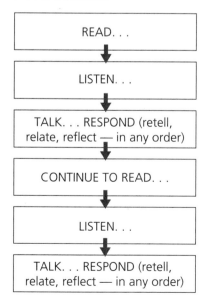

```
        READ. . .
           ↓
       LISTEN. . .
           ↓
 TALK. . . RESPOND (retell,
 relate, reflect — in any order)
           ↓
  CONTINUE TO READ. . .
           ↓
       LISTEN. . .
           ↓
 TALK. . . RESPOND (retell,
 relate, reflect — in any order)
```

Assessing and Evaluating

- Decide on a system of record-keeping and evaluation. (You may want to use Draft Planning Sheet 8, "Using the 3 R's Framework To Assess and Evaluate," to record your observations. See also Draft Planning Sheets 52 and 53, "Shared Reading Record" and "Guided Reading Record.")
- As you continue to watch and listen, ask yourself:
  - What books do the learners choose and why?
  - What places in the room did they choose for their reading and why?
  - What positions do they take as they sit together?
  - Who was the first reader? How did they decide?
  - Does the listener listen with text (follows along) or without text?
  - How do the learners examine the book before beginning?
  - Do the learners make comments about the illustrations?
  - How does the listener retell, relate, reflect (quality, depth of conversation)?
  - How much talk (length of conversation) is happening in between the reading of the chunks of text?
  - Are the learners able to take turns?
  - Who needs clarification or assistance during this process?
  - What happens when the book is finished? Do they continue to talk? Do they choose another book? Do they come to you for assistance, encouragement, reinforcement?
  - What are their questions? (You may wish to record these questions to use as a foundation for further teaching/learning.)

Continuing

- Encourage learners to work with other partners or with a group of 3 or 4. (You may wish to make overhead acetates, mini-posters for reference, or handouts of Draft Planning Sheets 10 and 11, "Group Read and Respond" and "Paired Read and Respond.")
- With the learners, choose different materials (e.g., student-made books, newspaper articles, computer information...) for other paired reading experiences.
- Invite the learners to set goals, respond and share in a variety of ways.
- Share reading and responding techniques with families and encourage them to read to and with their children each day. (If some of your learners' families do not read English, have your information translated and encourage the families to read to their children and talk about their shared reading in the family's first language.)
-

Figure 2.10 (opposite) provides an alternative and useful guide to paired reading. You may wish to give families copies of Draft Planning Sheet 9, "Paired Reading Guide," as reference.

Figure 2.10   Paired Reading Guide

Read for Enjoyment...Information...Meaning!
Don't correct if the meaning is retained!!

Before You Read...

- Talk about the title, characters, pictures...
- Predict what will happen in the story.
- Make connections... "This reminds me of another story, movie, etc."
- Ask questions... "I wonder why..."
-

Strategies to Use While Reading Together...

- Listen and make comments about the content of the reading.
- Point and follow along (for young children).
- When the learner cannot read a word, encourage:
  - guessing
  - skipping
  - looking at the pictures or diagrams
  - thinking about what went before and what might happen next (context)
  - reading ahead to find out more
  - rereading
  - sounding out (using phonics)
  - looking at the root words or word parts
- When the learner is still unable to read the word, then **give the word**.
- If you have given the word a number of times, this material may be too difficult. Try:
  - reading together with the learner
  - reading and the learner reads the last word of each sentence
  - reading one line and the learner reads the next
  - reading the first paragraph, poem, or line, and the learner reads the same again
-

During/After the Reading...

• **Retell**	• **Relate**	• **Reflect**
- This is about...	- I remember...	- I wonder if...
- I notice that...	- This reminds me of...	- I wonder why...
- I especially like...	- It makes me think of...	- What do you think
-	- It makes me feel that...	about...
	-	-

Note: Ask **genuine questions** to which you do not know the answers.

 # Practising the 3 R's in Literature Circles

Literature circles ideally refer to groups of three to five learners reading and talking in depth about the same book or related books (topic or theme related, same authors or illustrators, etc.). These resources, which have something in common, are often referred to as text sets. Literature circles involve sharing a selection with a group — retelling, relating, reflecting — talking and making connections about books, poetry, information, characters, events, experiences, feelings and reflections.

Literature circles are particularly effective with developing to fluent readers, but they can be modified and adapted to match the needs of beginning readers. The novel *Hare's Choice* by Dennis Hamley is an excellent selection to use with older readers and adults for an initial literature circle experience.

During literature circles, we model and demonstrate sharing interpretations, knowledge and questions. In literature circles, learners develop deeper comprehension and understandings of issues, events and themes. Literature circles foster talk, cooperation and independent small group work.

Literature circles should be scheduled over a period of time — over several consecutive days or weeks, at least once a term. We can often choose texts for literature circles that will tie in with a unit of study. Literature circles can be practised in all areas of the curriculum. Only the selection of text, the goals and the learnings may be different. Literature circles are particularly effective before, during or after an author/illustrator or guest presentation.

The following outlines one way to structure a literature circle experience.

Beginning

- Carefully select the text(s) and collect enough copies for everyone in each group.
- Present a short talk advertising the selection(s).
- Organize the groups yourself or invite your learners to choose their groups.
- Post a schedule, including the selection/book title, time for meeting, and the learners involved.
- Invite the learners to read the selection(s).

During the experience

- Discuss and post the expectations for talking about the selection — take turns, look at the speaker...
- Initiate the talk by inviting each learner to retell briefly.
- Encourage relating and reflecting. Model and demonstrate if it seems needed.
- Pose one (or more) broad, open-ended question(s) to initiate the talk, for example:
  - Why do you think the author wrote this book?
  - How does this book compare to other works by the same author?

Assessing and Evaluating

- Continue to watch, listen and record pertinent information.
- Decide on a system of tracking, record-keeping and evaluation. (Refer to Draft Planning Sheet 38, "Group 'Literature Circle' Reading Record.")

Continuing

- Encourage learners to respond in a variety of ways — dramatizing, writing, and/or creating. (Refer to Draft Planning Sheet 39, "Read, Respond and Create.")
- Invite the group to make decisions about responding to a selection.
- Value all varieties of response, including rereading, and reading another selection.
- Consider poetry circles as a similar format.
- Share with families the value and benefits of literature circles.

 # Practising the 3 R's in Language Experience

Language experience is a common teaching strategy used daily or when the need arises in which cooperatively composed stories that take the form of charts, labels, captions, diaries, lists, poetry, etc., are developed using the language of the learners, and this language is recorded by the teacher. The language may be theme, interest, or literature based. It is a strategy that can be used with the whole group, a small group, or an individual. Throughout the language experience, we invite and value conversations and connections — retelling, relating, reflecting.

We provide learners with demonstrations by creating with our learners cooperative charts and inviting the learners to observe how language is used in a variety of situations. The charts may include samples of letters, journal entries, lists, poems, charts, narrative stories, how-to explanations... The charts show models of how language is recorded, which helps learners understand the inter-relationships among talking, listening, writing and reading.

The language experience strategy creates natural opportunities for us to provide mini-lessons based on the needs of the learners. We model and demonstrate standard spelling. We model and demonstrate the process and functions of writing and thinking, and teach specific skills based on what learners know and need to know and on curricular expectations of the class, school and system. In language arts, language experience may be used to focus on specific areas of language instruction, such as cloze, sound letter patterns, phonics and spelling structures. For other areas of the curriculum, the specific skills focus will differ.

Here is one suggestion for structuring a language experience.

Beginning

- In large groups, small groups, or with individuals, invite learners to talk about a common experience or text.

During the experience

- Record the learners' talk and ideas on charts, posters, or overhead.
- Use these cooperatively written charts as models to teach specific skills or structures.
- Read and reread these charts to continue to teach and reinforce specific skills or structures.

- Create together on charts, posters or overheads a variety of formats and genres — letters, lists, advertisements, character sketches, experiments... to model different types of writing.

Assessing and Evaluating

- File a copy of each chart created.
- Notice and record what skills and concepts learners know and what they can read as the chart is read individually.
- Continue to watch and listen and ask yourself:
  - Are the learners able to retell the concepts or ideas?
  - How do the learners relate these ideas to personal experiences?
  - How do the learners demonstrate knowledge of skills or concepts?
  - Do any patterns from the chart reappear in their personal writing?
  - What are their questions?
  - What do they want to learn next?
  -

Continuing

- Provide a copy of each chart for learners to include in personal folders or scrapbooks. These collections of readings become practise reading material for them.
- Provide opportunities for learners to revisit their charts at the beginning, middle, and end of the year.
- Invite children to create their own charts individually or in small groups.
- Share charts and discuss experiences and accomplishments when conferencing with learners, families and other educators.
-

Practising the 3 R's in Journals

Journals are personal notebooks used specifically to record one's thoughts, ideas, feelings, questions and insights. The writing usually seems like speech or "thinking in draft." Journals are also labelled **logs** (*reading logs*, *learning logs*) or **diaries**, and are used for any form of expressive writing. Personal responses are recorded before, during or after a reading, classroom or outside-the-school experience. The writing in these notebooks may be in the form of narratives, letters, lists, diagrams, charts, sketches, drawings, art...

As teachers, we often practise *"written conversation"* by responding in writing in our learners' journals. We *retell* in writing, showing the learners that we are reading their writing and actively listening. We *relate* in writing, bringing ourselves closer to the learners who are interested and curious about us. We *reflect* in writing, asking questions, wondering, giving insights, and we nudge the learners on to further and deeper thinking. When we model and demonstrate the 3 R's framework in our written responses, our learners will be encouraged to use the framework naturally and automatically. Learners often respond, orally and in writing, with more enthusiasm, interest, and on a more personal level.

The following is one way to implement the 3 R's and response journals in your classroom.

Beginning

- Carefully select and practise a book or poem to read aloud.
- Organize materials for writing and demonstrating — chart paper and markers or overhead projector and acetate markers or blackboard and chalk.
- Provide age- and grade-appropriate journals and tools for writing — e.g., blank scrapbooks for young children.
- Provide date and draft stamps.
- Compose a letter to families to be kept in the front of the learners' journals explaining "thinking in draft" and the purpose of the journal. Have the letter translated if appropriate. Figure 2.11 provides a sample letter.

Figure 2.11 Journals: Sample Letter for Families

Dear Families,

Journals are used for children to express thoughts and feelings onto paper.

Children might write about books they have read or heard, about what they know or have learned, or about their experiences, memories, feelings, and how they connect these experiences and feelings with their lives. Children might record their questions and insights, draw pictures, make lists, write stories and poems, share feelings, design charts, sketch diagrams and/or explain experiments.

Please encourage independence and responsibility when children are writing. Journals are a place where children will "think in draft" — that is, they will write down thoughts and ideas quickly, sometimes in point form and sometimes by drawing. If children ask you for help, please help by discussing with them what they want to say, or by commenting on their ideas, order and flow of language. Please value their guesses about spelling and grammar. From their approximated spellings and grammar usage, I will see where to provide instruction and/or support. Therefore, in their journals, grammar and spelling will remain uncorrected. This journal is used as a vehicle to encourage understanding, thinking and reflecting.

It would be greatly appreciated if you would respond to your child's work by writing a letter in the journal. You might write about a part that you particularly liked, the connections or memories you have to similar experiences, and/or your questions, suggestions or insights gained from reading and sharing the journal. Remember to be supportive and encouraging.

Thank you for taking the time to show your continued interest and support.

Sincerely,

You may wish to make an overhead acetate, a mini-poster for reference, or a handout of Draft Planning Sheet 29, "Dear Families, Journals are used for..."

- Write a letter to the children inviting them to write to you about their reading and experiences. Figure 2.12 provides a sample letter.

Figure 2.12 (opposite) is reproduced as Draft Planning Sheet 30, "Dear Learners, When you write a response..." You may wish to make an overhead acetate, a mini-poster as reference, or a handout of this Planning Sheet.

During the experience

- Invite the learners to respond using the 3 R's framework.
- Read aloud the selected book or poem.
- Model the 3 R's framework by writing on a chart or board three statements to represent retell, relate and reflect respectively.
- Invite the learners to write a personal response to the reading and talk.
- Provide time for them to write — e.g., five minutes.
- Model by writing along with the learners.
- Model and demonstrate the 3 R's by sharing your writing.
- Invite the learners to share their writing.
- Write back to your learners using the 3 R's framework.
- Design a system to respond, based on your teaching style and timetable.
- Share the 3 R's framework with the learners to use as a reference. (Refer to Draft Planning Sheets 3, 4, 5, and 6, "The 3 R's Framework: Retelling, Relating and Reflecting," "Retell," "Relate," and "Reflect.")
-

Assessing and Evaluating

- As you continue to watch and listen, ask yourself:
  - Are any patterns emerging from the books they are choosing to read and write about?
  - How is their writing changing? Why?
  - Are they practising "retelling, relating, reflecting" when they write?
  - Are they learning more about questioning? In what ways?
  - Am I practising "retelling, relating, reflecting" when I write back to them?
  - Is my writing back to the learners encouraging them to write more competently, both in content of writing and attitude towards writing?
  - Am I becoming more proficient and effective at writing back to the learners?
  -

Figure 2.12 Journals: Sample Letter for Learners

Dear Learners,

When you write a response to the books you are reading or have finished, or to something you have just experienced (a movie, a trip, a guest speaker, etc.), you may find the following suggestions helpful.

RETELL
- Tell about the story or experience: "This story (experience) is about...", "The first thing that happened was..."
- Retell your favourite part(s): "The part I like best is..."
- Make lists to emphasize something in the story or experience.
- Draw pictures to share a part of the story or experience.
- Make an audiotape.

RELATE
- Make connections to other stories, poems, experiences or things you know or have seen: "This reminds me of...", "This makes me think of..."
- Share your memories: "I remember when..."
- Share your feelings: "I feel..."

REFLECT
- Ask questions: "I wonder why...", "I wonder if...", "Why do you think...?"
- Share insights: "Now I understand why..."
- Make predictions: "I think that..."
- State plans: "Now, I want to..."

Have fun reading, writing and thinking!

Fondly,

Continuing

- Continue this process using a variety of literature experiences.
- Invite the learners to write personal responses when they read independently.
- Provide time for learners to use cooperative or buddy reading journals when reading in small groups.

- Continue to respond in writing to the learners' writing, modelling and demonstrating the 3 R's framework.
- Extend this process to encourage responding to other experiences, such as trips, movies, speakers...
-

Practising the 3 R's in Reading Workshop

Reading workshop, also known as **readers' workshop**, is a block of time set aside daily during which we invite and expect our learners to practise reading. We expect them to make meaning from the materials they read. This block of time provides opportunities for learners and teachers to support one another. The learners choose their own selections and spend time practising reading, talking, and writing about their reading.

In reading workshop, we invite learners to become authentic readers, reading for real purposes and doing what real readers do, by making available to them a wide variety of materials that speak specifically to their emotions, their life experiences, their imaginations and their minds. When we encourage our learners to read daily and often for real purposes, they become involved in the process of reading. This process involves *pretending, memorizing, approximating, decoding, predicting, practising, understanding, responding, sharing and thinking* — retelling, relating, reflecting.

When learners **pretend and memorize**, they copy what they see readers doing in the world around them. We can picture the learner sitting on the floor, holding a book sometimes right-side up and sometimes up-side-down. This is the learner pretending to read. After read-aloud times at home or at school, learners, both young and old, often say, "Read it again." **Repetition** is an essential part of the reading process. Sometimes learners reread by themselves, sometimes with a small or large group, and sometimes they are reread to by another. We can see those learners who read from memory, holding the book properly, turning the pages at the right time, and repeating the text from memory as they look at the pictures. This memorizing is an important part of becoming a reader. We need to value both pretending and memorizing and give the learner credit as a reader. This is a critical stage.

The process of **approximating** — making guesses — is when learners move beyond relying on memory and begin to read bits and pieces of text accurately. They use these bits and pieces of the text as contextual clues to "read" other parts, often "reading" so close to the actual text that the meaning is retained. Sometimes this process is called "filling in the gaps." All readers approximate, especially if the text is new and/or challenging. As adult readers, we continue to use contextual clues to fill in the gaps when we come to words or small parts we do not know or meet words we find puzzling to pronounce. We just read on.

Decoding is one part of the reading process. Readers decode when they use their knowledge of consonant sounds, prefixes, suffixes, little words in big words... to figure out what a new word might be. Readers use these kinds of decoding strategies to help them make approximations that bring their reading of text closer and closer to accuracy. When they write, they use this knowledge of decoding to spell or sound out words they are including in their writing. This is why when learners use words in their writing that are beyond their age and grade levels, they sometimes use temporary or approximate spellings. Decoding skills learned in the context of reading and writing experiences are more naturally transferred to the reading process. Daily reading and writing experiences complement each other, are interwoven and integrated.

Predicting is when readers think about what comes next. They relate what they are reading to other ideas, topics, or experiences, imaginative or real. They organize their thoughts, connecting what has already happened to what might happen next. They continue to **practise** reading, confirming or adjusting their predictions. For young readers, predicting and practising is a way of playing with language as they become fluent, confident readers, willing to share what they have experienced and learned from their reading. As the learners practise their reading, they consider their audience — with whom they will share their knowledge of reading, both process and content.

Understanding occurs when readers have a variety of opportunities and ways to **respond** to what they are reading. We believe that when learners are invited to *retell, relate and reflect* as part of the reading process, using a wide range of materials and their own ideas, they develop **comprehension** and are able to demonstrate their understandings. We believe this process is essential to becoming an effective reader and thinker.

Responding and sharing are among the final stages of the reading process. **Thinking** about and *responding* to what we read is how we *share* our learning. Learners enjoy talking to others about what they read, and they share their responses to what they have read. Some of these responses can be published, presented as a script or play, displayed or recorded on audiotape or videotape. We add these "published" or "performed" presentations to the classroom library or reading corner for others to read and enjoy.

The authentic reading experiences learners enjoy in reading workshop involve them in a dynamic environment in which both the process and the product are valued. During reading workshop, readers talk and read aloud, they conference with one another and with us, they write about their reading, and they share insights. The room is alive with the buzzing hum of readers at work. In the reading workshop setting, learners make approximations, take risks and share responses to their reading as they become more independent learners and thinkers.

In order to organize reading workshop in the classroom, it is necessary to have a wide variety of quality resources available and accessible to learners. The learners should be immersed in a print-rich environment. Collections of reading material and a wide variety of resources are essential in order to match and value the many different learning and teaching styles.

Learners need to be encouraged to choose from a wide collection of selections, including predictable pattern books, poetry, non-fiction, novels, how-to's, dictionaries, thesauri, atlases, encyclopedias... These selections should be complemented by a variety of interesting and curious artifacts (e.g., globes, rocks, models, puppets) as well as audiovisual and technological resources (e.g., tape recorders, cameras, video cameras, computers).

We can brainstorm with our learners and colleagues the many ways to locate and access different resources. Many resources are age-less and grade-less. The same resource can be used in different ways for different age groups and grades. We believe that young learners as well as older learners are equally fascinated by a coffee table book about Beethoven or Monet. They gain different information for their age and interests. We make appropriate changes to our expectations and learning outcomes for different groups of learners and for individuals.

We need to discuss with our learners and develop with them appropriate ways to interact with the resources during reading workshop time in order to ensure predictable and successful learning experiences. We need to collaborate with our learners to develop routines and expectations, and design visual references. Our agreed-upon routines and expectations need to be clear, posted, reviewed, and practised in order to be effective. Learners can help compose and design classroom "expectation posters." These posters might include describing what a reader looks like and what a reader does when practising reading.

To gain ideas and topics for their continued reading, learners might brainstorm, discuss, or listen to book talks before choosing their selections. They might share with others and make individual or group lists for potential and possible ideas and topics. Providing choice encourages readers to be responsible for their own reading and encourages them to consider the why's and how's of making decisions. There are times when we give our learners parameters for making their choices; for example, we may have them choose a story, poem, or non-fiction book about "Living Things of the Night." We believe there needs to be a balance between personal choice with and without parameters. When learners are given choice, they are and continue to be excited about reading.

Learners and teachers glean many spontaneous ideas from reading — reading creates "I want to's" and "I wonder's." One effective way to give learners ideas for choosing reading selections is to read to them. Frequent read-aloud situations provide a bank of ideas, and allow us as teachers valuable opportunities to plan for appropriate instruction.

We believe that we do some of our most effective teaching when we read aloud.

During daily reading workshop time in the classroom, we recommend beginning with a read-aloud. For very young learners, we suggest considering having a work/play time at the different learning areas before practise reading time. This activity invites and encourages learners to read for information, confirmation, and for a specific purpose — e.g., to learn how to construct things. This is called *functional reading practice.*

We must be very careful to encourage learners to want to read in their earliest attempts. They need to see themselves as readers at whatever age. We must celebrate their efforts and encourage them to take risks with reading and to read independently. Often, when readers learn a selection, they feel it is an accomplishment, and that accomplishment should be celebrated.

When readers *perform* a reading selection, they realize that revisiting and practising are challenging and rewarding. During the reading process, learners benefit by talking, sketching, or rehearsing their understandings before responding. The rehearsal allows them to hear what they want to say or do, so when they begin, they know where they are going with the reading, and their confidence level is high. During this preparation, learners read what they have practised, and others listen to see if it is expressive and flows. They read to others and ask for suggestions and ideas, and they continue to practise and improve. In this way, they polish their reading and gain confidence.

Throughout reading workshop, we teach skills and strategies when we see the need. It is no longer enough to say that children learn to read by reading. We need to provide appropriate instruction throughout the reading process, so that reading strategies, comprehension, and the quality of reading and thinking continue to improve and progress. When, for example, learners confront unknown text and "get stuck," we remind/teach them of the various problem-solving strategies readers use when they read. These strategies include reread, check for picture clues, read ahead, remember and relate to similar text, and use phonic skills to check the sounds the consonants make. (Research shows knowledge of consonant sounds is an effective strategy to try when figuring out new words in context of the reading selection.) Throughout reading workshop, we continue to assess and evaluate the strategies our learners use and what strategies they need to be taught. We keep records of significant examples of growth over time. (See Draft Planning Sheet 44, "Reading Inventory," which asks children to articulate the strategies they use.)

During reading workshop, we conference with our learners in groups and individually, and our learners conference with one another. These planned and spur-of-the-moment conferences are an important component of the workshop. *Conferencing is the natural conversation that occurs when teachers and learners practise retelling, relating and reflecting.*

It is important to note that for reading workshop to be successful, a framework or system for the workshop needs to be in place. The following is one way to organize and run a reading workshop time.

Beginning

Read-Aloud (approx. 20 minutes)

- Carefully choose a selection — a story, poem, advertisement, non-fiction...
- Before, during or after the read-aloud, ask questions and make comments about the title, format, genre, cover, end pages, author, illustrations, copyright date, publisher, country where the read-aloud was published...
- Read aloud for enjoyment first.

Mini-Lesson (approx. 5-7 minutes)

- Select a focus lesson based on knowledge of your learners and appropriate needs.
- Begin with meaning-based mini-lessons — titles, leads (first words, first sentence, first paragraph or first illustration of a piece of writing), endings, main ideas...
- Consider using pre-reading strategies.

Plan and Share (approx. 3-5 minutes)

- Review routines and expectations.
  - Think to yourself, and/or turn to a reader close to you to share your thoughts and ideas. (This is called *think aloud*.)
  - Tell each other your plans for reading today.
  - Listen and help each other by suggesting, confirming or adjusting thoughts, ideas, plans... by retelling, relating and reflecting.

Status-of-the-Class (approx. 3-5 minutes)

- Invite readers to tell what they plan to do.
- Record on a class list — is continuing to read, rereading, choosing a new selection, reading to a peer, reading to another class, reading to/with teacher, responding to reading...
- Consider keeping or creating a format on which learners record what they read — title, date started, abandoned, completed... (See Draft Planning Sheet 40, "Independent Reading Record.")

During the experience

Practising Reading (approx. 20-40 minutes)

- Have a wide variety and number of print materials available.
- Include selections from all genres.
- Review routines and expectations.
- Invite readers to:
  - Choose 2 or 3 selections for reading time.
  - Record the titles of selections on a reading record sheet. (You may want to give each reader a copy of Draft Planning Sheet 40, "Independent Reading Record," to use for recording their reading.)
  - Print or write name or initial on the reading record sheet.
  - Date stamp reading record sheet.
  - Use strategies such as reread, read ahead, picture clues, look at consonant sounds, substitute, skip, ask another reader close by...
  - Store reading record in folder.
- Meet with and conference with the readers individually or in small groups.
- Encourage retelling: "Tell me about your reading, the author, illustrations, your responses..."
- Encourage relating: "That reminds me of..."
- Encourage reflecting: "I wonder why..."
- Provide individual instruction when appropriate.
-

Conferencing

Teacher "Roving-Conferences" take place during the practising reading time.

- Visit with the reader: "How's it going?" "Can I help?" "What do you plan to read next?"
- Listen carefully.
- Model and demonstrate retelling, relating, reflecting. "Oh, you are reading all about cats. I read about cats too, because I have one. I wonder how many other people in our class have cats as pets?"
- Move on to another reader.
- You may choose to work with a small group during part of this time.

Reader's Chair (approx. 5-10 minutes)

- Arrange a reader's chair at the front of your large group meeting area.
- Invite a reader to read aloud to the whole group.
- Invite individuals in the group to tell back (retell), make personal connections (relate), and/or ask questions (reflect). (Refer to Draft Planning Sheets 3, 4, 5, and 6, "The 3 R's Framework: Retelling, Relating and Reflecting," "Retell," "Relate," and "Reflect.")
- Encourage the reader or others to respond to the questions.

Value and Celebrate

- Consider having your learners be guest readers by having them visit other classrooms to read aloud.
- Have a "read-aloud" day — learners sign up to read aloud to one or two peers or invited visitors.
- Create with learners a list of ways to value and celebrate reading.
-

Assessing and Evaluating

- Continue to watch and listen, read with individuals, keep records and ask yourself:
  - Are the learners using appropriate strategies as they read?
  - Are they understanding what they read?
  - How are the readers handling the reading and sharing process?
  - Are the learners enjoying the reading process? Are they frustrated? confident?
  - What do the miscues they make tell me?
  - How can I best help the learners set goals?
  -
- Consider asking your learners to fill out Draft Planning Sheet 44, "Reading Inventory," at the beginning of each term, at the beginning and at the end of the year.

Continuing

- Continue the process.
- Review regularly the expectations for reading workshop.
- Reflect with learners on learning goals established by you, the learner, the school, the system...
- Provide appropriate instruction (mini-lessons) for the whole group, small groups and/or individuals.
- Select literature to build on the present skills of the learners and to introduce new strategies for reading.
- Provide many opportunities for learners to hear the sound of different genres by continuing to read aloud a wide variety of genres.
-

(For a one-page planning sheet for reading workshop, refer to Draft Planning Sheet 55, "Planning: Reading/Writing Workshop.")

Practising the 3 R's in Writing Workshop

We believe that when young learners begin school, they see themselves as writers. Writing is drawing, making marks, scribbling, and printing text. Telling and drawing stories are rehearsals for writing. The first word young learners usually attempt is their name. Learners who print their names have a background knowledge of what letters look like and how to make them, and they know that there is meaning in the writing.

Writing workshop, also known as **writers' workshop**, is a block of time set aside daily in which learners are invited and expected to practise writing. This time provides opportunities for learners and teachers to support one another as the learners become fluent writers. The learners choose their own topics and spend time practising writing, talking, and responding. Responding gives the learners an opportunity to practise retelling, relating and reflecting. (See Draft Planning Sheets 3, 4, 5, and 6, "The 3 R's Framework: Retelling, Relating and Reflecting," "Retell," "Relate," and "Reflect.")

When we encourage our learners to write daily and often, when we encourage them to become authentic writers — writing for real purposes that have meaning for them and doing what real authors do — they become involved in the process of writing. This process may involve *pre-writing, drafting, revising, proofreading and editing, and sharing/publishing.*

Pre-writing is when learners think about what they want to write — their ideas, topics, experiences, imaginative or real stories. They choose topics. (See Draft Planning Sheet 12, "Using the 3 R's Framework To Choose Writing Topics.") They organize their thoughts. They sequence what they want to say, thinking about what happens first, second, in the middle, at the end. They consider their audience — who will read their writing and why. They consider how they might present their writing — what formats they might use. Pre-writing benefits from play and having a variety of experiences in order to build a bank of ideas. This component of pre-writing is essential for young learners.

During this part of the writing process, writers benefit by talking, sketching, or rehearsing their stories before writing. (See Draft Planning Sheet 13, "Using the 3 R's Framework When Conferencing About Writing.") They might tell their stories many times to several audiences. The rehearsal allows them to hear what they want to say so that when they begin, they know where they are going with their writing, and their confidence level is high.

There are numerous and varied pre-writing strategies we can use in the classroom to encourage our learners to start writing. Figure 2.13 shows just a few. (Figure 2.13 is reproduced as Draft Planning Sheet 14, "Some Pre-Writing Strategies.")

Figure 2.13 Some Pre-Writing Strategies

> • Use the 3 R's framework to help you choose writing topics. Think about:
>   - the things you know a lot about, enjoy telling others about, and can talk about confidently (**retell**)
>   - the people, places and things you care about, like/love, and are passionate about (**relate**)

Figure 2.13 continued

- the people, places and things you are interested in, want to find out about, have questions about, know a little about and want to learn more about (**reflect**).

- Think about the books you have read, heard or discussed as possible ideas.
- Brainstorm possible writing ideas and record or list in chart form.
- Record lists of questions.
- Draw a picture and create a story in your mind.
- Talk your story through with a friend.
- Tell your story into an audiotape and listen to it play back.
- Reread books to examine specific patterns and techniques.
- Reread something you have previously read or written to think about it from a different point of view.
- Reread material and think about changing characters, setting, plots, formats...
- Brainstorm possible beginnings, endings, words, phrases.
- Create classroom reference lists from the brainstorming.
- Think about your audiences.

Note: Correcting spelling and checking grammar occur later when writers reread, proofread and edit their work.

Drafting, when learners begin their writing, is one part of the writing process. It is important for our learners that we collaborate with them to develop clear expectations for drafting. Our learners need to know that in the drafting part of the writing process, writers record their thoughts from their heads to the paper (or computer) as fast as they can. They need to realize that thoughts, clarity of content and meaning — not spelling and grammar — are important during the drafting part of the writing process. We need to urge our learners when they draft to write the letters they hear and know and not to stop to ask for help with spelling or grammar, since these functions will be addressed later through proofreading and editing. When we support our learners' approximations, they will become risk takers.

Together with our learners, we need to discuss expectations for drafting, record the expectations and post them for reference, either on the board or in individual writing folders. See Figure 2.14. (Figure 2.14 is reproduced as Draft Planning Sheet 15, "Expectations for Draft Writing.")

Figure 2.14 Expectations for Draft Writing

- Print your name or initial on each page.
- Date stamp every piece of writing. If you work on the same piece for three days, your writing should have three dates on it. Then everyone will know that this piece of writing is a three-day story/piece.
- Use a draft stamp on your writing so that anyone reading your writing will know this piece is "work-in-progress."

Figure 2.14 continued

- If you are stuck, rehearse or tell your story to yourself or to a partner. Ask for suggestions.
- Write on every other line, so that you can add words or phrases during revision.
- Work on one side of the paper, so that you can cut and paste, move parts around, take out or add words, phrases, sentences, paragraphs... during revision.
- Take one piece of paper at a time. Arrange and number completed pages.
- Cross out words or letters as you write, rather than erasing. This keeps ideas flowing since using an eraser slows down the writing process.
- Do your best with spelling by writing the sounds you hear, see, and remember.
- Store your writing in your folder.
- Decide whether you want to publish; and if you do, continue with revising and editing.

Note: Correcting spelling and checking grammar occur later when writers reread, proofread and edit their work.

When real writers complete a draft piece of writing, they soon realize that **revising** — revisiting the content of the writing — is quite challenging and rewarding. Before our learners revise as part of the writing process, we need to work with them to develop clear expectations for revising. We need to encourage them to reread what they have written to see if it makes sense and flows. We might encourage them to read their writing aloud to themselves or to others to hear questions, suggestions and ideas. We should encourage them to apply the 3 R's framework when they respond to one another's writing so that their comments/questions will help the writer see more clearly where revision is necessary.

It is during revision that learners add or take parts out. They rearrange words or ideas. They cut and paste. They change words or ideas, replace overused or unclear words, and work to make the content of their writing clearer. Learners who are proficient at keyboarding will find that using the computer greatly facilitates the revising process.

Revision for young writers may be adding a scribble, some letters, a word or a sentence, or adding details to a picture, or starting something new. *Revision for young writers may be leaving the first writing attempt — at this stage of development, this is their final draft.*

We must be very careful to encourage learners to *want to* write by valuing their understanding of writing. We must celebrate their efforts and encourage them to take risks with writing and to write independently. Often, when young writers complete a piece of writing, they believe it is finished, and it should be celebrated.

We need to post our agreed-upon expectations for revising for reference, either on the board or in individual writing folders. See Figure 2.15. (Figure 2.15 is reproduced as Draft Planning Sheet 16, "Expectations for Revising.")

Figure 2.15 Expectations for Revising

- Read and reread what you have written to see if it makes sense and flows. Make initial revisions.
- Read your writing aloud to others for their questions, suggestions, and ideas.
- Think about what others have asked you or suggested.
- Make revisions:
  - Add or take out parts.
  - Rearrange words or ideas — cut and paste.
  - Change words or ideas to better ones.
  - Replace overused, unclear, and/or unnecessary words.
  - Use a variety of resources — other people, books, thesaurus — to find more interesting words.
  - Reread to another.
- Make final changes.
- Remember that correcting spelling and checking grammar occur when writers reread, proofread and edit their work.

Note: When you are responding to someone else's writing, remember to use the 3 R's framework — *retell* what the writer has written; *relate* — what does the writing make you think of?; *reflect* — what questions does the writing raise in your mind? Using the framework in this way will help you to help the writer make thoughts clearer and more meaningful.

Proofreading and editing is only necessary when writing is "going public" — being published or performed. During proofreading and editing, learners proofread carefully in order to address spelling, capitalization, punctuation, grammar and sentence structure. They may use dictionaries, thesauri, or computer spell-check programs to check the spelling of unfamiliar words. During editing, we encourage them to work with a partner — peers, learning partners, teachers and/or families — to make editing changes.

Learners who are involved in the process of writing know that some of their writing will be seen by an audience, and therefore they want this published work to be the best it can be. As writers, they request a final edit, knowing that the editorial ("red") marks are part of the editing process. We point out that published authors also make errors and receive help with editing. Therefore, teachers, adult volunteers and/or families need to be the final editors, pointing out last-minute editing changes that learners may have missed. It is helpful to have an editing box in the writing workshop area into which learners can put their pieces for *final* editing.

Editing for young writers needs to be approached carefully. For many learners, editing too early may create anxiety and unnecessary attention to mechanics and spelling. Such anxiety may be damaging to young writers who need continued encouragement to want to write and to take risks.

We believe that very young writers see the writing of their name as their beginning attempt at writing and reading. This is their signature and it changes as they grow and develop. Their signature should be treated with respect and dignity.

We should provide direct instruction to our young writers when we believe that an individual learner is ready for a particular skill or concept.

Early in the writing process, we need to collaborate with our learners to discuss, record and post the expectations for editing for reference, either on the board or in individual writing folders. See Figure 2.16. (Figure 2.16 is reproduced as Draft Planning Sheet 17, "Expectations for Proofreading and Editing.")

Figure 2.16   Expectations for Proofreading and Editing

This is when writers, peers, teachers, editors...correct spelling and/or check grammar by rereading, proofreading and editing.

- Read and reread your writing.
- Check the structure of your sentences, verb tenses, plurals, endings of words...
- Check capitalization, punctuation and grammar.
- Circle words you feel need to be checked for spelling. Use a dictionary, computer spell check, or other sources.
- Work with another to make shared editing changes.
- Consider rereading your piece aloud as a final "proofread."
- Put your work in the editing box.
- Final editing is completed by the teacher or volunteer.

The final part of writing is **sharing and publishing**. Learners enjoy sharing their writing in the author's chair. Some of these pieces can be published in book format, or presented as a script or play, on a poster, as a visual display, etc. These "published" pieces should be added to the classroom, library or reading corner for others to read and enjoy.

Again, we need to collaborate with our learners to establish expectations for sharing and publishing. These expectations should be recorded and posted for reference. A chart using pictures can be used for young learners. See Figure 2.17. (Figure 2.17 is reproduced as Draft Planning Sheet 18, "Expectations for Sharing/Publishing.")

Figure 2.17   Expectations for Sharing/Publishing

- Decide how you will publish — e.g., in book format, poster, mural, experiment, diorama, play...
- If you decide you want to publish a book, choose the format and cover — e.g., hard cover, spiral binding, accordion book, pop-up, book-in-a-box, character on a string, puppet book...
- Collect the materials you will need to put your book together.
- Choose the print size and font, and the number of pages.
- Make decisions about chapters, table of contents, index...
- Choose the materials and the styles you will use for illustrations.
- Put your story into final form — e.g., reprint the piece yourself, ask your teacher or a volunteer to input onto the computer, send to the in-school "publishing house"...

Figure 2.17 continued

- Complete your illustrations, title page and cover. You may wish to cut and paste your original illustrations.
- Write the dedication page and an "About the Author" page. You may wish to include your photograph.
- Finalize your title.
- Share your published effort, and display for others to read.

Note: Remember, authors and illustrators have an editor do *their final edit*. Ask a teacher, family member or volunteer to be your editor.

Authentic writing involves learners in a dynamic learning experience where both process and products of writing are valued. During writing workshop, writers talk and write, they read their writing out loud, they conference with one another and with us, they rewrite, and they share insights. In the writing workshop setting, learners make approximations, take risks and share responses to their writing as they become more independent.

In order to organize a successful writing workshop time in the classroom, we need to make readily available to our learners a wide choice of writing materials — pencils, coloured markers, sharpeners, pens, erasers, rulers, various kinds, sizes and colours of paper (plain, lined, construction paper, etc.), writing folders for the learners to keep their writing together, date and draft stamps, ready-made booklets, wallpaper covers, etc. The workshop area should include a variety of magazines, newspapers, and books — predictable pattern books, poetry, non-fiction, novels, how-to's — that the learners can refer to for ideas for writing topics and formats. The writing workshop area should also have dictionaries, thesauri, atlases, and encyclopedias readily accessible. These resources should be complemented by interesting and curious artifacts (e.g., globes, rocks, models, puppets...) and audiovisual and technological resources (e.g., tape recorders, cameras, computers...).

We need to discuss with our learners and develop with them appropriate ways to interact with the resources surrounding them during writing workshop. Together, we need to develop routines and expectations, and design visual references. Our agreed-upon routines and expectations need to be clear, posted, reviewed, and practised in order to be effective. Learners can help compose and design classroom "expectation posters." The posters might include descriptions of what a writer looks like and what a writer does when practising writing.

When learners choose their own writing topics, they are eager to write. Providing choice encourages learners to be responsible for their own writing and to consider the why's and how's of making decisions. When learners are given choice, they are and continue to be excited about writing.

There are times when we may give the learners parameters for making their choices; for example, we may ask them to write a story, poem, or report about "Endangered Species." We believe learners need to be encouraged to write in a variety of modes: **personal writing** — letters, journals, chart stories...; **imaginative writing** — stories, poetry, plays...; and **functional writing** — lists, memos, recipes, business letters, reports... . We believe there needs to be a balance between personal choice with and without parameters so that learners experience all kinds of writing. It is important that different styles of writing are read, examined and modelled as part of pre-writing before learners practise these writing styles.

Learners might brainstorm with others and make individual or group lists for possible ideas for writing topics. To gain ideas and topics for their writing, they might draw or sketch to see their stories in concrete form as they create. They might draw on the 3 R's framework for topic ideas: they can think about what they know a lot about, enjoy telling others about and can talk about confidently (retell); they can think about the people, places and things they care about, like/love, and are passionate about (relate); and they can think about the people, places and things they are interested in, want to find out about, have questions about, know a little about, and want to learn more about (reflect). (See Draft Planning Sheet 12, "Using the 3 R's Framework To Choose Writing Topics.")

An obvious way to provide a bank of ideas for writing is to read aloud. Frequent read-aloud experiences allow us as teachers valuable opportunities to provide appropriate instruction. Here is how and when we introduce learners to different *modes* of writing and writing styles. During writing workshop, we recommend beginning with a read-aloud each and every day. For very young learners, we recommend read-aloud in small groups and allowing a work/play time at different learning areas before or as part of writing.

In writing workshop, we teach skills through direct instruction and many demonstrations or mini-lessons as we see the need. We teach our learners decoding strategies and encourage them to use this knowledge of consonant sounds, prefixes, suffixes, little words in big words... to approximate spellings of unfamiliar words or to choose new words to use in their writing. We recognize that when learners use their decoding skills to spell words beyond their age and grade levels, the result may be temporary or approximate spellings and we accept these approximations. Children learn to write by practising writing and by receiving appropriate instruction throughout the writing process. This process of writing and teaching is how they continue to improve their writing skills and the quality of their writing. We continue to assess, evaluate and keep records of significant examples of growth over time.

Throughout writing workshop, we conference with our learners and they conference with one another. These planned and spur-of-the-moment conferences are an important component of the workshop. Conferencing is the natural conversation that occurs when teachers and learners practise retelling, relating and reflecting.

It is important to note that management strategies need to be in place in the classroom to achieve success in a writing workshop. The following is one way to organize and run a writing workshop time.

Beginning

Read-Aloud (approx. 20 minutes)

- Carefully choose a selection — a story, novel, poem, non-fiction...
- Before, during and after reading aloud, observe and make comments about the cover, title page, dedication, illustrations, format, genre, end pages...

Mini-Lesson (approx. 5-7 minutes)

- Teach a mini-lesson or point of instruction before, during or after the read-aloud experience.
- Keep the mini-lesson short and clear.
- Begin with "content" or "meaning-based" mini-lessons — e.g., beginnings, endings, titles, exciting parts, problems in story, characters...
- Encourage learners to use books as models or patterns for their own writing — word structure, story lines, characters, setting, genre, vocabulary, author's style, format...

Plan and Share (approx. 3-5 minutes)

- Review routines and expectations:
  - Think to yourself, and/or turn to a writer close to you to share your thoughts and ideas. (This is called *think aloud*.)
  - Tell each other your plans for writing today.
  - Listen and help each other by suggesting ideas, asking questions — retelling, relating, reflecting.

Status-of-the-Class (approx. 3-5 minutes)

- Ask writers what they plan to do.
- Record what each writer is working on — e.g, drawing, beginning text, continuing, conferencing, publishing...
- Consider recording what each learner is writing about — e.g., topic, idea, genre — or invite learners to keep their own records. (See Draft Planning Sheet 41, "Independent Writing Record.")

During the experience

During the Practising Writing Time (approx. 20-40 minutes)

- Review routines and expectations. (See Figures 2.13, 2.14, 2.15, 2.16 and 2.17, also reproduced as Draft Planning Sheets 14, 15, 16, 17 and 18, "Some Pre-Writing Strategies," "Expectations for Draft Writing," "Expectations for Revising," Expectations for Proofreading and Editing," and "Expectations for Sharing/Publishing.")
- Demonstrate through role playing how learners ask one another for help, and/or solve problems during practising writing time.
- Help learners understand and value the need for you to be free to work with individuals or small groups while they practise writing.
- Have available a variety of writing tools and paper for learners to choose — e.g., pens, pencils, blank paper, coloured paper, booklets, accordion, shapes, lined paper with blank space for illustrations...
- Learners practise writing (pre-writing, drafting, revising, proofreading and editing, sharing/publishing) while you conference with individuals and/or small groups.
- Move about the room and have short talks with writers — roving conferences.

- Use and model *retelling, relating, reflecting*:
  - "Tell me about your writing (or picture)…"
  - "You are writing about your pet cat." (retell)
  - "I have had pet cats for many years." (relate)
  - "Do you know about the different kinds of cats?" (reflect)
- Encourage learners to use and practise retelling, relating and reflecting. (Refer to Draft Planning Sheets 3, 4, 5 and 6, "The 3 R's Framework: Retelling, Relating and Reflecting," "Retell," "Relate," and "Reflect.")
- Invite learners to share and talk together about their writing and/or ideas.
- Encourage learners to focus on meaning/composing during revision.
- Value and encourage approximation and risk taking.
  (Remember that over-emphasizing surface features with young learners can cause them to become anxious.)
-

Sharing in the Author's Chair (approx. 5-10 minutes)

- Arrange an author's chair near your large group meeting area.
- Invite the whole class to the author's chair presentation.
- Invite someone to sit in the author's chair to share his or her writing (in idea, draft or published form).
- Encourage the audience to tell back (retell), make connections (relate) and ask questions (reflect).
- When a piece of writing is shared at the idea or draft stage, record significant questions on Post-its and give to the writer for consideration when revising.
- Develop a system for author's chair presentations for your class — by volunteering, request, schedule date…
- Value and celebrate these "authors" by adding published work to the class and/or school library or even local community offices.
-

Assessing and Evaluating

- Continue to watch and listen, keep records, and ask yourself:
  - How are the learners doing throughout the writing process?
  - How can I assess the process and product — e.g., What can I see in the content and composition of each learner's piece of writing regarding sequence and plot development, ideation, coherence, imagination, maturity of writing…? What are the strengths regarding the mechanics of writing — e.g., punctuation, capitalization, grammar?
  - What do the miscues in spelling tell me?
  - How can I best help the learners set their goals for continuing to learn about their writing?
  -

Continuing

- Continue the process. (Refer to Draft Planning Sheet 55, "Planning: Reading/Writing Workshop.")
- Review regularly the guidelines and expectations for the writing process.
- Continuously read and review learners' pieces in progress — daily, weekly, monthly...
- Reflect on learning goals established by learners, you, school, system...
- Provide appropriate instruction (mini-lessons) for the whole group, small groups and/or individuals.
- Select literature to build on the present skills of the learners and to introduce new techniques for writings.
- Model/demonstrate new forms and formats of writing.
- Invite learners to try these new forms.
- Continue to read aloud a wide variety of genres to enable learners to write in different genres based on these models.
-

(You may wish to make overhead acetates, mini-posters or handouts using Draft Planning Sheets 12, 14, 15, 16, 17, and 18, "Using the 3 R's Framework To Choose Writing Topics," "Some Pre-Writing Strategies," "Expectations for Draft Writing," "Expectations for Revising," "Expectations for Proofreading and Editing," and "Expectations for Sharing/Publishing." For a one-page planning sheet for reading/writing workshop, refer to Draft Planning Sheet 55, "Planning: Reading/Writing Workshop.")

Practising the 3 R's When Choosing Writing Topics

Our 3 R's framework of retelling, relating and reflecting provides us as teachers with an ideal framework for valuing what our learners know, their experiences, and what they want to know. The 3 R's also provide an effective framework for enabling learners to choose topics for their writing experiences. Learners write confidently and comfortably about their "retell" and "relate" topics throughout the year. The "reflect" topics offer opportunities for us to teach, model and demonstrate a variety of research skills and writing strategies.

The following process of choosing and recording topics works effectively when practised and completed over three or more consecutive days.

Beginning

- Carefully select and practise a book or poem to read aloud.
- Invite the whole class to gather in the large group meeting area.
- Share the read-aloud.
- Talk with learners about why they think this author chose to write on this topic.
- Share with your learners things you know a lot about, enjoy telling others about, and can talk about confidently — *retell*.

- Encourage learners to think about the things they know a lot about, enjoy telling others about, and can talk about confidently — *retell*.
- Invite them to turn to the person closest to them and share their topics.

- Share with your learners people, places and things you care about, like/love, and are passionate about — *relate*.
- Encourage learners to think about the people, places and things they care about, like/love, and are passionate about — *relate*.
- Invite them to turn to the person closest to them and share their topics.

- Share **people, places** and **things** you are interested in, want to find out about, have questions about, know a little about and want to learn more — *reflect*.
- Encourage learners to think about the people, places and things they are interested in, want to find out about, have questions about, want to learn more about — *reflect*.
- Invite them to turn to the person closest to them and share their topics.

- List and record on charts the *retell* topics generated — this information and knowledge provides insights into the **cognitive** domain.
- List and record on charts the *relate* topics generated — these personal stories and experiences provide insights into the **affective** domain.
- List and record on charts the *reflect* topics — these wonderings and questions provide insights into **research** possibilities.

During the experience

- Invite the learners to brainstorm and collaboratively compose their lists (individual or group) of retell, relate and reflect topics.
- Post the lists in the classroom or have the learners place them in their writing folders for reference. (See Draft Planning Sheet 12, "Using the 3 R's Framework To Choose Writing Topics.")
- Encourage learners in groups of two to tell and/or draw some of their retell topics as rehearsal for writing.
- Encourage learners in groups of two to tell and/or draw some of their relate topics as rehearsal for writing.
- Encourage learners to talk with teacher-librarians, families and other resource people to collect information to read and review as rehearsal for reflect topics — research.

Assessing and Evaluating

- Make notes of similar topics of interest.
- Make a master class list of possible writing topics for reference.
- Keep a record of individual topic choices.
- Encourage learners to keep their own records.
- Observe changes in writing in all curriculum areas.
- Continue to watch and listen, and ask yourself:
  - Are the learners using their topic list for writing ideas?
  - Which topics are they writing about most often?

Continuing

- Use the 3 R's framework to choose writing and research topics for other curriculum areas.
- Think about how this process connects to other curriculum areas and to life-long learning.
- Examine published works through literature studies.
  - Notice when and how real writers write about what they know, what they care deeply about, and their research or new knowledge.
  - Create lists of tips and techniques to invite learners to imitate real writers and what they use and do.
- Practise writing using personal retellings, relatings and reflections.
- Share this writing with learners throughout the process — pre-writing, draft, revision, proofreading/editing, sharing/publishing.
- Use your own writing for mini-lessons, demonstrations and as models.

(You may wish to make an overhead acetate, a mini-poster as reference, or a handout by using Draft Planning Sheet 12, "Using the 3 R's Framework To Choose Writing Topics.")

Practising the 3 R's When Conferencing

Conferencing in the sense we are using it here is a brief conversation between the teacher and an individual learner. (Conferences can occur between the teacher and a small group of learners, and/or learners can conference with one another.) These conversations happen when learners are practising language skills — during reading, writing, experimenting or creating. We visit and invite our learners to talk about their learning and their work.

Conferencing experiences need to be positive, purposeful, and supportive. The learner needs to be the initiator and direct the flow of the conference. We need to listen carefully and respond using a balance of retelling, relating and reflecting statements, questions and appropriate suggestions. We respond first to content and ideas. We need to know, understand and keep in mind the age/grade appropriate skills and concepts, based on individual, class, school and system expected goals. We need to value the self-esteem of every learner and practise fostering and nurturing learner-confidence. *Conferencing is really a natural conversation to help learners learn and teachers teach.* Conferencing provides us with opportunities to give specific individual instruction.

Beginning

- Design a format for learners to schedule a weekly conference.
- Consider using a calendar where learners sign up for their conference time or day.
- Develop a conference schedule for yourself with learners. Tell learners that you will "visit" them.
- Think about possible relate and reflect statements for conferencing.
- Prepare for these individual conferences.

- Prepare a "conferencing packet" to use during conferencing — Post-its, pen, highlighter, record sheets, class list... (See Draft Planning Sheet 8, "Using the 3 R's Framework To Assess and Evaluate.")

During the experience

- Visit and talk with a number of individual learners.
- Listen to each learner talk about his/her work.
- Retell what the learner says.
- Make a connection related to what the learner says.
- Extend the learner's thinking by beginning with "I was wondering...", "What if...", "How come...", "Do you think...", "How can I help..."
- Use a Post-it note to remind the learners of the "nudge" comment, idea or question given during sharing so it can be included in the revision.
- Thank the learner for sharing.
- Move on to another learner.

(You may wish to make an overhead acetate, mini-poster as reference, or a hand-out using Draft Planning Sheet 13, "Using the 3 R's Framework When Conferencing About Writing.")

Assessing and Evaluating

- Record and date the things learners can do.
- Continue to watch and listen and ask yourself — How do I allow the learners to:
  - initiate the conversation
  - practise questioning strategies
- How do I continue to reflect on scheduling methods in order to:
  - invite the learner to choose a conference time
  - visit and listen to every learner over a period of time
  - allow time for me to study "the work" of each learner
- How do I practise the strategies of:
  - careful listening
  - retelling
  - relating
  - reflecting
  - appropriate recording
- How do I watch and listen for learning potentials in order to capture appropriate teaching moments?
- How do I review the learning on a regular basis?
- How do I keep a cumulative record of learner growth and development?
- How do I practise conferencing regularly in all areas of the learning environment?

Continuing

- Record and date the things learners can do.
- Share specific strategies with the whole group.
- Revise the conference schedule when needed.

- Keep a record of longer conferences — record with whom, why, and the date.
- Make note of where to begin conferencing the next day.
- Review work folders to schedule necessary longer conferences.
- Invite learners to schedule conferences based on need.
- Record the learners' goals — what learners want/need to learn next.
-

Practising the 3 R's When Creating

When they read or listen to a reading, learners respond by thinking, talking, or writing, and often, they respond by creating a product using a variety of materials. Literature provides links to the arts, the sciences, mathematics — any subject area — and encourages the processes of creating, constructing, investigating, and problem solving.

Learners create products to express their interpretations, feelings, ideas and experiences in many diverse and creative ways. Through the creating process, they develop appreciation and joy for the arts. We need to foster and encourage an understanding of "beauty" in the arts, and invite and value conversations and connections (retelling, relating, reflecting) about creative products.

When we invite and value individual interpretations and creations, our learners create — a painting, a drawing, an experiment, a diorama, a block structure, a sand table display — in response to literature and experiences. Often, we invite learners to work cooperatively, to use any learning area to create their responses. They might produce a cooperative book, a mural, a readers' theatre, a play, a block structure, a sand table display — a group response to literature.

Beginning

- Collect and have accessible a wide variety of materials.
- Invite learners to choose and design the format and/or form.
- Invite learners to choose the necessary materials and tools.
- Provide blocks of time for learners to work on their creations.
-

During the experience

- Respond to the creations by modelling and demonstrating the 3 R's framework: "Oh, you've built a castle that's at the top of the beanstalk" (retell). "It makes me think of the castle that I saw when I was travelling in England" (relate). "I wonder how you decided on which blocks to use when you were creating the drawbridge?" "How will you label your creation" (reflect)?
- Listen to learners talk about their work.
- Add materials when requested or appropriate to enhance creativity.

Assessing and Evaluating

- Continue to watch and listen.
- Decide on a system of record keeping and evaluation.
(Refer to Draft Planning Sheet 39, "Read, Respond and Create.")

Continuing

- Invite learners to re-create by changing a previous creation based on a different literature experience.
- Invite learners to write about their creations, describing and explaining the creation process.
- Provide opportunities and time for learners to share their responses with others.
- Share and celebrate process and products with families.
-

Practising the 3 R's in Professional Reading and Writing

When the 3 R's framework of retelling, relating and reflecting becomes automatic and natural, it gives us a tool to use in reading, responding, discussions, writing, and for creating. Using the 3 R's framework heightens comprehension by encouraging us — and our learners — to make connections to our own experiences and beliefs, and it encourages us to think.

When we practise the 3 R's framework, we find that retelling occurs frequently and naturally. Relating in particular situations happens fairly frequently and intentionally. Reflecting regularly is more challenging, and needs to be incorporated consciously into learning situations and experiences. In our thinking, reading, writing, and conversations, and in our classrooms, we need to work to achieve a balance of the 3 R's. Maintaining this balance is a continuous challenge.

The following illustrates the process we use at in-service courses to introduce the 3 R's framework. We invite the participants to practise and internalize retelling, relating and reflecting to help them when they have conversations with learners, model/demonstrate for learners, write daily journal entries for professional courses, and respond in conversation and in writing to a partner, to a family member, or to learners in their classrooms.

Beginning

- Select a reading that is short, topical, interesting, informative, thought-provoking, and invites discussion.
- Organize participants into groups of two.
- Provide copies of the reading for each participant.
- Present the 3 R's framework.
- Provide a copy of this framework for each participant. (See Draft Planning Sheets 3, 4, 5, and 6, "The 3 R's Framework: Retelling, Relating and Reflecting," "Retell," "Relate," and "Reflect.")
- Model/demonstrate for the group using the framework of retell, relate and reflect by reading the first two sections of the reading with a volunteer.
- A volunteer reads aloud a chunk.
- The leader listens and responds by retelling, relating and reflecting.
- The leader reads aloud the next chunk.
- The volunteer responds by retelling, relating and reflecting.
- Each group of two decides where they will read and who will begin reading.

During the experience

- One person reads aloud a chunk of the material.
- The other listens and responds using retell, relate and reflect as a response strategy.
- Take turns reading aloud, listening and responding.
- Continue this process until the end of the reading.
-

Assessing and Evaluating

- Continue to watch and listen, and record exactly what you see and hear — quotes, ideas, questions, actions.
- Ask yourself:
  - Where do the learners choose to read and write?
  - How do they use pencils, highlighters, Post-its?
  - How do they sit?
  - What are their physical behaviours?
  - What strategies are they using?
  - What do they do when they are finished?
  - How do they retell, relate, reflect?
  - How long do they talk in between reading?
  - What are their conversations/comments about?
  -

Continuing

- Share observations with the group.
- Share recorded comments and questions.
- Continue to share the 3 R's framework.
- Invite reactions, feelings and ideas.
- Discuss the implications for recording journal entries about course readings, speakers, presentations, content.
- Brainstorm other applications for personal and/or professional use.
- Encourage participants to use the 3 R's when they write to their partners in their dialogue response journals.
- Encourage participants to consider using the process used in this in-service in their classrooms.
- Create a large reference chart for the participants to use in their classrooms. (See Draft Planning Sheet 11, "Paired Read and Respond.")
- Provide a smaller copy for each learner.
- Consider a variation of this activity called "Group Read and Respond" (see Draft Planning Sheet 10, "Group Read and Respond").
-

Practising the 3 R's in Action Research — "Teacher as Researcher"

Action research is a process of professional development whereby we as educators learn through engaging in our own inquiries in our classrooms and schools. It is a thought-provoking, systematic and ongoing learning process that evolves and changes, shifts and bends, as we become researchers, and question, observe, reflect and analyze our own observations and actions.

Action research is conducted by teachers individually, in partnerships or in groups. As well as gaining insights into teaching and learning and providing continuous ongoing personal and professional growth, action research often leads us to develop alternative instructional practices or new approaches to programming and curriculum implementation.

Becoming involved in this type of inquiry process can change our practice, thinking and learning. We can be affected on a professional and a personal level. We become learners as we question and reflect upon our own teaching and learning. The focus changes as we become more "reflective practitioners" (Nancie Atwell).

The 3 R's play a role in action research by helping us to describe what is happening (retell), make connections to our own knowledge base and experiences (relate), and question and gain insights on our findings (reflect).

The following outlines one way to approach an action research study. (The steps are adapted from Judith Green's guidelines to help teachers conduct research in their classrooms as discussed in Dorothy S. Strickland's article "The Teacher as Researcher: Toward the Extended Professional" (*Language Arts*, Vol. 65, No. 8, December 1988).

Beginning

- Choose an area of interest or concern.
- Write what you know about the area (retell), your experiences (relate), and your questions — what you want to know (reflect).
- Read related professional books and articles, view videos, talk with colleagues and speakers, attend conferences, write pertinent notes...
- Watch and listen to your learners and collect baseline information.
- Review your questions and reflect on the collected data.
- Choose, refine and rewrite *one* specific research question.
- Plan appropriate learning experiences related to this question.
- Develop a time line — when to begin the investigation and an approximate time span to conduct the study — one month, one term, one year... . (This time span may change as your research expands and extends into other areas.)
- Implement the learning experiences.

During the study

- Continue to look for, read and think about any related readings and studies, particularly in the area of "teacher as researcher" and "action research."
- Talk with colleagues and experts about your particular area of study and your classroom observations and happenings.
- Continue to keep a professional journal (or write letters to a colleague) retelling, relating and reflecting about activities, readings, dialogues, experiences, feelings, and findings.
- Share observations, writings, ideas, questions with colleagues orally and in writing.
- Remember to date your writing, and save for rereading and reflection to note growth and changes over time.

- Reread the journal (or letters) and review the data, continuing to reflect on the learnings and outcomes.
- Continue to watch, listen and record observations, questions and other pertinent data.
- Revise the plan by reflecting upon and modifying your actions.
- Share your results with colleagues, family and friends either formally in a presentation, display or paper, or informally through conversation.

Assessing and Evaluating

- Observe and listen carefully.
- Record observations, reflections and other pertinent data.
- Reflect on the observations and data collected.
- Modify what you are doing in order to plan what to do next.
- Continue to watch, listen and record observations, questions and other pertinent data.
- Reread your learning log or journal.
- Invite a colleague to read and respond to your journal or talk together about your study.
-

Continuing

- Share your findings and questions with colleagues, staff members, administrators, course participants...
- Consider recording your findings and questions in written form.
- Consider submitting your writing to a professional journal for publication.
- Meet with interested teachers practising this research model.
- Choose another issue, concern or question to pursue.
- Continue to read and make connections to related professional material.
- Go to conferences to hear "teacher as researcher" presentations, or professional talks in your area of interest.
- Take a course.
- Invite a partner to participate in a shared research project.
- Listen to and value your personal questions, wonderings, reflections.
-

Practising the 3 R's in a Homework in a Bag Program

HOMEWORK IN A BAG Meaningful homework activities help to involve families as partners in their children's education. Such activities provide a window into the classroom and help families to continue to be knowledgeable and better acquainted with their children's in-school learning experiences. Families, teachers and learners collaborate in learning as they talk, read, write, dramatize, draw and create together. Everyone helps and encourages one another. Successes are celebrated and ideas and experiences are shared. A community of learners is created.

Homework in a Bag is a creative and novel way to package and encourage home and school learning experiences. This program encourages families and their children to participate in shared reading, talking and creating. Through modelling, demonstrating and information sessions, as well as through letters sent home, we encourage the use of the 3 R's as a framework to guide thinking, talking, reading, writing, and doing.

With this homework program, mini-libraries of books and a variety of theme-centred learning materials are brought into the home regularly for almost a week by the learners, and families are helped to understand the value of homework and shared learning. They become learners and models for their children, and children begin to shine as experts when they explain about the materials in the bag. Literacy and life-long learning are encouraged and fostered.

Before you begin implementing this homework program, it is a good idea to communicate with your administrators for support and funding. Some teachers have approached businesses in their neighbourhood or their Home and School Associations for funding. The bags need to be purchased, donated or collected, as do the books and materials to be put into the bags. These materials include a variety of reading materials and artifacts — shells, toy cars..., and tools — magnifying glass, thermometer... Journals are important and should be included in each homework bag. You need to give some thought to preparing or buying these items. Notebooks, paper in duotangs, handmade wallpaper covers with paper inside, or spiral bound booklets all serve as effective journals. Some homework bags include things to write with (pencils, markers) and/or consumable materials such as blank or lined paper, construction paper, paper bags, ready-made booklets.... These supplies are especially important and necessary in areas where these items are not commonly found in the home.

The following outlines a possible process to follow.

Beginning

- Make decisions about the type of bags to use for your Homework in a Bag program. Homemade cloth bags with a tie string, holiday gift bags, plastic bags, or backpacks are some possibilities.
- Talk with learners about the Homework in a Bag concept and the idea of different themes in one bag.
- Brainstorm with learners about possible topics for these theme bags. Some topics might be Bugs, Dinosaurs, Babies, the Sea, etc.
- Select one or two themes to start.
- Buy or organize from your classroom collection, the library, children's homes..., books and other reading materials pertaining to the selected themes (fiction, non-fiction, poems, magazines, newspaper articles...).

> **Note:** You may have some students who do not read English well and/or whose families do not speak much, if any, English. In this case, have your letters explaining the Homework in a Bag translated into the families' first languages. Encourage them to read to their children in their first language, and to talk about what they read together in the first language. If possible, include in the bags books, tapes and/or newspapers in the first language.

- Title and decorate each bag.
- Add related concrete materials — puppets, artifacts, etc.
- Include things to write with, things to write on and some samples of arts and crafts materials.
- Include a completed art or craft sample with "how-to" directions.
- Add tapes and a cassette recorder for families where more than one language is spoken.
- Include a page or card explaining the program. See Figure 2.18. (Figure 2.18 is reproduced as Draft Planning Sheet 31, "Homework in a Bag: Learning Experiences.")

Figure 2.18   Homework in a Bag: Learning Experiences

What is Homework in a Bag?

- It is a bag of learning materials based on one topic or theme to be used at home and shared at school.

When does Homework in a Bag come to your home?

- It comes at least once a month.
- It arrives on a specific day of the week, e.g., Wednesday.
- It stays in your home for almost a week.
- It returns to school about 5 days later, e.g., Monday.
- It stays at school for one full day for reorganization.

Why is Homework in a Bag important?

- It provides a new and fun way to do homework.
- It is cooperative learning.
- It encourages making time for shared learning.
- It provides opportunities for making choices and decisions.
- It brings a variety of learning materials and topics into your home.
- It encourages talking, reading, writing, doing and thinking.
- It encourages literacy and lifelong learning.

How do you use Homework in a Bag?

- You and your child and/or other family members examine and use the materials in the bag to share and learn together by:
  - exploring
  - reading
  - talking
  - drawing
  - making
  - creating
  - writing
  -

- Include a homework journal. At the front, add a letter to families (on the first page or on the inside cover) inviting everyone to write in the journal. See Figure 2.19. Note the 3 R's framework embedded in the letter. (Figure 2.19 is reproduced as Draft Planning Sheet 32, "Homework in a Bag: Journals.")

Figure 2.19   Homework in a Bag: Journals

Dear Families,

Please use this special journal to record your comments and reactions about the reading and activities you have done with your child during the Homework in a Bag learning experiences.

- You might write/print your comments or make drawings about:
  - what you already knew and what you have learned
  - what you remember from your own experiences
  - your questions or understandings.

We invite both you and your child to use this journal. Please feel free to write in your first language.

Enjoy learning together.

Sincerely,

- Suggest activities that can be done at home with the materials in the bag. See Figure 2.20. (Figure 2.20 is reproduced as Draft Planning Sheet 33, "Homework in a Bag: Things To Do.")

Figure 2.20   Homework in a Bag: Things To Do

Read together.
Talk about the reading materials together.

- *Retell*
  - Tell about the story or information: "This story is about...", "I learned that..."
  - Retell your favourite parts: "The part I liked best is..."

- *Relate*
  - Make connections to other stories, poems, experiences or things you know about or have seen: "This reminds me of...", "I remember when..."
  - Share your feelings: "I feel..."

- *Reflect*
  - Ask questions: "I wonder why...", "I wonder if...", "Why do you think..."
  - Share insights: "Now I understand why..."
  - Make predictions: "I think that..."

Figure 2.20 continued

Try an activity you have read about in one of the books or magazines.

Dramatize the story.

- Act out a part of the story (with or without the use of props).
- Create a character — a paper-bag puppet, a finger puppet, a simple mask, a hat that a character wears, etc.

Illustrate your favourite scene.

- Use wax crayons, pencil crayons or coloured markers you may have at home.

Design, create and complete a new activity based on this same theme or topic... or create a bag of your own.

- Add blank materials for learners to use to write on, such as eight-page booklets (write on some pages — as a sample of what the children/families might write in the journal — and leave some pages empty to encourage writing). Sample writing you might put in the booklets might be:
  - **Retell:** "What we know about Bugs..."
  - **Reflect:** "What questions we have..."
  - **Relate:** "These bugs remind me of the time when we were camping and..."
  - **Retell:** "After reading the books in this bag, and doing some activities, the new things we learned about Bugs are..."
  - **Reflect:** "What we still want to find out..."
- Include an inventory page at the back of each journal to ensure that all materials are returned each time. A good idea might be to print this page very small so that it fits into a library pocket which can be stored at the back of the journal. See Figure 2.21 (next page). (Figure 2.21 is reproduced as Draft Planning Sheet 34, "Homework in a Bag: Inventory.")

During the experience

- Invite the learners to explore the materials in one bag.
- Discuss the learning and management expectations.
- Talk about the variety of materials — books, objects, activities.
- Model/demonstrate the learning and management experiences in class.
- Be enthusiastic.
- Send home an introductory letter to families explaining the Homework in a bag program. See Figure 2.22 (page 97). Have the letter translated if necessary. (Figure 2.22 is reproduced as Draft Planning Sheet 35: Homework in a Bag: Description.")

Figure 2.21 Homework in a Bag: Inventory

Dear Families,

To help us keep track of the materials in this bag, we have included a list of the items in the bag. Please check off the RETURNED column as you put materials back in the bag to be returned to school.

Thank you.

HOMEWORK IN A BAG CHECKLIST

_____

(Child's Name)

Check YES if the item has been returned.
Check NO if the item has not been returned.

ITEM	SENT OUT	RETURNED	
		Yes	No
_____	_____	_____	_____
_____	_____	_____	_____
_____	_____	_____	_____

List the things you added to this bag.

_____

_____

Thank you for your participation!!

- Carefully choose the group of children who take the bags home for the very first time. You may want to call their families before the bag goes home to ensure understanding. Remember, the journal entries remain in the bag for others to see and read, and will serve as a model.
- Talk with families and highlight the Homework in a Bag program — at a curriculum night in the early fall, during conferences, by telephone... throughout the year.
- Distribute a limited number of bags to be taken home each week.
- Create a schedule.
- Ensure that the Homework in a Bag is "special" — "It's my turn to take a bag this week!"
- Schedule time each week for learners to share their experiences and activities when they bring the bag back to school.

Figure 2.22   Homework in a Bag: Letter for Families

Dear Families,

This year, your child will be using and sharing **Homework in a Bag**. These bags of learning materials will be arriving in your home at least once a month for almost a week at a time — home on Wednesday and back to school the following Monday. Each bag will contain different learning materials based on a topic or theme.

With your child and with other family members, examine and use the materials in the bag. Different reading materials have been included. Some of these books or magazines or newspaper articles may be appropriate for your child **to read to you.** Some you might **read together,** and some are included for **you to read to your child.** Research has shown that children who are read to regularly become confident readers. By reading to or with your child, you:

- help them see the importance that you place on reading and literacy.
- let them hear quality literature that they cannot yet read easily on their own.
- have an opportunity to share knowledge (retell), personal connections and feelings (relate), and wonder and ask questions (reflect).
- show your child by doing the activities together that you care about his/her learning.

A **Homework in a Bag journal** or **diary** is included in the bag for recording any comments, drawings, experiences, stories, questions and understandings. Please feel free to write in your first language.

Information with ideas for **things you and your child might do together** is included.

Please feel free to add to this bag.

These **Homework in a Bag** learning experiences will help you, as families, and me, as teacher, learn about your child. Enjoy learning together.

Sincerely,

- Create one or two "new" bags every few months. Brainstorm with the learners for other topics.
- Encourage learners to put together their own bags at home and share them with the class.

Assessing and Evaluating

- Discuss with learners (and informally with families when you see them) how they feel about the Homework in a Bag program.
- Reflect on the dated journal entries.
- After an interval of time, find out from families how they feel about the Homework in a Bag program by sending out a written questionnaire. See Figure 2.23 (next page). (Figure 2.23 is reproduced as Draft Planning Sheet 36, "Homework in a Bag: Questionnaire.")

Figure 2.23   Homework in a Bag: Questionnaire

Dear Families,

Please complete the following and send the form to school with your child. Your feedback is very important and greatly appreciated.

1. How did the **Homework in a Bag** help you and your child learn and share together? Please give an example.

   _____
   _____
   _____

2. How did brothers, sisters or other family relatives become involved in the **Homework in a Bag** experiences?

   _____
   _____
   _____

3. When would your family like to receive **Homework in a Bag**?

   ❏ every other week
   ❏ weekly
   ❏ other

4. How long does your family need to have the **Homework in a Bag** at home?

   ❏ one week
   ❏ two weeks
   ❏ less than one week
   ❏ more than two weeks

   Please add any comments, suggestions, ideas or questions about the **Homework in a Bag** experience.

   Thank you for your time and participation.

                                        Sincerely,

Continuing

- Invite the learners to choose a particular bag and then tell or write about why they made the choice.
- Consider creating mathematics or science bags using hands-on material and related literature. Consult professional references for additional ideas. Examples are *Family Math* by Jean Kerr Stenmark, Virginia Thompson and Ruth Cossey (Lawrence Science, 1986) and *Sign Out Science: Simple Hands-On Experiments Using Everyday Materials*, by Silvana Carletti et al (Pembroke Publishers Limited, 1993).
-

Assessing and Evaluating

"We believe all partners — teachers, learners, families, school, system — need to be involved in conversations (retelling, relating and reflecting) about assessment and evaluation in order to better understand the connecting threads to learning and teaching."
(page 104)

"We believe self-confidence and self-image are at the heart of assessment and evaluation, both for teachers and for learners."
(page 105)

In this chapter, we share our ideas about assessment and evaluation — what assessment and evaluation are, and what we personally value and evaluate. We talk about the importance of getting to know our learners and establishing a base of information about each of them — learning what the learners know and can do, what they want to know about and where they need help. We discuss how using the 3 R's framework can help to establish this baseline knowledge, which is a clear example of diagnostic assessment and evaluation, and we illustrate how effectively the 3 R's framework can be used for formative and summative assessment and evaluation.

ASSESSMENT AND EVALUATION

Ultimately, what is taught in the classroom will be determined by the assessment and evaluation programs used, and if changes are to be made in educational practises, evaluation procedures must also change.

— Robert J. Anthony, Terry D. Johnson, Norma Mickelson, Alison Preece, *Evaluating Literacy — A Perspective for Change*, pages 21-22

We believe that assessment and evaluation are integral and essential parts of the teaching and learning process and that the ultimate purpose of assessment and evaluation is to enrich learning and teaching practices. Assessment and evaluation and curriculum are closely connected, interwoven, and consistent with what is valued about teaching and learning. Continuity or change in teaching practices and learning experiences emerge and evolve from ongoing assessment and evaluation practices.

When we **assess** and **evaluate**, we use the information to plan and implement programs and to select appropriate materials to meet the needs of the learners. Through assessment and evaluation, we find out which learners experience difficulty, and which learners need enriched programs. Through assessing and evaluating, we are encouraged to reflect on how well our program and teaching practices are working for the entire group of learners and for individual learners. Through assessment and evaluation, we articulate to families, learners and colleagues what we are doing and why, and how well the learners are doing.

By **assessment**, we mean the gathering, recording and interpreting of information and data over a period of time. This data provides information about a learner's progress and achievements, or about a particular program's implementation and effectiveness.

By **evaluation**, we mean analyzing and making judgements based on the collected information and data, in order to place a value on the progress or achievement of learners, or on the effectiveness of programs.

Assessment and evaluation are both process and product oriented. As teachers observe, collect information, and reflect upon, analyze, interpret, and utilize the information they have gathered in their work with children and parents, they provide demonstrations of growth and development.

— Robert J. Anthony, Terry D. Johnson, Norma Mickelson, Alison Preece, *Evaluating Literacy: A Perspective for Change*, page 3

Evaluation is **evaluating what is valued**. As teachers, we begin with what we know, believe and value in education. What we value determines what and how we teach. What and how we teach reflects our beliefs about teaching and learning.

We use our beliefs and values about teaching and learning, our knowledge about school and system expectations and goals, and our understanding about how people learn as our baseline for evaluating what we value. We have conversations with families, learners and colleagues. We state clearly our learning and teaching expectations and goals. These shared understandings and educational goals provide us with a base for establishing assessment and evaluation strategies and procedures.

Before we discuss strategies for using the 3 R's framework of retelling, relating and reflecting in assessment and evaluation, we invite you to read our lists of what we personally value. These lists continually change and grow as we read, talk and learn — as we retell, relate and reflect.

Susan and Maxine :

We value:

- knowing what teachers believe
- establishing a baseline of information about each of our learners by recording what our learners already know and can do
- encouraging approximations and risk taking
- observing by learner-watching and learner-listening
- recording and evaluating by using the same criteria at the beginning, middle and end of the year — continuously retelling, relating and reflecting
- collecting and organizing a variety of concrete samples (products) chosen by learners and/or by us at different times throughout the year to show growth and development over time
- negotiating what the learner wants to have evaluated — goal setting
- evaluating for a specific purpose
- defining together with our learners and posting expectations and learning outcomes
- listening carefully to questions and responses
- developing a system for assessing and evaluating on a daily basis
- using self-evaluation regularly — both for ourselves and with our learners
- using personal understanding and knowledge to connect teaching and learning
- sharing the same information with teachers, learners and families — no secrets or surprises
- inviting and valuing conversations and connections — retelling, relating, reflecting
-

We believe families are the learners' first teachers and evaluators, and that as teachers we should have ongoing conversations with them about their children. We need to invite families to share with us how much their children have grown and changed over time. We value this information because it helps us know even more about the learners.

We value:

- family-teacher-child conferences — retelling, relating and reflecting
- listening to family-shared observations
- listening to family-shared developmental background information
- viewing concrete learning samples from home
- hearing and recording families' questions
- negotiating together with families to establish educational goals
- sharing current and relevant information to ensure common understandings of appropriate educational practices
- keeping families well informed — no secrets or surprises
- inviting and valuing conversations and connections — retelling, relating, reflecting
-

We believe all partners — teachers, learners, families, school, system — need to be involved in conversations (retelling, relating and reflecting) about assessment and evaluation in order to better understand the connecting threads to learning and teaching.

We invite you to have conversations with your learners and their families about what you know and value, and how you plan to evaluate what you value. We invite you, by yourselves or with others, to create your own lists of what you value.

Asking and answering questions is the cornerstone of effective educational assessment and evaluation.

— Robert J. Anthony, Terry D. Johnson, Norma Mickelson, Alison Preece, *Evaluating Literacy — A Perspective for Change*, page 5

Asking and answering questions is also the cornerstone of effective educational programming and instruction. Educational systems have questions, administrators have questions, teachers have questions, learners have questions, and families and the public have questions. As teachers, our questions about learning and teaching needs and directions continually emerge from the process of assessment and evaluation. We need to reflect, research, collect data and information continuously, in order to formulate effective answers to questions about program, assessment and evaluation.

To assess and evaluate effectively means that we as teachers need to know ourselves, as well as knowing our learners and knowing about learning. Self-evaluation is one of the driving forces behind the learning and teaching process. The ultimate purpose of self-evaluation is to invite and support learners and teachers as they continue to take responsibility for their own growth and development. We continue to collaborate with our learners to design, develop and implement a variety of strategies to assess and evaluate our learnings and teachings. The ultimate goal is to have learners and teachers reflect, assess their own work and outline future teaching and learning objectives.

> *Before we can become expert observers, we have to be expert learners.* We have to be able to observe and value strengths more than deficits. We have to know what to look for; what are the developmental markers we are seeing or not seeing?
>
> *We have to be expert listeners*: what does the student really mean? We have to be able to recognize an individual student's learning patterns and use them to take the child further. We also have to know how to set up the learning environment to maximize student development. Most of all, we need to value observation as integral to evaluation and be willing to risk adding it to our literacy programs.
>
> *None of this is easy, and most of us take many years to make our evaluation processes more consistent with our beliefs about learning.*
>
> — Regie Routman, *Invitations*, page 303 (Emphasis is ours.)

USING THE 3 R'S FRAMEWORK IN ASSESSMENT AND EVALUATION

The 3 R's framework of retelling, relating and reflecting is clearly evident in **diagnostic assessment and evaluation** when we find out what learners know (their knowledge — when they retell), when we find out about their experiences (when they remember, relate and make connections), and when we see their reflections, questions and insights (when they wonder or talk/write about what they want to know about). The 3 R's framework is evident in **continuous formative assessment and evaluation** when we watch, listen and record (when and how learners retell, relate and reflect). The 3 R's framework is evident in **summative assessment and evaluation** when we reflect on what learners can do and know, what they relate to and remember, and what they need and want to learn. (See Draft Planning Sheet 19, "Using the 3 R's Framework in Assessment and Evaluation.")

We use our professional judgement, knowledge of our learners, school, systems, goals, experience, and sensitivity to assess and evaluate in order to encourage our learners to take greater responsibility for their own learning and thus to feel successful and confident. We believe self-confidence and self-image are at the heart of assessment and evaluation, both for teachers and for learners.

There are a number of practices that many of us commonly use when assessing and evaluating learners in our classrooms. These include:
- observation
- inventories and surveys
- conferences with learners
- conferences with families
- self-evaluation
- portfolios
- children's literature

We show below how the 3 R's framework is interwoven into each of these assessment and evaluation practices and provide practical strategies for using the 3 R's to implement the practices in the classroom setting. But first, we will examine the role of the 3 R's framework in baseline assessment and evaluation — where we believe assessment and evaluation begins.

Beginning With the Learners: Using the 3 R's Framework for Baseline Assessment and Evaluation

One of the most important understandings in experience-based, learner-centred education is that teaching and learning begins with the learners. John Dewey, an American philosopher and earliest advocate of experience-based education, in his book *Experience and Education* (1945) talks about learner-centred learning when he discusses a learner's **experience** as being extremely important in shaping that individual. He argues that an individual's experiences is the starting point for all further learning.

We, too, believe that an individual's experiences strongly impact on that person's knowledge, stories, questions and insights. We believe, therefore, that it is essential that any time we teachers begin with a new group of learners, we need to collect information about our learners. This need is particularly important today when our learners may come from a variety of backgrounds. Some children starting school may come from a home situation; others may come from a daycare situation. Some learners may come from other parts of the province or from a different province; others may come from a different part of the world. We need to find out what our learners know (their knowledge), what they remember or relate to (their personal stories), what they want to know (their questions) and what they understand (their insights and reflections). This information establishes the starting point, the **baseline of information** that forms the foundation blocks necessary for creating a learner-centred curriculum. Figure 3.1 (opposite) illustrates this "baseline" and its connections to the 3 R's framework.

Collecting baseline data is, we believe, an essential component in the assessing and evaluating process. **In the last section of this chapter, "Getting To Know You," pages 117-143, we provide strategies you can use in the classroom with your learners to collect this baseline information about the learners.** The strategies in the "Getting To Know You" section are examples of **diagnostic assessment and evaluation.**

Throughout the process of collecting baseline information, we watch and listen, and keep records of what we see and hear. We are involved in continuous **formative assessment and evaluation.** We consider what we discover in order to plan appropriately and effectively to meet the needs and interests of the learners. Our knowledge of school and system expectations and goals, and the baseline information we collect about our learners become important planning and instructional data, and assessment and evaluation data.

Many of the "Getting To Know You" strategies are most effective if repeated in the same or similar ways during the year. We may use these experiences during the first few weeks of the year and again at the end of the year. We compare the observations and work samples, and help to illustrate, in a concrete way, growth over

Figure 3.1 The 3 R's Framework and Baseline Information

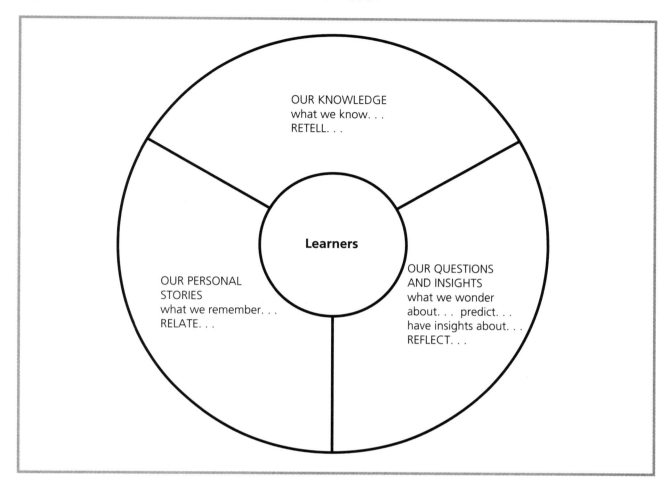

time. This data then helps to inform **summative assessment and evaluation** and the reporting process. This information connects curriculum instruction and teaching decisions, and addresses individual differences.

Using the 3 R's framework to establish baseline data becomes an important first step in ongoing assessment and evaluation procedures.

 ## Using the 3 R's in Observation

Observation — "learner-watching" and "learner-listening" — is an essential strategy for gaining information about our learners, and for providing us with an objective source of information for writing report cards and for sharing with families, administrators, and colleagues. Observation can be spontaneous or it can be scheduled at specific times each day.

Some of the strategies we can use when we practise observation are
- Look for growth and development signposts or indicators. Refer to *Observing Children, Observing Adolescents*, available from the Toronto Board of Education, Toronto, Ontario.
- Understand clearly what the learner is doing and saying.

- Ask learners "Why?" and "What if...?"
- Recognize individual learning patterns.
- Record observations in a systematic way.
- Record notable events or significant changes.
- Have pen, notebook, Post-its, and file folders available.
- Retell and record exactly what the learner says and does.
- Record learner behaviours — postures, gestures, voice qualities, facial expressions...
- Use pertinent or significant information to add to portfolios. (See Draft Planning Sheet 57, "Possible Items for Portfolios.")
- Use anecdotal records as signposts for noting progress and setting instructional goals.
- Include sample pieces from portfolios to share with families to support written records, e.g., report cards, checklists, mark sheets...
- Invite and value conversations and connections — retell, relate, reflect.
- Base the assessment and evaluation on sections of curriculum documents, research, system policies... that refer to child development and stages of learning.

When we observe, we objectively record or **retell** on paper what our learners can do and say. It is important to keep in mind when we record that:

> Observing and recording do not, by themselves, constitute assessment. Teachers must reflect on WHAT they have observed and recorded in relation to program goals and objectives for each child.
>
> — Tynette W. Hills, *Assessment in Context, Teachers and Children at Work*

We must **relate** our prior knowledge and past experiences, our understanding of child development, and our knowledge of program goals, objectives and expectations to our recorded observations. We **reflect** on our collected data and make decisions for appropriate programming and teaching strategies.

Through observation and retelling, relating and reflecting, we discover who needs assistance and/or reinforcement, and when it is most appropriate to intervene with an idea, suggestion or question. Our observations and reflections provide us with insight into each learner's interactions with people, places and things. We date our notes and file them so we can refer to and reflect on the comments. We include the information and data from our observations in our portfolios for each learner. (See Draft Planning Sheet 57, "Possible Items for Portfolios.")

Figure 3.2 (opposite) illustrates the role of the 3 R's in observation, assessment and evaluation. The 3 R's framework is particularly useful as a record sheet for observation and notetaking during the assessment and evaluation of any learning experience. It helps to structure observing, thinking and writing. It is also an effective device for giving constructive and personal feedback, which values the learners' presentations, performances and products. The framework is useful for those of us who work with children of all ages, for course directors who work with adults, and for administrators who work with teachers and must evaluate process and product. (You may want to use Draft Planning Sheet 8, "Using the 3 R's Framework To Assess and Evaluate," to record your observations.)

Figure 3.2 The 3 R's Framework in Observation, Assessment and Evaluation

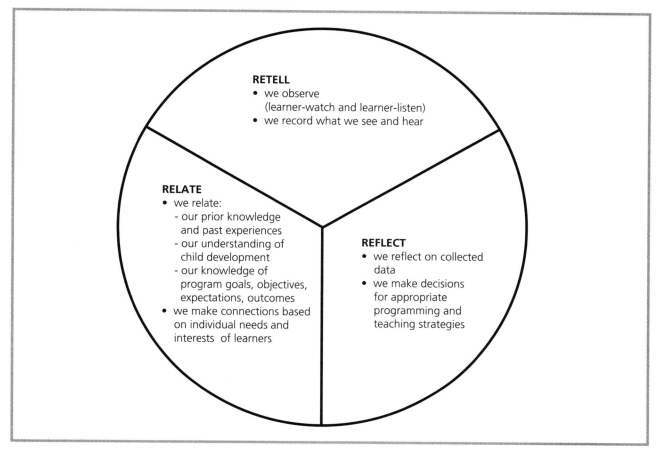

Practising Using the 3 R's Framework as a Tool for Observation and Record-Keeping

- Tell learners you will be using the 3 R's framework as a tool to help you record what you see, hear and think during a presentation, performance, or evaluation of a product. (You may want to show your learners overheads of or hand out copies of Draft Planning Sheets 3, 4, 5 and 6, "The 3 R's Framework: Retelling, Relating and Reflecting," "Retell," "Relate," and "Reflect.")
- During the experience, watch and listen carefully, and record on a page divided into 3 columns (Figure 3.3) or on a circular model of a blank 3 R's framework

Figure 3.3 The 3 R's Framework in Observation, Assessment and Evaluation: In Chart Form

Retell	Relate	Reflect

(Figure 3.4; Draft Planning Sheet 8, "Using the 3 R's Framework To Assess and Evaluate").

- In the "retell" column or section, describe what you see and hear. (See Draft Planning Sheet 4, "Retell.")
- In the "relate" column or section, make connections to your own experiences. (See Draft Planning Sheet 5, "Relate.")
- Consider recording only the "retell" and "reflect" information as "relate" may occur in your mind as you observe.
- In the "reflect" column or section, write questions or suggestions, e.g., "I wonder if you could have...", "I wonder why you thought to...", "You might think about..." (See Draft Planning Sheet 6, "Reflect.")
- Share your draft notes and discuss individually with learners.
- Add or delete recorded information based on this discussion.
- Encourage learners to use the 3 R's framework to self-evaluate and to make peer evaluations.
-

Figure 3.4 The 3 R's Framework in Observation, Assessment and Evaluation: A Circular Recording Sheet

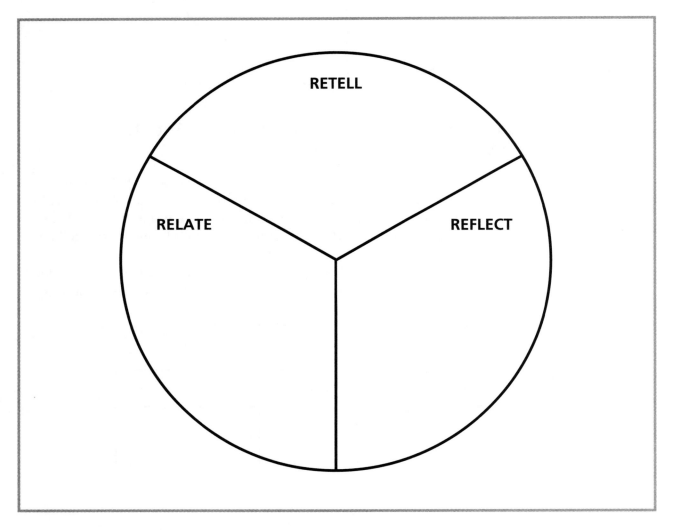

Using the 3 R's in Inventories and Surveys

Inventories and surveys consist of sets of questions or sentences for learners to complete. They are usually in written form about a specific area or topic. They become a sharing of experiences and information, and provide specific information about different learning areas and interests, what learners can do and know (retell), what experiences they have had (relate), and what they want or like to do or learn (reflect). The inventories and surveys are completed by learners, families and/or teachers. For younger learners, teachers and families ask the questions and act as the scribe. (See Draft Planning Sheets 42 and 43, "Learner Résumé" and "Learner Interest Survey.")

Inventories and surveys are useful early in the year to help establish baseline information about our learners. Inventories and surveys are useful before a unit of study, when reviewing collected work samples, when preparing for formal reporting, or when organizing groups. They are also useful at the end of the year to inform the summative evaluation process.

Through the use of inventories and surveys, we find out important information. We can find out about attitudes and behaviours and how learners view themselves. We use the information to set and/or adjust learning goals, collect appropriate learning materials and to plan or revise programs.

Practising Using the 3 R's in Inventories and Surveys

- Review the 3 R's framework. (You may want to make overheads of or hand out copies of Draft Planning Sheets 3, 4, 5 and 6, "The 3 R's Framework: Retelling, Relating and Reflecting," "Retell," "Relate," and "Reflect.")
- Provide copies for individual learners and/or groups of learners.
- Provide an appropriate place for learners to work.
- Allow time for learners to complete the inventory or survey.
- Act as recorder for young learners.
- Invite and value all responses.
- Use information to add to portfolios. (See Draft Planning Sheet 57, "Possible Items for Portfolios.")

Using the 3 R's in Assessment and Evaluation Conferences With Learners

Conferences with learners are conversations — when we and our learners retell, relate, and reflect. These are times to share information from inventories and surveys, or to talk about collected work samples from any area of the curriculum. Conferences are times when we meet together in large and/or small groups to set goals.

We get to know individual learners when we talk one-on-one with them. We discover and review attitudes, interests and learning styles, and collect and establish baseline information. We nurture the development of self-image and self-confidence by focussing on what learners can do and need/plan/want to learn next.

Conferences with learners happen regularly, informally or at scheduled times, depending on the needs of the learners. Conferences with learners are especially helpful before formal reports are shared with families or when we or our learners specifically request or need a conference.

Practising Using the 3 R's in Assessment and Evaluation Conferences With Learners

- Schedule sufficient time for conversations.
- Set up an inviting place to talk — round table, chairs facing one another, carpet area
- Review the 3 R's framework. (You may want to hand out copies of Draft Planning Sheets 3, 4, 5 and 6, "The 3 R's Framework: Retelling, Relating and Reflecting," "Retell," "Relate," and "Reflect.")
- Share concrete samples and data.
- State and show what the learner can do.
- Listen to the learner's point of view.
- Listen to the learner's questions.
- Establish together one or two future learning goals.
- Invite and value conversations and connections — retell, relate, reflect.
- Consider including significant information in portfolios.
-

Using the 3 R's in Conferences With Families

Conferences with families are conversations — when families and teachers retell, relate, reflect, sharing experiences and information. Family conferences are times to review and talk about collected work samples. These are times to talk about what learners know, what their experiences have been, and what they have learned and understand. They are also times to share and encourage any questions and concerns.

Conferences with families help to provide us with valuable and purposeful information, and help us to collect and establish baseline information. We need to value the knowledge families can provide about their children. From them, we discover what our learners can do outside the school setting, and we understand how they react in numerous and varied situations. Conferences with families provide us with a chance to view and value concrete learning samples from home, to hear families' and learners' questions, share beliefs about education, and negotiate common understandings of expectations, goals, and appropriate educational practices. Conferences provide us with ideal opportunities to be informed and involved, and to develop close partnerships.

Conferences should occur regularly and often. They usually occur at the beginning of the year, at some point each term, and when initiated by families, teachers and/or learners.

Practising Using the 3 R's in Conferences With Families

- Contact families to schedule a time.
- Schedule sufficient time for conversations.
- Set up an inviting place to talk — round table, chairs facing one another.
- Offer beverages and/or snacks.
- Be prepared and have all information ready to share.
- You may want to have copies of Draft Planning Sheets 3 and 7, "The 3 R's Framework: Retelling, Reflecting and Reflecting" and "The 3 R's Framework in an 8-Page Book Format," on hand to give out as references.
- State and show what the learner can do.
- Listen to observations shared by families.
- Listen to developmental background information shared by families.
- Listen to and value the questions posed by families and children.
- View and value concrete learning samples from home and from school.
- Establish together one or two future learning goals.
- Share professional information and resources.
- Start and finish on time.
- Invite and value conversations and connections — retell, relate, reflect.
- Consider including significant information in portfolios.
- Continue to communicate regularly and often throughout the year.
-

 ## Using the 3 R's in Self-Evaluation

Self-evaluation is an evaluation practice whereby learners examine themselves, their actions, their learning processes, and/or their performances. They think, talk or record what they can do (retell), what their experiences are (relate), and what they want to learn next (reflect). We encourage them to set learning goals for themselves.

When learners self-evaluate, they examine and reflect upon their growth over time. They review their successes and accomplishments. They think about the changes in their attitudes, skills and knowledge. They become more aware of their learning styles and needs, and they become more reflective and perceptive about themselves. When we encourage our learners to monitor and evaluate their personal growth, they often become more independent, motivated and focussed on their own progress.

When learners practise self-evaluation, we are provided with insights into how they make use of people, places and things. The information from self-evaluation is valuable when included in portfolios. This information is also valuable for us as teachers for assessing and evaluating our own teaching and programs.

Self-evaluation can be used any time throughout the year. It is useful at the beginning and end of a unit of study, or at the end of an instructional time. It is also useful before, during or after a teaching/learning strategy — e.g., after a read-aloud, after a special class experience (e.g., visitor, trip...), or just before report cards are shared with families.

Practising Using the 3 R's in Self-Evaluation

- Review the 3 R's framework. (You may want to make overheads of or hand out copies of Draft Planning Sheets 3, 4, 5 and 6, "The 3 R's Framework: Retelling, Relating and Reflecting," "Retell," "Relate" and "Reflect.)
- Think about a variety of ways to introduce self-evaluation to learners, for example:
  - Invite learners to talk to one another and share one or two things they know, are expert in, or can do (retell).
  - Have them recall and talk to one another about a previous learning experience (relate).
  - Suggest they record their thoughts in a personal response journal (retell, relate, reflect).
  - Have them respond to a series of purposeful questions. (See an example for teachers in Draft Planning Sheet 56, "Personal Assessment: Reflections")
  - Invite them to review and reflect on collected work samples and/or learning records (reflect).
  - Ask them to choose their best pieces of work for formal evaluation (reflect).
  - Invite them to write a personal draft report card (retell, relate, reflect).
- Invite the learners to be part of the process when deciding what pieces of work to collect in portfolios (see Draft Planning Sheet 57, "Possible Items for Portfolios").
- Implement self-evaluation practices when appropriate.
- Think about including self-evaluation as an essential and ongoing part of the teaching/learning process.

Using the 3 R's and Portfolios

Portfolios are files containing materials that reflect the learner — that show the depth and range of the knowledge, growth and ability of the individual. They are concrete records of each individual's learning and/or teaching journey. They illustrate examples of retellings, relatings and reflections. Portfolios may include dated samples of work chosen by learners, teachers, peers and/or families, inventories and surveys, records of conferences, observations and checklists, anecdotal notes, teacher, peer and self-evaluations, information from other teachers, learners, peers, families — collections of many snapshots of learning compiled over time. (See Draft Planning Sheets 37 and 57, "Creating Personal Portfolios" and "Possible Items for Portfolios.") Portfolios are a way to select and remember moments of approximations, risk taking and excellence.

Portfolios are similar to reading a favourite book — the more we read, reread and reflect, the better we understand. They are similar to watching videos of growth and development, windows revealing the potentials of learners. They are learning albums that individuals view together, portraits of learners and their growth as learners — individual masterpieces. Portfolios are an integral part of assessment and evaluation.

We believe there is no one way to use portfolios. How they are structured and how they are used depends on who the learner is and what the learner is working towards.

One way to introduce our learners to the use of portfolios is for us to create our own portfolios. We might include a letter explaining why we chose to include the items we did. We might include a personal reading log listing the professional books, children's literature, and pleasure reading we have read or are in the middle of reading. Our portfolio might include copies of our favourite books and magazines, the newspaper we read regularly, rough drafts of any articles, letters or curriculum writing we are working on, photographs and/or drawings. We might even include wrappings of our favourite candy bar or chocolate. By sharing our portfolios with our learners, we model and demonstrate to learners that we are real people who possess knowledge, memories, and questions, and who are continuing to learn and grow.

We then invite learners to design and create their own portfolios. (You may want to brainstorm possible items or discuss some of the items in Draft Planning Sheet 57, "Possible Items for Portfolios," with your learners before they start their portfolios or you may decide to post the sheet for your learners to refer to throughout the year.) We need to provide large group, small group and individual time for learners to share and discuss their growth and development. Portfolios become celebrations that value and evaluate learning and teaching in a natural and authentic way. As confidence and self-image grows, learners begin to value and develop self-assessment and self-evaluation processes. They become more critical of their own progress, and they set goals for what they need or want to do next. They develop lifelong skills necessary in today's society.

Portfolios become personal collections, valuing what learners can do over time. They reflect what learners are all about — their attitudes, skills and knowledge — their growth.

Practising Using the 3 R's in Portfolios

- Read and review professional information about portfolios.
- Think about your expectations for creating and using portfolios with learners and families.
- Review your board/system curriculum documents and resources, and utilize any checklists, developmental charts, etc., for possible portfolio inserts.
- Review and consider how you will use the 3 R's framework.
- Make your own portfolio and share with learners.
- Discuss and collect or provide materials for creating portfolios, e.g., box, file folder, binder, scrapbook...
- Decide with your learners the inserts to be included in the portfolios and when they are to be included — beginning and end of year, each term... (Refer to Draft Planning Sheet 57, "Possible Items for Portfolios.")
- Present mini-lessons throughout the year on choosing samples to be included in the portfolios.
- Invite learners to select and comment on significant work samples.
- Provide time for learners to examine their responses and reflect on their growth and development over time.
- Provide time for learners to review and talk about portfolio contents.

- Value the contents, and base formal evaluation (report card comments) on information contained in the portfolios.
- Value and use portfolios as an integral part of teacher-learner-family conferences.
- Discuss portfolio assessment with your colleagues and/or staff.
- Choose which pieces will remain in the learner's portfolio and which will be taken home.
- Invite the learner and family to be part of this decision.
- Pass the portfolio on to the next teacher of that learner.
- Review and discuss with all partners the process of using portfolios — think about what went well and what needs to be changed.
- Monitor, assess and evaluate this process on a continual basis.

 Using the 3 R's in Literature-Based Assessment and Evaluation

We can use a variety of carefully selected picture books or a single book in read-aloud experiences as vehicles to help us assess and evaluate what learners know and can do. This approach is most effective with individual learners, but it can also be used with small groups or with the whole class, depending on the age and grade. Adding real objects from the book(s), such as a letter, toy or artifact, will complement the experience and will promote conversations and connections — retellings, relatings and reflections.

This experience is effective when used with very young learners and their families as part of an initial assessment and evaluation process. For example, by listening and observing carefully, we and the children's families find out which colours the learners are able to recognize when they use a picture book with a colour theme. Learners point out and talk about the illustrations and colours, and their talk and questions about colours are natural and authentic. Similar observations illustrate mathematical knowledge and skills when we select from numerous examples of books that integrate mathematical and literacy concepts. (See the list of titles on pages 124–125 in this chapter and the "Literature Bibliography" on pages 189-198 for titles that integrate mathematical and literacy concepts.)

When we watch, listen, and record what learners of all ages say as they listen to or read a book, we learn pertinent information for assessment and evaluation. Literature selections and real objects are natural vehicles for stimulating spontaneous conversations. They enable us to ask authentic questions to gain deeper insights into what learners know and can do. Making these literacy connections values what learners know and can do and helps us to use authentic assessment and evaluation practices for appropriate programming.

Practising Using the 3 R's in Literature-Based Assessment and Evaluation

- Select and use a book to read aloud, such as *Jasper's Beanstalk* by Mick Inkpen and Nick Butterworth.
- Collect objects that complement the book — a bean, watering can, dirt, piece of hose...

- Arrange a time to meet with the learner and family.
- Review the 3 R's framework. (You may want to make overheads or hand out Draft Planning Sheets 3, 4, 5 and 6, "The 3 R's Framework: Retelling, Relating and Reflecting," "Retell," "Relate" and "Reflect.")
- Read aloud the story to the learner and family using the objects. Invite conversations.
- Ask questions when necessary and/or appropriate.
- Observe and record learner responses — record exactly what you see and hear. (You may want to use Draft Planning Sheet 8, "Using the 3 R's Framework To Assess and Evaluate," to record your observations.)
- Review the recorded observations, examining what the learner knows and can do.
- Based on this initial assessment and evaluation, plan appropriate program.
- Repeat this experience at a later time in the year using the same book and materials.
- Observe and record growth and changes over time by comparing to initial assessment and evaluation information.
-

"GETTING TO KNOW YOU": STRATEGIES FOR USING THE 3 R'S FRAMEWORK IN BASELINE ASSESSMENT AND EVALUATION

We believe that when any of us begin to work with new learners, we need to collect baseline information about those learners.

Lucy McCormick Calkins in her book *Living Between the Lines* outlines many suggestions for "getting to know" our learners. She says we need to:

> ...fill the classroom with children's lives. Imagine the message we would convey if we began the year by asking everyone to bring photograph albums from home and spend an hour in twos and threes sharing the moments and people in our lives.... Instead of beginning the year by asking children to take turns reading aloud from a textbook, we might ask them to read their favorite poems and books aloud, and especially to read in their native languages. Imagine the message we would convey if children began the year by surveying each other about topics of real concern and then making bar graphs depicting which children read the front page of the newspaper, which native languages are represented in the classroom, who believes in boycotting tuna fish companies, and how many in the class are only children.

> — Lucy McCormick Calkins, *Living Between the Lines*, pages 12-14

We invite you to try some of the following **"Getting To Know You"** strategies with the purpose of collecting baseline information about your learners. These are examples of **diagnostic assessment and evaluation**. Through the "Getting To Know You" strategies you will find out what your learners know and how they came to know (retell), what they remember and have experienced (relate), and what their questions are (reflect). This information is focussed on what learners can do and know. For a particular unit of study, you may want to record the information you gather on charts, and date and post the charts for learners to refer to as they seek answers to their questions.

Many of the "Getting To Know You" strategies are most effective if repeated in the same or a similar way during the year. You might use these experiences during the first few weeks of the year and again at the end of the year. These collected samples, when dated and repeated, illustrate growth and development of learners over time.

We believe it is important to share the information collected from the "Getting To Know You" experiences with learners and families. This sharing helps us as teachers to articulate, in a concrete way, what we are doing and why, and it focusses on what learners can do and know, what their plans and needs — goals and objectives — are, and what they have learned. By practising baseline and finding out what learners know, growth and development over time is clear.

When using the following strategies, you may decide to begin slowly, with the whole class, or with one small group at a time. With young learners or when modelling and demonstrating for older learners, you may wish to act as the recorder.

What We Know and Want to Know: The Donut Model

In this experience, we invite learners to share what they already know about a particular topic, theme, or unit of study — retelling, relating, reflecting. To help learners, we developed the donut model (Figure 3.5). We call it the "donut" model because when we used it with a group of younger learners, they thought it looked like a donut because of its circular shape and they named it for us. (Figure 3.5 has been reproduced as Draft Planning Sheet 45, "The Donut Model.")

In the centre of the circle, we ask learners to indicate what they already know about the topic, theme, or unit of study (retell), and in the outer circle we ask them to indicate what questions they have about the subject (reflect). We value the collective knowledge of the whole class, and invite learners to form questions to illustrate what they want to find out. We as teachers reflect upon school and system expectations and add our own questions to fill in any gaps. Once the strategy is completed, all involved have a better understanding of what is known by the group, and important questions are brought to light. Curiosity and interest are fostered as learners and teachers strive to answer these questions through reading, researching, interviewing, talking, writing, drawing and creating.

The donut model can be used with a large group, small groups or individuals, depending on the age and experience of the learners. Older learners can work in small groups. With younger learners, it is best for you or an adult volunteer to act as recorder.

This experience provides initial and important baseline information and is a beginning step in negotiating curriculum with learners.

Figure 3.5 The Donut Model

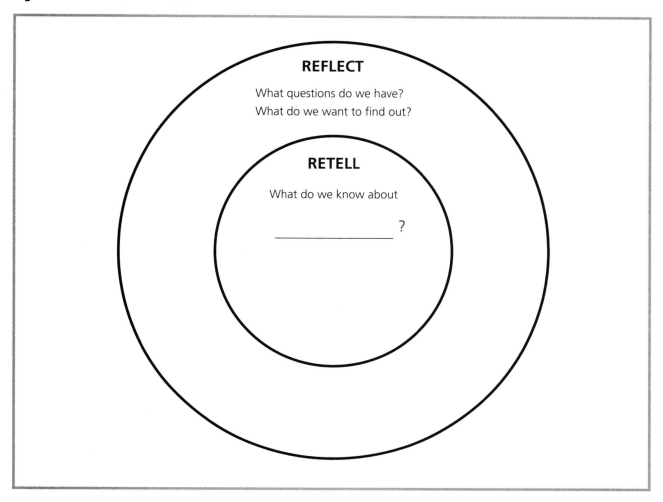

Beginning

- Read aloud an appropriate selection to introduce a unit of study, topic or discussion about a particular issue. For example, read *Crinkleroot's Guide to Walking in Wild Places* by Jim Arnosky.
- Find out what the learners know and want to know about the topic and record on the donut model. (See Draft Planning Sheet 45, "The Donut Model.")
- Use a green marker to record what learners know — or think they know (retell).
- Use a red marker to record what learners want to learn — their questions (reflect).
- Encourage learners to relate their memories and personal stories. Listen and value these stories, but for this experience, do not record them as part of the baseline model.
- If the learners are working in small groups, invite learners to share with others in the group and/or with other groups.
- If you know of a particular issue, curriculum guideline that needs to be addressed, or if you want to move the learning forward in a particular direction, add your own knowledge and questions to the information in the donut model, and discuss when appropriate.

During the experience

- Date stamp and post the donut model(s) for reference.
- After listening to a non-fiction read-aloud, film or speaker presenting information that relates to the topic, refer to the donut model(s) with your learners. Check off the facts in the "retell" part of the model when they have been confirmed — or proven wrong. Highlight questions in the "reflect" part of the model when answers are found.

  This experience encourages learners to confirm or negate what they think they know, and it fosters interest and motivation as learners strive to find answers to their questions. It makes the listening and learning more focussed and directed.

Assessment and Evaluation

- Continue to watch, listen and notice what learners do know.
- Observe and record who contributes.
- Date the donut model(s) and keep until the end of the unit.
- Refer to often throughout the unit to confirm or negate what learners know or think they know.
- Refer to at the end of the unit to see if learners can now answer the questions.
- Share information with learners, families and other educators.
-

Continuing

- Invite the learners to reflect on their progress over time, on their thinking and learning, and on the process they were involved in.
- Repeat this experience at the end of a unit, topic, discussion, or reading, and compare with the original donut model(s) developed at the beginning of the unit.
-

Other titles you might use:

- *Sun Up, Sun Down* by Gail Gibbons
- *Block City* by Robert Louis Stevenson
- *No Problem* by Eileen Browne
- *Why Mosquitoes Buzz in People's Ears* by Verna Aardema
- *Sarah, Plain and Tall* by Patricia MacLachlan
- *How To Eat Fried Worms* by Thomas Rockwell
-

We Draw What We See

In this experience, we find out how learners follow directions, how teacher-dependent or independent they are, and how self-confident they feel. At the same time, the activity encourages creativity, imagination and expression of artistic talents.

The book *Frosted Glass* by Denys Cazet in a read-aloud situation encourages a discussion about many issues. The main character is a dog named Geoffrey, who, when asked by his teacher to draw a still life (a vase with flowers) turns his drawing upside down and ends with a colourful spaceship blasting into space. Knowing that he created a drawing different from the drawings of everyone else in the class, Geoffrey is quite worried about his teacher's reaction to his piece of art.

Frosted Glass lends itself to an in-depth character study of the main character Geoffrey who sees pictures and stories in everyday situations, is creative and imaginative, daydreams, forgets directions, and appears to need extra guidance and support from his classmates and teacher. At the same time, this book illustrates the teacher's role as builder of self-esteem and character. This book provides many issues and insights to use as points of discussion with learners of all ages.

Beginning

- Bring in a vase with fresh flowers.
- Organize the materials — paper or Post-its, crayons...
- Invite the learners to become artists and draw the "still life" vase and flowers (just as the teacher in the read-aloud did).
- Ask them to add their signature — like real artists!
- Invite them to place their completed paper or Post-it drawings on a large piece of Bristol board.
- Fold the Bristol board in half and create a model of the end pages in *Frosted Glass*.

During the experience

- Read aloud the book *Frosted Glass* by Denys Cazet.
- Stop part way through the story, before the learners find out what the teacher thinks of Geoffrey's drawing.
- Invite and record predictions about how the teacher will react to Geoffrey's drawing.
- Finish reading the story.
- Revisit the predictions and encourage further responses.
- Invite the children to examine their drawings and signatures to notice and appreciate individual differences and styles.
- Discuss creativity, imagination, following directions, drawing what you see, being an artist...
- Discuss Geoffrey's character.
- Brainstorm and list possible words to describe Geoffrey.
- Study the end pages of the book, examining the drawings and the signatures.
- Encourage learners to compare the drawings on the end pages of the book with their own drawings.
- Listen to the conversations and note the connections the learners make.

Assessing and Evaluating

- Watch, listen and record some of the children's responses and behaviours during the drawing experience. Ask yourself:
  - Who starts immediately?
  - Who appears frustrated?
  - Who helps others?
  - Who follows directions?
  - What colours of crayons do they use?
  - How many draw the colours they see?
  - How do they add detail?
  - Do they add other objects or people to their pictures?
  - Do they change the vase to another shape?
  - How do they place the paper — vertically? horizontally? on an angle?
  - How do they view and respond to the drawings of others?
  -
- Reflect on your observations and notes:
  - How did the learners respond to teacher direction?
  - Was anyone dependent on another and why?
  - Was anyone frustrated and why?
  - How did creativity emerge?
  - How did learners demonstrate their artistic talents?
  -
- Encourage the learners to date stamp their work.
- Display their drawings and/or store as a sample of independent drawing.

Continuing

- Reread the same story again at another time.
- Repeat this experience or a similar one at the end of the month, term, or year to observe growth over time.
- Share the assessment and evaluation information with learners, families and other educators.
-

Other titles you might use:

- *The Art Lesson* by Tomie de Paola
- *Alice The Artist* by Martin Waddell
- *No Good In Art* by Miriam Cohen
- *All I See* by Cynthia Rylant
- *The Young Artist* by Thomas Locker
-

We Can Print and Write

In this experience, we find out how learners follow directions, and how they record onto paper the letters that they know. Using an alphabet book in a read-aloud situation helps to reinforce and value the learners' concepts of letters, names and the alphabet.

Beginning

- Read aloud an alphabet book — e.g., *The Wildlife A·B·C·* by Jan Thornhill.

During the experience

- Invite learners to print the letters and words they know.
- Invite them to copy letters, words, sentences, stories, or poems.
- Invite them to compose anything they wish — marks, drawings, symbols, letters, words, sentences, stories, poems...
- Invite learners to print/write their name.
- Encourage them to date stamp their work.
- Encourage them to print the best they can.

Assessment and Evaluation

- Store this printing as a sample of independent printing/writing.
- Reflect on your observations and notes:
    - How did the learners respond to the directions?
    - Did learners choose to copy or compose?
    - Who needed more time to complete the activity?
    - Who asked for help and why?
    - Who appeared to be frustrated or to have difficulty and why?
    - What stage of development appears to be evident?
    - How can I help the learner at this stage of development?
    -

Continuing

- Repeat this activity or a similar one at the end of the month, term, or year to observe growth over time.
- Use the book you read aloud in this activity to teach specific skills and concepts, such as names, initial consonants, alphabetical order...
- Create a cooperative class book patterned after the word structure in the read-aloud, using the names and favourite foods of the learners in the class.
- Share the assessment and evaluation information with learners, families, and other educators.
-

Other titles you might use:

- *ABC* by Jan Pieńkowski
- *A B C* by Brian Wildsmith

- *Jambo Means Hello: A Swahili Alphabet Book* by Muriel and Tom Feelings
- *Albert's Alphabet* by Leslie Tryon
-

We Know Our Numbers

In this experience, we find out how learners follow directions, what they know about numbers and how they record numbers. Using the book *From One to One Hundred* by Teri Sloat in a read-aloud situation helps to reinforce the learners' concepts of numbers and demonstrates the connections between literature and mathematics.

Beginning

- Read aloud the book *From One to One Hundred* by Teri Sloat.

During the experience

- Invite learners to record all the numbers they know.
- Invite them to tell you about the numbers they have recorded.
- Invite them to print/write their name.
- Encourage them to date stamp their work.

Assessment and Evaluation

- Store this printing as a sample of number recognition and formation.
- Reflect on your observations and notes:
  - How did the learners respond to the directions?
  - Who needed more time to complete the task?
  - Who asked for help and why?
  - Who appeared to be frustrated or to have difficulty and why?
  - What stage of development appears to be evident?
  - How can I help the learner at this stage of development?
  -

Continuing

- Repeat this experience or a similar one at the end of the month, term, or year to observe growth over time.
- Read other books to reinforce mathematical concepts — see below for some suggested titles.
- Provide time for practising number recognition and formation.
- Share the assessment and evaluation information with learners, families and other educators.
-

Some additional titles that highlight math concepts:

- *Anno's Counting Book* by Mitsumasa Anno
- *One Watermelon Seed* by Celia Lottridge
- *Numblers* by Suse MacDonald

- *Moja Means One* by Muriel Feelings
- *Helen Oxenbury's Numbers of Things* by Helen Oxenbury
-

We Know About Names

In this experience, we find out what learners remember about their first days at school and what they know about names. Using the book *Chrysanthemum* by Kevin Henkes in a read-aloud situation helps to bring out the learners' experiences with names. They become more familiar with the names of people and flowers. As well, they engage in conversations about name calling, making fun of others, friendship, beginning school experiences and other points of interest.

Numerous examples of teaching and learning stem from this book — e.g., learners see an example of an *epilogue* and often begin to use epilogues in their own writing. They see examples of *alliteration* such as "blushed, beamed, bloomed," and *metaphors* such as "she wilted and bloomed," just like a flower. They see examples of interesting ways to illustrate picture books with many shaped boxes on different pages — horizontal, vertical, square... They learn that characters can be drawn to look like their names, such as Mrs. Twinkle, the music teacher, who has a tail shaped like a treble clef and musical notes on her dress. This picture book has many possibilities for teaching and learning.

Beginning

- Invite learners to turn to the person closest to them to talk about their own name — their first, middle and family name.
- Encourage learners to discuss where their names come from, what they mean, how they received their names, and other information or stories about their names or the names of others in their family.
- Invite learners to share with the large group.

During the experience

- Read aloud the book *Chrysanthemum* by Kevin Henkes.
- Model and demonstrate by sharing a personal response: *"In this story,* Chrysanthemum *is teased by the other children in the school because her name is the name of a flower (retell). I always feel sad when children in school make fun of others because they are different (relate). I wonder why the children acted this way (reflect)?*
- Invite learners to respond to the story:
    - What did they like about the story and why?
    - What did it remind them of?
    - What did they predict or wonder about?
    -

Assessment and Evaluation

- Watch and listen to the learners' talk and behaviour during this experience. Ask yourself:
  - Who followed directions well?
  - Who related stories about their own names and families?
  - How did individual learners react to the discussion on name calling, being different, etc.?
  - What did I learn about each learner?

Continuing

- Brainstorm with the learners for other things to do with names, e.g.,
  - Research the history and meaning of specific names.
  - Interview families and others about their names.
  - Graph the names that are the most common in the class or school.
  - Research the names of dogs, cats, streets, cities, countries, stores...
  - Note names in environmental print, e.g., street names, store names, billboards, cereal boxes...
  - Note differences in print in books, in environmental print, on products — e.g., names in cursive versus printed, lower-case letters versus block letters...
  - Do some art activities involving names — e.g., designs, bubble letters...
  -
- Repeat this activity or a similar one at the end of the month, term, or year to observe growth over time.
- Share information with learners, families, and other educators.
-

Other titles you might use:

- *Six-Dinner Sid* by Inga Moore
- *My Name Is Alice* by Jane Bayer
- *The Day of Ahmed's Secret* by Florence Parry Heide
- *Potluck* by Anne Shelby
- *Alison's Zinnea* by Anita Lobel
- *There's an Ant in Anthony* by Bernard Most
-

We Learn About One Another

In this "Getting To Know You" experience, we observe and gather information about the learners. Using a personal favourite, *Laura Charlotte* by Kathryn O. Galbraith, as a read-aloud sets the stage for the experience. In this picture book, we learn about the central character and her stuffed elephant. This invites readers and listeners to recall memories and share their common experiences.

Beginning

- Read aloud a book where personal information about a central character is given — e.g., *Laura Charlotte* by Kathryn O. Galbraith.
- Invite listeners to respond by having conversations and making connections.
- Model/demonstrate by sharing a personal response: *"In this story, <u>Laura Charlotte</u>, I learned many things about the little girl in the story and her relationship with her mother and a stuffed elephant. It makes me think of the story of <u>The Velveteen Rabbit</u> and my son's 30-year-old-stuffed cow Bessie. I wonder how many families have similar treasures that are passed on from generation to generation?*

During the experience

- Invite learners to:
  - Arrange themselves into groups of four.
  - Select a recorder.
  - Fold a piece of chart paper into four equal parts and draw a big circle in the centre; put each group member's name at the top of one of the squares and label the circle "Things in Common" (see Figure 3.6), or use Draft

Figure 3.6   We Learn About One Another

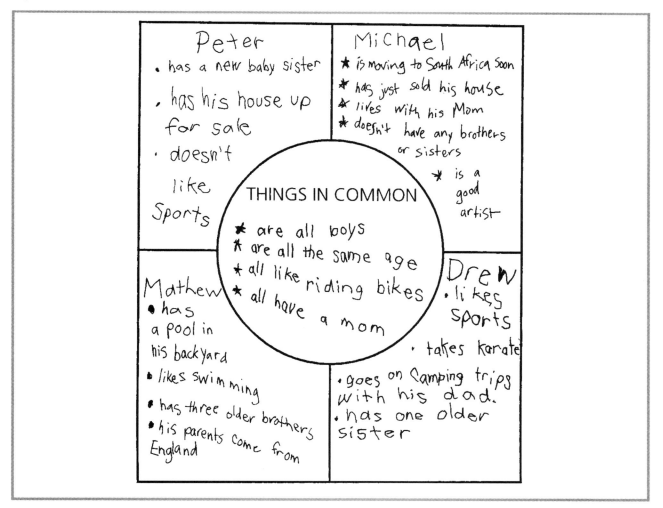

Planning Sheet 46, "We Learn About One Another."
- Talk about themselves and discover things they have in common.
- Record these similarities inside the circle.
- Talk about themselves and discover things that are different.
- Record each person's special characteristics on the quarter of the chart paper that has his/her name.
- Present the information to a small or large group.
- Post these chart "mini-biographies" for rereading and reviewing.

Note: You may want to consider organizing your classes into small groups and completing this experience with one group a day. This approach provides an opportunity for you to be part of the group and to learn and share with the learners.

Assessment and Evaluation

- Watch and listen to the learners and take note of significant shared information. Some of the conversations you will hear will tell about:
    - interests
    - talents
    - background knowledge
    - experiences
    - families
    - friends
    - pets
    - favourite books, movies, TV shows, foods...
    - likes and dislikes
    - needs
    - strengths
    - social interactions
    -
- Use these conversations to plan and develop your program based on the interests and strengths of the learners.

Continuing

- Read other books and discuss (compare, contrast) the characters.
- Collect books based on the interests of the learners.
- Repeat this activity or a similar one at the end of the month, term, or year to observe growth over time.
- Share the assessment and evaluation information with learners, families, and other educators.
-

Other titles you might use:

- *Rosie and Michael* by Judith Viorst
- *Tom* by Tomie de Paola
- *My Favourite Person* by Byrd Baylor

- *Brenda and Edward* by Maryann Kovalski
- *The Most Beautiful Place in the World* by Ann Cameron
- *The Very Best of Friends* by Margaret Wild
-

We Share Our Treasures

In this experience, we select personal treasures (artifacts) to share with our learners. In this way, we model/demonstrate personal sharing, become "real" for our learners, as in *The Velveteen Rabbit*, and encourage learners to share with others. Everyone begins to show and share some things that are valued and explains why these items are valued.

This experience provides opportunities for learners to handle and experience learning and storytelling by using real objects from everyday lives. It encourages and values talk and builds literacy connections. It provides a natural vehicle for practising the 3 R's.

Beginning

- Read the poem "What's in the Sack?" by Shel Silverstein

> What's in the sack? What's in the sack?
> Is it some mushrooms or is it the moon?
> Is it love letters or downy goosefeathers?
> Or maybe the world's most enormous balloon?
> What's in the sack? That's all they ask me.
> Could it be popcorn or marbles or books?
> Is it two years' worth of your dirty laundry.
> Or the biggest ol' meatball that's ever been cooked?
> Does anyone ask me, "Hey, when is your birthday?
> "Can you play Monopoly?" "Do you like beans?"
> "What is the capital of Yugoslavia?"
> Or "Who embroidered that rose on your jeans?"
> No, what's in the sack? That's all they care about.
> Is it a rock or a rolled-up giraffe?
> Is it pickles or nickels or busted bicycles?
> And if we guess it, will you give us half?
> Do they ask where I've been, or how long I'll be stayin',
> Where I'll be goin', or when I'll be back,
> Or "How do?" or "What's new?" or "Hey, why are you blue?"
> No, all they keep asking is, "What's in the sack?"
> "What's in the sack?" I'm blowin' my stack
> At the next one who asks me, "What's in the sack?"
> What?
> Oh no. Not you, too!"

> — From *Where the Sidewalk Ends: Poems and Drawings* by Shel Silverstein, page 111, © 1974 by Evil Eye Music, Inc. Courtesy HarperCollins Publishers.

- Encourage conversation and responses.

During the experience

- Bring in a bag in which you have placed several different items, each one of which is important to you in some way. The items can be artifacts, souvenirs, photos, books...
- Share some of the items using the 3 R's framework. Tell what the treasure is (retell), why it has special meaning for you (relate), and possibly what you are still wondering about (reflect).

> "Here is a sack — a bag that was given to me by one of the teachers in my course this summer. Inside, there is a little stuffed monkey. Kerry-Lynn gave me this monkey after I talked about my son's monkey collection and read the pattern book I wrote, *A Bedful of Monkeys*. This stuffed monkey will always remind me of that course and the stimulating discussions we had.
>
> "You're probably wondering what else is in my bag.
>
> "Here is a boala tie that I bought when I was in Phoenix, Arizona, this past summer. The boala tie became the official neckwear in the State of Arizona in 1971. This piece of jewellery brings back fond memories of my trip. I wonder why people in Arizona wear boala ties more often than people in Canada?
>
> "Here is a pebble from Sedonna that I picked up the day that I went to see the Grand Canyon in Arizona. The thing that really amazed me was all the different colours of the rocks in Sedonna and the Grand Canyon. I wonder if we could find rocks like this around here?
>
> "This is a baseball card and it has my son Michael's photo on it and information about him. It reminds me of all the baseball games I attended this summer with him. I wonder how many of you play baseball with an organized league?"

- Invite the learners to bring in their own bags and artifacts to share.

Assessment and Evaluation

- Continue to watch and listen.
- Record pertinent information.

Continuing

- Continue to share other treasures (artifacts), poems and books that hold personal memories for you.
- Continue to use real objects for as many learning experiences as possible.
- Create a collection of books with artifacts from each story — e.g., a Madeline doll for the story *Madeline* by Ludwig Bemelmans, a red pebble for *Sylvester and the Magic Pebble* by William Steig, a stuffed koala bear for *Koala Lou* by Mem Fox.
- Invite learners to create their own collections of stories and artifacts.
- Repeat this activity or a similar one at the end of the month, term, or year to observe growth over time.
- Share collections and information with learners, families, and other educators.
- Consider inviting families and other interested people to a celebration — everyone who comes will bring a "treasure" to tell about.
-

Other titles you might use:

- *Five Secrets in a Box* by Catherine Brighton
- *Sam's Surprise* by David Pelham
- *Tales of a Gambling Grandma* by Dayal Kaur Khalsa
- *William's Doll* by Charlotte Zolotow
- *Grandma's Jewelry Box* by Linda Milstein
- *Galimoto* by Karen Lynn Williams
- *The Gift* by John Prater
- *What's in Fox's Sack?* by Paul Galdone
- "Hector the Collector" by Shel Silverstein in *Where the Sidewalk Ends*
- *The Pumpkin Blanket* by Deborah Turney Zagwyn
-

We Collect and Share Books

In this experience, we model and demonstrate how much we value books and reading. The activity provides us with an opportunity to talk about the books we care about and why. It fosters positive attitudes and encourages sharing.

Beginning

- Select and bring in some books from your personal collection.

During the experience

- Read the title, names of author(s) and illustrator(s), and tell (by retelling, relating, and reflecting) why each book is special:

  "All the books in my bag are personally important to me. This book, *Wilfrid Gordon McDonald Partridge* by Mem Fox and illustrated by Julie Vivas, is about a little boy who helps an elderly woman remember. It is one of my favourite books because it makes me think of my own memories. I have shared this book in many workshops, with many audiences. It helps encourage people to remember and tell their own stories. It makes me want to read all the stories written by Mem Fox.

  "This book, *The Desert Is Theirs* by Byrd Baylor and illustrated by Peter Parnall, makes me think of the summer I heard Byrd Baylor in Arizona. Later, I had the opportunity to tour through the desert on my way to the Grand Canyon. I wonder when I will visit Arizona again?

  "This book, *Take Time To Relax* by Nancy Carlson, is about a family who are seen rushing from one activity to another. One winter day, they are snowed in and rediscover family life. This book makes me think about my own family and our busy lives. It makes me wonder about how to keep the balance that is so necessary between family and career.

  "This book, *Classroom Events Through Poetry,* by Larry Swartz, talks about poetry as a vital part of the classroom. It has confirmed for me the importance of poetry. I wonder how to share this book with more people so that poetry will find its way into classrooms and homes. This book makes me think of the author. I remember the course we took together, his presentations I attended, and his recent presentation on poetry at my school. Perhaps you will get a chance to meet him this year."

- Invite conversation.
- Invite the learners to bring in a favourite book of their own, read the title, give a mini-book talk and tell why the book is a favourite.
- Display the books for everyone to enjoy.

Assessment and Evaluation

- Record the title each learner reads or tells about.
- Continue to watch and listen.
- Record information based on the book selections shared.
- Date and file.

Continuing

- Take time each term to ask learners to bring in favourite books.
- Invite learners to talk about their books and create a display.
- Record additional information to assess and study growth over time.
- Continue to share other pieces of literature that hold personal memories for you.
- Find books that are similar to the books the learners brought in and draw them to the learners' attention.
- Consider reviewing and using Draft Planning Sheets 50 and 51, "Literature: A Year-at-a-Glance" and "Balancing a Literature-Based Program."
- Share information with learners, families, and other educators.
-

Other titles you might use:

- *The Wednesday Surprise* by Eve Bunting
- *I Like Books* by Anthony Browne
- *The Bee Tree* by Patricia Polacco
- *Little by Little* by Jean Little
- *You Read to Me and I'll Read to You* by John Ciardi
-

We Design a Coat of Arms

In this experience, learners find out about and create a personal coat of arms. We encourage them to review the illustrations in their coat of arms and think about and record the literature they know that relates to something in their coat of arms. We invite them to research books that connect in some way to their lives. Throughout this process, they read, talk about and share literature that is meaningful and related to their personal experiences.

Beginning

- Read aloud *The Medieval Feast* by Aliki.
- Encourage conversations and responses.
- Reflect on the coat of arms in the story.
- Design and model/demonstrate with the whole group your personal coat of arms.
- Record titles of books that relate in some way to the illustrations in your coat of arms. See Figure 3.7.
- Model/demonstrate how you decided which books you thought connected with the different sections of your coat of arms. See Figure 3.7.
- Invite responses — statements and questions.

Figure 3.7   Coat of Arms

During the experience

- Invite learners to draw a crest and divide it into four parts.
- Invite learners to draw something important to them in each part.
- Encourage learners to share their coat of arms with others.
- Invite learners to work with a partner or small group to brainstorm titles of familiar books that they think have some connection to the illustrations in each section of their crest.
- Provide time for learners to discuss how the books they chose relate to their interests and strengths as depicted in their coat of arms.
- Encourage learners to review the classroom book collection and/or visit the school and community libraries and their personal book collections at home for additional titles.

Assessment and Evaluation

- Continue to watch and listen.
- Record pertinent information in order to plan next teaching steps.
- Encourage the learners to date stamp their coat of arms.
- Consider as a portfolio insert.

Continuing

- At a later date, invite learners to reexamine their coat of arms and add new titles that relate to the illustrations in each of the squares.
- Model/demonstrate by adding new titles to your coat of arms.
- Invite learners to reflect on their experiences and learning.
- Continue to share related literature.
- Use the information gained from this experience as one way to organize and select materials and resources to complement the interests of your learners.
- Use this experience as a cooperative learning strategy to encourage working together in groups of two, three or four. You might want to invite the learners to complete a group crest.
- Invite learners to redo this experience at the end of the year and, together with your learners, compare the new coat of arms to the previous one.
- Share information with learners, families and other educators.
-

Other titles you might use:

- *Harold the Herald: A Book About Heraldry* by Dana Fradon
-

We Make and Can Read "A Bookful of Bags"

This experience highlights bags as an important source of environmental print. It has endless possibilities and potential. The bags that learners bring in usually tell something about their home, interests, trips or shopping habits. The activity encourages learners to notice the wide variety of bags — the sizes, shapes, colours, materials, designs, pictures, print... This strategy encourages learners to read and to notice the environmental print on bags and in the environment around them. For younger learners, when they "read the bags," they see themselves as readers and this increases their sense of achievement and self-confidence. This experience illustrates and enhances the literacy abilities of learners, and provides us with important information. The reusing of bags is also one way to create and demonstrate a new purpose for used materials.

Beginning

- Collect a variety of store bags and make a bookful of bags — your personal collection of bags taped together in the form of a book.
- Read the book *The Signmaker's Assistant* by Tedd Arnold. This book is about a boy who, when the signmaker is away, plays tricks on people by painting unusual signs and leaving them around the neighbourhood. This story can generate a great deal of discussion about environmental print.
- Share your bookful of bags. See Figure 3.8. Remind the learners that shopping bags are not toys, and should be used with adult supervision.

Figure 3.8 Bookful of Bags

During the experience

- Ask questions throughout as you read your bookful of bags aloud, inviting your learners to make predictions:

    "I found all of these bags in my home and decided to put them all together to make a book. This book tells a story about my husband and me. I'd like you to read it. Who can help me read this bag?

    Sandy: "It says Bill's Pet Store. There's a picture of a bird on it. I bet you have a pet bird at home."

    John: "This says 'recyclable' — that means you will use it again."

- Talk with the learners about making a class bookful of bags.

    "How many children are there in this class? If each one brings in a bag, how many 'pages' will there be in our class book of bags?"

- Invite learners to bring in their own bags from home.
- Place one bag on top of the other.
- Arrange in sequence — by colour, shape, size, etc.
- Staple along the edge, or tape one bag at a time to the others.
- Tape over stapled or taped edges to make a spine.
- Encourage the learners to take turns reading the bookful of bags aloud to the group, with each learner talking about their bag — Where did it come from? What was in it? What material is it? What words are on it?

Assessment and Evaluation

- Continue to watch and listen.
- Listen and record words learners can read and some words that might be useful for them to learn to read.
- Record pertinent information.

Continuing

- Leave the bag at the reading corner for children to read independently.
- Continue to share examples of environmental print from home and in the classroom, as well as other pieces of literature about environmental print.
- Invite learners to share their bags and read in pairs.
- Invite learners to go on an environmental print walk, and using a clipboard or pad of paper, record words, signs, logos they see and recognize.
- Invite learners to redo this experience at the end of the year and, together with your learners, compare to the previous one.
- Share information with learners, families and other educators.
-

Other titles you might use:

- *I Read Signs* by Tana Hoban
- *I Read Symbols* by Tana Hoban
- *How Do You Make a Bubble?* by William H. Hooks, Joanne Oppenheim, Barbara Brenner
- *We Read A to Z* by Donald Crews

- *The Legend of Slappy Hooper*, retold by Aaron Shepard, pictures by Toni Goffe
- *Mr. Pine's Mixed-Up Signs* by Leonard Kessler
-

We Cooperate: "Line-Ups"

In this cooperative learning experience, we learn about our learners' problem-solving strategies and their tolerance levels (who gets frustrated easily, who perseveres). We note the social interactions and leadership qualities (who organizes, who leads). This experience easily leads into valuable mathematical connections, such as linear measurement (height, distance between) and time (months, days, years), as well as language opportunities (descriptive words, sayings, favourites...) and ideas about the types of language used — mathematical, scientific, technological, etc.

Beginning

- Read the book *The Line-Up Book* by Marisabina Russo, which is about a young boy who uses objects in the house to make a line from his bedroom to the kitchen.

During the experience

- Invite learners to form a line in order of birthdays, beginning with September and ending with August.
- Consider doing this task with and/or without talking. Doing it without talking adds to the challenge.
- Have ready a long piece of mural paper taped on the wall at about the height of the tallest person in the class, and ask learners to trace the outline of their neighbour's head with a marker onto the mural paper.
- Invite learners to fill in their features on their own outline.
- As a group, brainstorm words that can be used to describe people in the class.
- Invite learners to write one or two words that best describes them above their outline. See Figure 3.9.

Figure 3.9 Line-Ups

Assessment and Evaluation

- Continue to watch and listen.
- Record pertinent information.
- Observe how the learners interact and work together problem solving.

Continuing

- Use the "line up" strategy to line up alphabetically by first letter or last letter in name(s).
- Use this strategy in other ways, e.g., line up from tallest to shortest, by birthdays, etc., and observe growth over time.
- Invite learners to line up materials or objects as part of the math/science program, e.g., collections of buttons, keys, shells, rocks, hockey cards...
- Share assessment and evaluation information with learners, families and other educators.
-

Other titles you might use:

- *Madeline* by Ludwig Bemelmans
- *Mr. Gumpy's Outing* by John Burningham
- *The Name of the Tree* by Celia Lottridge, Ian Wallace
- *The Camel Who Took a Walk* by Roger Duvoisin
-

We Design Character Cubes

With this strategy, we invite learners to think about personal characteristics after listening to a read-aloud selection. This experience provides them with an opportunity to respond to literature, illustrate their understanding of characterization, and relate to their lives. It encourages learners to use their creative arts ability to illustrate their special attributes. They can use this strategy to illustrate the traits of other characters.

Beginning

- Read the book *Rosie and Michael* by Judith Viorst.
- Model/demonstrate for learners by drawing and creating a "Rosie" cube and a "Michael" cube using the information in the book.
- Invite responses — statements and/or questions.

During the experience

- Invite learners to create or cover their own box or cube.
- Have the learners draw six pictures (one for each side of the cube) that tell something about themselves. These pictures are then glued onto the cube.
- Invite learners to work together in pairs or in groups rolling the cubes and talking about the pictures that come up. These stories, which can be taped and/or written, provide information about the learners. See Figure 3.10.

Figure 3.10 Character Cubes

Assessment and Evaluation

- Continue to watch and listen.
- Listen to the learners' spoken language styles and structure as they tell about the cubes.
- Record pertinent information.
- Listen and notice the responses to the read-aloud.
- Observe and record what kinds of things learners can do as they express themselves in arts and crafts.

Continuing

- Continue to share related pieces of literature.
- Use different books and make some character cube mobiles, building on the initial cube designing experience.
- Offer to place some completed cubes in the foyer, library...
- Share information with learners, families and other educators.
-

Other titles you might use:

- *Miss Maggie* by Cynthia Rylant
- *Miss Rumphius* by Barbara Cooney
- *Emily* by Michael Bedard
- *Mary of Mile 18* by Ann Blades
- *Mufara's Beautiful Daughters* by John Steptoe
-

 # We Write Letters

In this experience, we encourage learners to practise letter writing. This strategy gives them opportunities in the classroom to understand and use a form of writing that will be useful throughout their lives.

Beginning

- Read the book *Dear Annie* by Judith Caseley.
- Share a letter you have received and a letter you are about to send. Discuss some of the features (address, salutation, paragraphing) of the letters and share why you and the person who wrote to you chose to write the way you did.
- Bring in some addressed envelopes and share with your learners different ways envelopes may be written.
- Organize a variety of writing notepaper and envelopes.
- Think about setting up a mailbox for the class on the wall or on a stand, or individual boxes for each student. (Empty boxes with sections that hold bottles or glass make an excellent mailbox for each learner in the class.)

During the experience

- Invite learners to select notepaper and envelopes.
- Invite learners to write a letter to a friend, penpal, book or TV character, author or illustrator, family member…
- Invite learners to address their envelopes and send the letter.
- Invite learners to write letters to class members or staff and post them in the class mailboxes.

Assessment and Evaluation

- Continue to watch and listen.
- Keep a copy of this first letter and envelope.
- Observe and record pertinent information regarding the learners' letter-writing abilities.

Continuing

- Repeat this experience and, together with your learners, compare to the initial letters. Note the progress over time.
- Continue to encourage, provide demonstrations, and practise letter writing and various types of letter forms whenever appropriate, e.g., after a guest or speaker visit, to thank someone… .
- Continue to have available and accessible a variety of paper and stationery for letter writing purposes.
- Share growth and development with learners, families and other educators.
-

Other titles you might use:

- *Messages in the Mailbox: How To Write a Letter* by Loreen Leedy
- *Dear Mr. Henshaw* by Beverly Cleary
- *Don't Forget To Write* by Martina Selway
- *Dear Greenpeace* by Simon James
- *Sea Swan* by Kathryn Lasky
- *Dearest Grandmama* by Catherine Brighton
-

We Play "Interview Bingo"

This experience helps teachers and learners learn more about one another. As learners talk together during the experience, they find out about one another's strengths and interests. Later, they may remember and say: *"Here's a book about cats. I know John likes cats. Maybe he'll like this book."* Or *"I want to make a spaceship. I know Jill likes to read space stories. Maybe she'll work with me."*

Beginning

- Introduce this experience by singing the familiar song B-I-N-G-O.
- Invite your learners to ask you questions about yourself.
- Put your answers to their questions in point form.
- Model/demonstrate how this information can be recorded on a square on a bingo page.
- Share and talk about the above information with the class.
- Invite responses — comments and questions.

During the experience

- Provide one blank bingo page for each learner. (This activity is particularly effective if the bingo card has the same number of squares as the number of learners in the class plus a square for you.)
- Invite learners to move around the classroom and interview their classmates.
- Invite each person interviewed to record their name and something about themselves in a square on the form — one square per person. Invite learners to move around, interview and record others in order to complete the form.
- Provide time for learners to share their completed bingo cards with another person.

Assessment and Evaluation

- Continue to watch and listen.
- Record pertinent information.
- Notice the learners' signatures
- Observe the wide variety of ways they record information.

Figure 3.11 Interview Bingo

has a dog named Teela	went to Florida in August	loves to dance and take jazz	plays piano	loves baseball and went to camp	hit 10 home runs this summer
had family from the Philippines come to visit	saw "Home Alone" six times	has a best friend named Matthew	has two black cats	loves to eat pizza	loves to read "Curious George"
loves to read mysteries	has moved to our community from Nova Scotia	loves horses	has four sisters and a new brother	has a pet bird	loves painting best of all in school
is really a good helper on the computer	can sing very well	loves to watch "The Flintstones" on T.V.	wants to be a library helper	loves to do math	just arrived in Canada from Jamaica

Continuing

- Invite learners to repeat this experience at the end of the year.
- Compare the form from the beginning of the year to the end of the year and notice likenesses and differences.
- Share growth and development with learners, families and other educators.
- Consider another variation of this bingo experience:

    - In advance, prepare the same bingo card for every learner. Put information about each learner in one of the squares, based on information you have gathered about each learner. (This activity is particularly effective after you and the learners have completed a number of the "Getting To Know You" experiences. As you watch, listen and keep records, you build up a wealth of information about your learners and you use this information to create the bingo card. The bingo card becomes personal to that particular group of learners. See Figure 3.11.)
    - Invite learners to find the owner of each information square and collect signatures.
    - The first learner to find the owners of all the information squares shouts "Bingo."
    -

-

Other titles you might use:

- *Wilfrid Gordon McDonald Partridge* by Mem Fox
- *Are There Any Questions?* by Denys Cazet
- *The Furry News* by Loreen Leddy
- *Extra! Extra! The Who, What, Where, When and Why of Newspapers* by Linda Granfield
-

In summary, we believe it is critical to implement baseline learning experiences to begin and end each school year. The "Getting To Know You" experiences we have provided are extensive, yet not exhaustive. We invite you to select the activities you feel most comfortable with, keeping in mind a balance of curriculum areas and the needs of your particular learners.

Perhaps the activities you choose will be validations or extensions of present practices. Perhaps your choices will provide you with opportunities to try new experiences. Regardless of the activities you choose, it is important that you repeat the experiences and records in order to illustrate growth and development over time.

What do all the baseline experiences we have provided have in common?

1. They intentionally invite teachers to know more about their learners.
2. They value growth and development as an integral part of curriculum and instruction.
3. They are organized and invitational, yet flexible.
4. They show how the teacher can model and demonstrate the process and the product.
5. They encourage confidence because what learners and teachers know is valued, recorded and celebrated.
6. They give learners opportunities to interact, do, read, listen, write, design, create, experiment, choose, decide, think — learners see themselves learning.
7. They allow teachers to schedule time wisely at the beginning and end of the year.
8. They invite and encourage teachers to treat learners with respect, value their ideas, thoughts, knowledge, choices and interests.
9. They provide opportunities for teachers to get to know their learners so that program goals and expectations are valid and appropriate.
10. They are enjoyable for teachers and learners.

Based on the information about learners collected from these kinds of experiences, we can begin and continue to assess and evaluate effectively. The results of these experiences form the basis for planning and programming. They guide the curriculum, enrich teaching practices, and open windows into many areas of understanding.

Negotiating Curriculum

"Celebrating the joys and achievements of learning is a vital part of the process of negotiating and planning curriculum with our learners."
(page 151)

"We believe that integrated, learner-centred and process/product-balanced programs are most effective when we are actively involved in planning and working cooperatively and productively with our learners and with others — when we negotiate curriculum together."
(page 152)

In this chapter, we discuss planning and negotiating curriculum with our learners. We show how our 3 R's of retelling, relating and reflecting provide a natural framework for the processes of negotiating curriculum, planning programs, and integrating curriculum. We discuss the need for balance between the learning process and the products of that learning. We provide a personal illustration as well as a theory-based understanding of the main requirements and conditions that we, as lifelong learners and teachers, need in order to continue to understand and reflect upon the teaching/learning process. We provide practical examples for you to use and modify when planning and implementing curriculum with your learners.

CREATING A LEARNER-CENTRED CURRICULUM

In creating a learner-centred curriculum, it is important that we **begin** with our learners. We believe that when we negotiate curriculum with our learners and with our learners' families, we establish a collaborative and personalized learner-centred curriculum and environment.

Negotiating curriculum with learners allows us to create programs and learning experiences collaboratively with our learners. They share the ownership, and their learning becomes more meaningful. Throughout the negotiating curriculum and program planning processes, we include what we know about our learners, their knowledge, ideas, feelings, and suggestions. We invite learners to add their questions, which provide insight into what the learners are interested in learning more about. We include our personal questions and make links to curriculum expectations to ensure that we address the appropriate areas of the curriculum and follow pertinent guidelines. We model and demonstrate wondering, and together, we search for answers to everyone's questions. These questions usually match important learning outcomes and curriculum guidelines. Where there are gaps, we add further questions and statements to ensure appropriate instruction and learning experiences. Thinking and inquiry are encouraged and fostered as important aspects of the learning and teaching process. A holistic learning and teaching process grows and develops collaboratively.

Our 3 R's of retelling, relating and reflecting provide an excellent framework for negotiating curriculum. In order to negotiate and plan curriculum with our learners, it is essential that we first find out what the learners already know and can do and what they want to know — their retellings, relatings and reflections. Working with our learners and their families, we need to gather baseline information about each learner.

To negotiate curriculum effectively, we also need to hear the questions posed by families, share with them beliefs about education, and negotiate with them common understandings and expectations, goals and appropriate educational practices — we need to hear their retellings, relatings and reflectings.

Our role as teachers is critical to the negotiating curriculum process. Negotiating curriculum depends on setting clear goals and expectations that complement the expectations, goals, and policies of the school and system. We need to combine the information we gather from our learners and their families with what the learners **need** to know. We must bring to the process our knowledge — our retellings, relatings and reflections — of:

- curriculum guidelines and policies
- child development
- current teaching/learning theories and research
- the school and system expectations and goals
- what learners know and want to learn
- expectations of families
- our own personal and professional experiences
- our questions and wonderings

When we negotiate curriculum in this way, planning and implementing curriculum becomes a shared responsibility among teachers, learners and families. Together, we decide how learners will find out, how they can demonstrate their learning, and how they came to know. This process makes learning and teaching a truly active/interactive process for everyone.

When we demonstrate that we have confidence and trust in our learners' ability to be part of the decision-making process and that we value their contributions, we encourage the learners' sense of ownership and responsibility for their own learning.

> Learners will work harder and learn better, and what they learn will mean more to them if they are discovering their own ideas, asking their own questions, and fighting hard to answer for themselves. They must be educational decision makers. Out of negotiation comes a sense of ownership in learners for the work they are to do, and therefore a commitment to it. Learning is an active process.
>
> - Garth Boomer, *Negotiating the Curriculum*, page 134

FOCUS ON PROCESS AND PRODUCTS

 ## Process

When learners interact with *people*, *places* and *things*, they become involved in an ongoing and natural process of making connections and learning. It is through this learning process — this constant retelling, relating, reflecting — that learners continually develop their understandings of the world.

We work collaboratively with our learners to plan experiences and instruction in response to everyone's knowledge, personal stories and questions. Together, we make decisions, look for information, research and collect data to find answers to the questions raised. We encourage our learners to use their environment and surroundings when they search for answers. They learn by making connections and asking questions, while interacting with, examining and exploring the *people, places and things* in the world around them. They have experiences, and develop their knowledge, stories and questions by watching, listening and talking with *people*, visiting and exploring *places*, and discovering and examining *things*.

Figure 4.1 illustrates some of the people, places and things learners may connect with in their homes, school or environments outside their homes and school.

Figure 4.1 People, Places, Things

Some of the people with whom learners continually talk:	Some of the places learners continually visit and explore:	Some of the things learners continually seek out and examine:
• families • friends • peers • siblings • relatives • teachers • community residents • others in the world around them •	• homes • other classrooms • camps • arenas • parks • movie theatres • libraries • museums, galleries • other places of personal and/or educational interest •	• literature • other print materials • audiovisual resources • artifacts • manipulatives • pieces of music • theatrical presentations • performances • works of art • other related objects of interest •

Using what the learners know (retellings), their personal stories (relatings) and their questions (reflections), we brainstorm with our learners to create cooperative lists to decide:

- what "people, places and things" resources are available
- what "people, places and things" resources the learners will use
- how they will use "people, places and things" resources

Products

In presenting and celebrating their learning, learners use a variety of resources and ways to **practise, perform, present, share and publish ("go public")** with different audiences. These presentations and celebrations become the **products** of what the learners have learned. Again using our 3 R's baseline knowledge about our learners (what they know, personal stories and questions), we brainstorm with the learners to create cooperative lists to decide:

- how they will practise what they have learned
- how they will perform, present, share or publish what they have learned

Balance of Process and Product

Our 3 R's framework for negotiating curriculum with learners and their families elaborates and expands upon the concepts of **process** and **products**. Both are important and need to be given equal value in order to provide a balance in any program. This balance is necessary to address individual learning styles and the needs of the learners. See Figure 4.2. (See Draft Planning Sheet 47, "The 3 R's Framework and Negotiating the Curriculum.")

Figure 4.2 The 3 R's Framework and Negotiating Curriculum: Learners, Teachers, Families

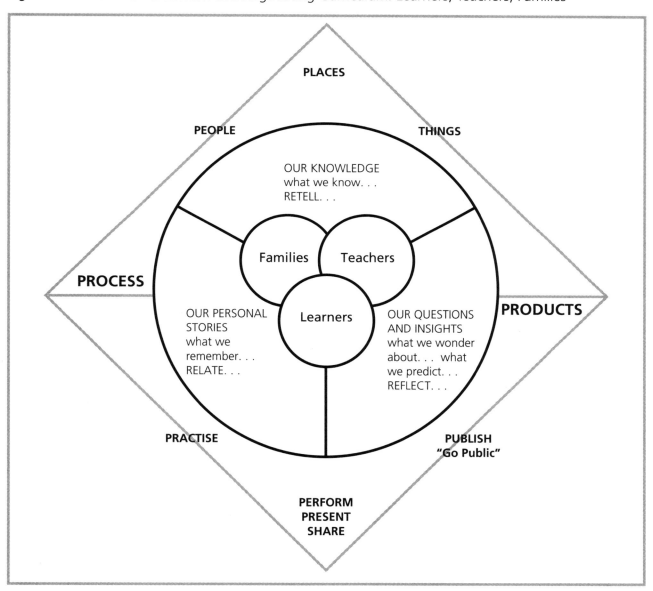

Negotiating curriculum and planning to balance process and products are integral parts of learning and teaching, and often transcend and connect many subject areas, themes and disciplines. The curriculum becomes integrated and meaningful. The negotiated and integrated curriculum grows out of collaboration, respect, natural inquiry, knowledge and problem solving. It develops by everyone continuously retelling, relating and reflecting. Negotiating and integrating the curriculum depends upon everyone — teacher, learners, families — continuously acquiring knowledge and experience.

Negotiating curriculum and integrated learner-centred learning encourage making connections and the meaningful pursuit of learning. Figure 4.3 represents the negotiated and integrated learner-centred curriculum. When you look at the diagram, imagine the diamond shape in the large circle — the **process** and **products** — as mobile, revolving around its axis end points. As it moves, it connects with meaningful active experiences and many subject areas, themes, topics, concepts, skills... This image illustrates meaningful, involved, integrated and authentic learning.

Figure 4.3 The 3 R's Framework and Negotiating and Integrating Curriculum

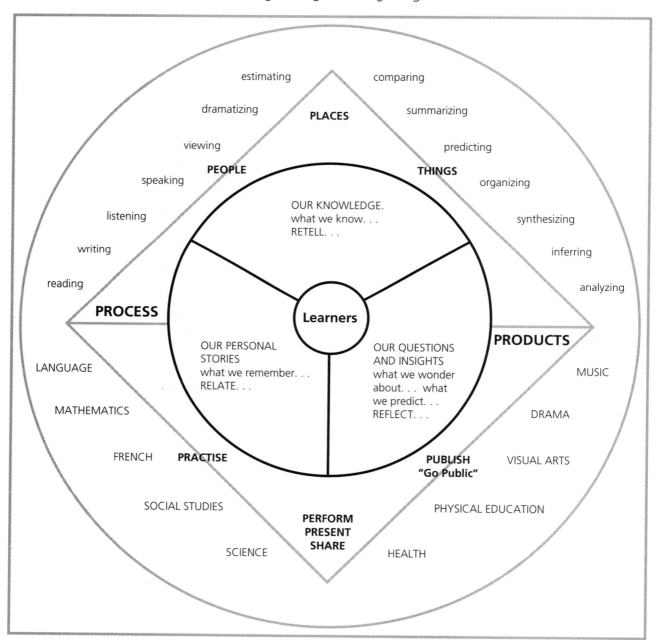

The greater the variety of resources and ways to acquire and to demonstrate knowledge that we can provide, the better able we will be to meet the different learning styles and needs of our learners.

CELEBRATING LEARNING

Celebrating the joys and achievements of learning is a vital part of the process of negotiating and planning curriculum with our learners. Celebrating learning involves practising , performing, presenting, sharing and publishing — "going public." Learners enjoy sharing and applying new information in unique and creative ways. We need to provide them with as many models as possible of how they can share what they have learned. We invite our learners to choose from these models or from other models of their choice, and we expect them to be responsible for making appropriate choices. It is important for learners to learn to choose and make these decisions. They gain ownership of their products and take responsibility for practising their learning when they decide for themselves what they will make and how they will use what they make to present their knowledge.

To ensure that all learners have the tools to be able to choose for themselves how they will **practise, perform, present, share, and/or publish ("go public")**, we need to provide **"how-to" mini-lessons** throughout the year. In these mini-lessons, we encourage our learners to practise, perform, publish or "go public" in different ways using a variety of resources. We model and demonstrate by talking about and providing examples of many of the different ways information is shared in the world — book jackets, record jackets, posters, paintings, bookmarks, t-shirts, letters, diaries, stories, biographies, experiments, constructions, inventions... By providing direct instruction in small and large groups, we ensure that learners know how to create and complete products before they choose the way(s) to share their information.

Some of the ways to practise, perform, present, share, and/or publish ("go public") that we might model and demonstrate for our learners are
- letters
- stories
- poems
- riddles
- albums
- scrapbooks
- dioramas
- booklets
- 8-page book (See Draft Planning Sheet 7, "The 3 R's Framework in an 8-Page Book Format")
- overhead acetates
- cooperative class books
- Plasticene/clay models
- paintings
- quilts
- dramatizations
- plays
- maps

- pop-up books
- audiotapes
- pamphlets
- alphabet books
- collections
- posters
- wordless stories
- cartoons
- comic strips
- videos
- commercials
- inventions
- experiments
- constructions
- structures
-

Learners are continually investigating new areas of study. Although the content of what they are learning changes throughout the year, a variety of ways of presenting their learning may remain the same. Some learners are confident and comfortable sharing their knowledge about the different areas of study through paintings and other art forms (sculpting, cut and paste, drawings...). Some learners are confident and comfortable sharing their knowledge through writing (diaries, letters, stories, poems...). We need to value every product equally. When we encourage our learners to make different products and we value every product equally, we foster and value individual differences and creativity.

At first, learners will use the method(s) for practising and/or presenting their learning with which they are most comfortable. Over time, we need continuously to invite them and expect them to use a variety of resources to celebrate their learning.

We believe that integrated, learner-centred and process/product-balanced programs are most effective when we are actively involved in planning and working cooperatively and productively with our learners and with others — when we negotiate curriculum together. We have conversations and make connections about learning and teaching. We negotiate our learning and we celebrate that learning.

Susan and Maxine: EXAMINING OUR LEARNING PROCESS

*The following story is an example of natural and authentic learning. It illustrates the **3 R's and baseline frameworks** and **the natural negotiation of process and products.** It describes our personal learning in response to our experiences when we attended an educational conference in Phoenix, Arizona.*

*We examined our baseline knowledge and our questions on the plane to Phoenix. We interacted with **people, places and things** trying to find the* *answers to our questions, and we purchased and produced a variety of **products.** This story highlights the **balance** between process and product and illustrates learner-centred lifelong learning.*

At the last minute, we decided to attend the "Many Voices, Many Cultures" Conference in Phoenix, Arizona. Before we left, we were teaching university courses and didn't have much time to think about our upcoming experience.

On the plane, we chatted about what we knew about Arizona and what we thought we might learn. We knew how much we had enjoyed and learned from attending a similar conference the previous year in St. Louis, Missouri. We knew Ken and Yetta Goodman worked at a university in Tucson, Arizona. We had been told it would be extremely hot in Phoenix. These were the things that immediately came to our minds about Arizona and the conference.

We realized we had many questions about our trip and this experience. We wondered where we were headed. Exactly where is Phoenix? How long would it take to get there?

Our ticket told us that we would arrive at 8 p.m. — that seemed to be only one hour away from Detroit, but when we found and looked at a map of the United States in the Airline Magazine, we realized that Phoenix is very close to California. We thought about the time zone changes and realized that the flight had to be considerably more than one hour. Later we asked the flight attendant and were told that it was a three-and-a-half-hour flight plus the time of the flights from Toronto to Buffalo to Detroit. We would be on this journey with the time change and wait-overs for nearly one whole day.

By chatting with other people on the plane, we learned more about Phoenix and the climate. There were still many unanswered questions, and we decided the first day to go on a bus tour of Phoenix to find out more about the city. On the last day, we toured the Grand Canyon to further expand our knowledge of Arizona.

A week later, we found ourselves watching a television production about some of the environmental issues in the state of Arizona, and what we were seeing and hearing was now more meaningful. Before our trip, we would not have watched this program with the same interest or understanding. Because of our trip, our baseline of knowledge had changed, as had our learning. We believe this is what lifelong learning is all about. By continually examining our knowledge and our questions, we are constantly informed about learning and teaching.

As we chatted and reflected about our experiences, we realized that we were indeed involved in a natural and authentic learning process that at the time did not require an immediate product (although when we returned from our trip, we put together several products of our learning — a scrapbook of photos, post cards, maps and travel brochures, as well as a "Bookful of Bags" (see Chapter 3, "We Make and Can Read 'A Bookful of Bags'" pages 135-137) collected from the conference and shopping in Arizona.)

We went from what we knew, and became involved naturally and spontaneously with people, places and things in order to find out about some of the things we wanted to know and to seek answers to our questions. The appropriate curriculum evolved through our experiences with people, places and things and the personal responses that emerged. We had become engaged and had taken responsibility for our own learning.

We used our 3 R's framework to create a visual to illustrate our personal "negotiated curriculum" and our learning experiences. See Figure 4.4.

By recording our learning on a framework, we were able to assess and evaluate our own learning. In this way, Figure 4.4 becomes our negotiated curriculum

Figure 4.4   Using the 3 R's Negotiating Curriculum Framework to Examine Our Learning

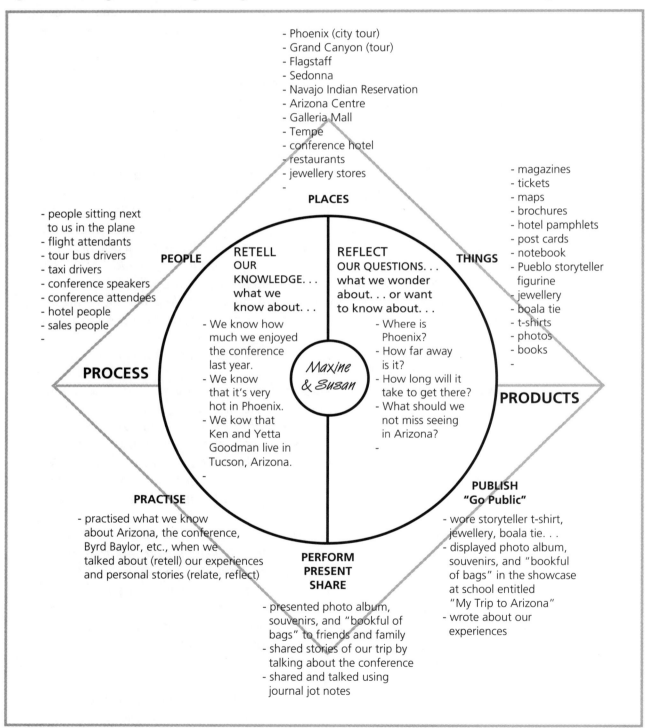

PLACES
- Phoenix (city tour)
- Grand Canyon (tour)
- Flagstaff
- Sedonna
- Navajo Indian Reservation
- Arizona Centre
- Galleria Mall
- Tempe
- conference hotel
- restaurants
- jewellery stores
-

THINGS
- magazines
- tickets
- maps
- brochures
- hotel pamphlets
- post cards
- notebook
- Pueblo storyteller figurine
- jewellery
- boala tie
- t-shirts
- photos
- books
-

PEOPLE
- people sitting next to us in the plane
- flight attendants
- tour bus drivers
- taxi drivers
- conference speakers
- conference attendees
- hotel people
- sales people
-

RETELL OUR KNOWLEDGE. . . what we know about. . .
- We know how much we enjoyed the conference last year.
- We know that it's very hot in Phoenix.
- We kow that Ken and Yetta Goodman live in Tucson, Arizona.
-

REFLECT OUR QUESTIONS. . . what we wonder about. . . or want to know about. . .
- Where is Phoenix?
- How far away is it?
- How long will it take to get there?
- What should we not miss seeing in Arizona?
-

Maxine & Susan

PROCESS

PRODUCTS

PRACTISE
- practised what we know about Arizona, the conference, Byrd Baylor, etc., when we talked about (retell) our experiences and personal stories (relate, reflect)

PERFORM PRESENT SHARE
- presented photo album, souvenirs, and "bookful of bags" to friends and family
- shared stories of our trip by talking about the conference
- shared and talked using journal jot notes

PUBLISH "Go Public"
- wore storyteller t-shirt, jewellery, boala tie. . .
- displayed photo album, souvenirs, and "bookful of bags" in the showcase at school entitled "My Trip to Arizona"
- wrote about our experiences

and report. Notice in this visual representation the balance between process and products. It is also interesting to note that:

- Some of our products we shared immediately, while others we shared weeks and months later.
- Some of the products we created from resources we collected, while others were commercial (t-shirts, jewellery...)
- Some of the learning continues to emerge and evolve as time passes.

Since we returned from Phoenix, we have had several conversations about Jerome Bruner's statement:

> "Knowledge is a process, not a product."

*As we reflect on our own learning, we realize that our knowledge comes from what we know and our new experiences. Any products that come out of our learning are the vehicles for sharing our knowledge — **how we learn** as well as **how we share what we learn.***

We invite you to think about the process behind the products, to think about the balance needed between process and product, and the value given to each. We believe it is essential to continue to examine often our beliefs, practices and attitudes about learning and teaching. We believe it is essential for us to know ourselves as learners — to ask ourselves what we know and how we came to know — in order to establish our own baseline. It is through this process of self-examination that our questions evolve and emerge, and that we develop our action plans. It is through this process that we integrate our philosophy of teaching and learning to design an effective, learner-centred curriculum and environment. And it is through this process that we develop appropriate assessment and evaluation frameworks.

We find that using our 3 R's framework when we examine ourselves as learners helps us to clarify our thoughts. When we think about learning and teaching, we ask ourselves these three questions:

- **Retell:** What do we know about learning and teaching?
- **Relate:** How did we come to know about learning and teaching?
- **Reflect:** What are the implications of these two questions for the classroom and for learning, teaching, assessing and evaluating?

We invite you to join us in experiencing and internalizing this process. Once we internalize the process, we will understand how to recreate and practise the same process with the learners we teach.

PRACTISING THE 3 R'S AND NEGOTIATING CURRICULUM

We use the 3 R's negotiating curriculum framework with individuals, small groups, or large groups to initiate and plan a unit of study.

 # Negotiating a Unit of Study Using Fiction

You may want to write the information gathered in this activity on a large circle on a chart or on an overhead so that everyone can read along as the activity proceeds. Consider using different coloured markers to differentiate between previous knowledge, questions, new knowledge, resources... Someone — you, a volunteer, an older student — may need to record for younger learners.

Beginning

- Read aloud the book *Owl Moon* by Jane Yolen or another carefully selected book of your choice.
- Invite learners to talk to the person closest to them about what they know or think they know about nighttime, the moon or owls.
- Invite learners to share with the large group.
- Ask them where they found their information (did someone tell them, did they read it in a book, read it in the newspaper, study it last year, see a movie about it...)
- Record in the circle in point form <u>with a green marker</u> **what the learners know about nighttime, the moon or owls.** (This strategy is a variation of the "donut model." See Chapter 3, "What We Know and Want To Know: The Donut Model," pages 118-120.) See Figure 4.5.

Figure 4.5   Retell: What Do We Know About. . . ?

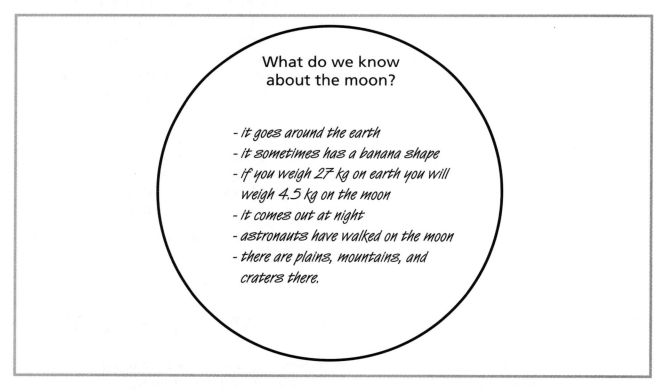

What do we know about the moon?

- it goes around the earth
- it sometimes has a banana shape
- if you weigh 27 kg on earth you will weigh 4.5 kg on the moon
- it comes out at night
- astronauts have walked on the moon
- there are plains, mountains, and craters there.

- Invite learners to tell the person closest to them what they want to find out — their questions about nighttime, the moon or owls.
- Invite learners to share with the large group their questions or the things they want to find out.

- Record in point form <u>with a red marker</u> the learners' **questions.** This information can be written around the first circle. See Figure 4.6.

Figure 4.6   Reflect: What Questions Do We Have?

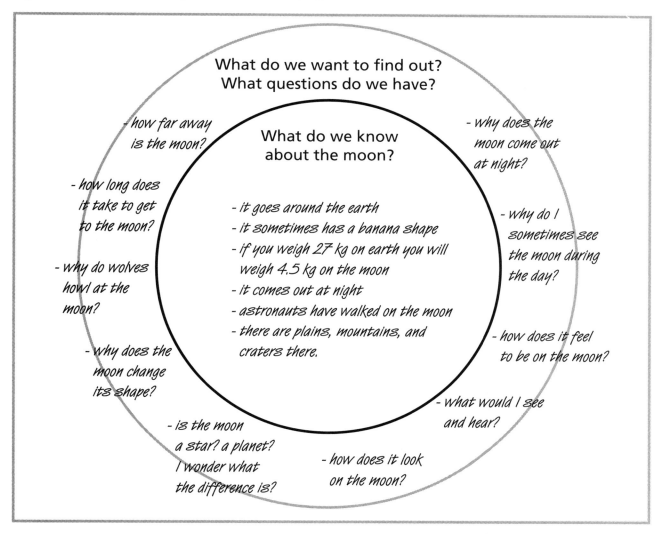

During the experience

- Invite the learners to brainstorm all the possibilities they can think of for **how they can find answers for their questions (research).**
- Record these possibilities <u>in blue marker</u> on little strips of paper or on Post-its.
- Invite the learners to categorize and paste the strips or Post-its into resource lists of **people, places and things.** See Figure 4.7 (next page)(Draft Planning Sheet 48, "People, Places, Things").
- Invite the learners to brainstorm all the possibilities of **how they will practise, perform (present/share) and publish ("go public") what they are learning and have learned.**
- Record these possibilities <u>using a black marker</u>. Date and post the chart paper or overhead for continuous reference. See Figure 4.8, next page (Draft Planning Sheet 49, "Practise, Perform, Publish").

Figure 4.7 People, Places, Things

People	Places	Things
People we can invite, call, listen to, interview, ask opinions of, talk with...	Places we can go to:	Things we can explore:
• families • librarians • experts at the planetarium and science centre •	• planetariums • science centre (space section) • libraries •	• models of spaceships • models of planets and moons • movies • books •

Figure 4.8 Practise, Perform, Publish

Practise	Perform Present, Share	Publish "Go Public"
• paintings • writing moon stories or poems • building using blocks • experimenting with flight • writing information about the moon • keeping a moon journal • studying the phases of the moon •	• a play about the book (Reader's Theatre) • moon facts • paintings • experiments • block constructions • problems and solutions • poems, raps or songs about the moon •	• a chosen piece of writing • a painting • a photograph of a construction • a list of favourite books • experiments for others to try •

- Together, plan and implement the experiences for this unit of study appropriate to the needs and interests of the learners.
    - Explore the materials and resources available in the classroom.
    - Visit the library resource centre and collect possible resources.
    - Check at home for possible materials and resources.
    - Contact the people resources.
    - Collect the related literature.
    - Write any necessary letters to invite visitors, speakers...
    - Check the film/video catalogue and order films or videos.
    - Organize and book any excursions.
    - Organize the materials necessary to do the presentations.
    - Design and use any necessary planning charts, such as webs, charts...
- With the learners, make decisions about and organize their information and learning for this unit of study:
    - how they wish to present, share and/or publish
    - where they will begin

- how they will begin
- who will be involved, who will do what (assign jobs to be done)
- what materials they will need
- when are the appropriate "finish" dates and sharing times (develop a presentation and sharing schedule)
- what assistance they will need
- how they will assess and evaluate their learning

Assessment and Evaluation

- Continue to watch and listen.
- Record pertinent information for ongoing assessment and evaluation purposes.
- At the end of a unit of study, find out what the learners now know, what questions have been answered, and what questions are still left to be answered, and compare this information to the baseline (the knowledge and questions recorded at the beginning of the experiences). Refer again to Figures 4.5 and 4.6.
- Use this information as part of ongoing assessment and evaluation.
-

Continuing

- Read other stories and have other resources available about the nighttime, the moon, or owls, depending on the chosen topic.
- Encourage learners to use this strategy independently or before any group project.
- Practise using this experience before each new unit of study.
- Use this experience as the first step in all research studies.
- Try this process before beginning a chapter book, an author study, going on a field trip...
-

Other related titles:

- *The Moon Is Following Me* by Philip Heckman
- *Architect of the Moon* by Tim Wynne-Jones
- *Moonflute* by Audrey Wood
- *The Moon Came Too* by Nancy Karlstrom
- *Moonlight* by Jan Omerod
- *Grandfather Twilight* by Barbara Berger
- *Goodnight Moon* by Margaret Wise Brown
- *Moon Man* by Tomi Ungerer
- *Through Moon and Stars and Night Skies* by Ann Turner
- *Many Moons* by James Thurber
- *Papa, Please Get the Moon for Me* by Eric Carle
-

# Negotiating a Unit of Study Using Non-Fiction

Non-fiction picture books are effective when used to initiate research. By research we mean delving into an already known topic of interest or beginning to learn about a totally new topic. Research provides real purposes for practising reading in the content areas.

Before reading aloud the selected book, establish what learners already know and what you/they want to find out. This activity can be done in a large or small group or groups. It is an effective way to use the read-aloud strategy to explore content at the older levels. The experience reinforces cooperative learning and provides an authentic purpose for notetaking. This learning experience takes place over several days or weeks depending on the group.

This outline illustrates one way to use non-fiction literature to initiate research.

Beginning

- In preparation, read *The Great Northern Diver: The Loon* by Barbara Juster Esbensen, illustrated by Mary Barrett Brown.
- Think about four or five main headings or sub-topics from the story such as:
    - the calls
    - the movement — flight, diving, swimming
    - the mating, the nest construction, the birth and care of young
    - the appearance
    - the habitat — where the loons live
- Decide how you will arrange the learning environment.
- Choose the sub-topics and make a label for each one.
- Organize paper and recording tools for each group.
- Consider how you will organize the learners into groups.
- Organize the groups.
- Introduce the topic.
- Invite each group to select a sub-topic.
- Give each group a label for the sub-topic.
- Encourage each group to choose a recorder.
- Invite each group to record known facts about the loon and their particular sub-topic. (This is a retelling of previous knowledge).
- Invite each group to brainstorm and record their questions.

During the experience

- Read aloud *The Great Northern Diver: The Loon*. Invite each group to study the illustrations as they listen to the text.
- Invite the learners to **relate** the story information to their prior knowledge, e.g., "Loons are at the cottage during the summer", "I've read the book *The Loon's Necklace*", "Babies ride on the adult loon's back..."
- Encourage the learners to listen for any information that answers or relates to their questions.
- Invite the learners to take notes, make jottings, sketches, diagrams — use whatever ways to help them remember and/or record pertinent information about their sub-topic.

- Invite learners to record or remember an interesting new fact.
- Invite each group to present the new knowledge and questions and to share the information from the read-aloud pertaining to their sub-topic.
- Encourage the learners to listen to all the groups and notice any overlap in information.
- Invite learners to listen to see if any other group provides information to answer their questions.
- Invite the groups to work together and decide how they will present their information and what materials they will need.
- Provide time for the groups to work together to complete their presentations.
- Encourage each group to decide how the members will share the completed product(s).

Assessment and Evaluation

- Continue to watch and listen.
- Notice how each group organizes and records information and questions.
- Observe how learners work in groups — who leads, records, listens...
- Select strategies for self, peer, group, and teacher assessment and evaluation. (See Draft Planning Sheets 8, 19 and 56, "Using the 3 R's Framework To Assess and Evaluate," "Using the 3 R's Framework in Assessment and Evaluation," and "Personal Assessment: Reflections.")
- Record pertinent information for ongoing assessment and evaluation purposes.
- At the end of the unit of study, find out what the learners know, what questions have been answered, and compare this information to the baseline (the knowledge and questions recorded at the beginning of the experiences).
- Use this information as part of ongoing assessment and evaluation.

Continuing

- Select books, articles, excerpts, poems for other curriculum topics and use the same process.
- Work with one group to address a specific area of curriculum, need or interest.
- Invite learners to practise this process independently or with peers to consolidate notetaking skills, enhance comprehension and extend knowledge and attitudes.
-

Other related titles:

- *The Loon's Necklace* by William Toye
- *For the Love of Loons* by Kate Crowley
- *Two Ways To Count to Ten* by Ruby Dee
- *The Wall* by Eve Bunting
- *Wolf Island* by Celia Godkin
-

Note: The above two approaches also provide a framework for studying other genres, such as folk tales, legends, poetry, mystery...

Family-Teacher Partnerships

"We emphasize the involvement and valuing of families as a necessary and vital part of the teaching/learning process."
(page 164)

"In the two workshops outlined in this chapter, we use the 3 R's of retelling, relating and reflecting as a framework for clearly demonstrating and illustrating 'how we talk and listen,' and 'how we learn and teach.'"
(page 164)

In this chapter, we outline two workshops you can use with families to illustrate in a concrete, hands-on, active/interactive way, many of the ideas in this book. We emphasize the involvement and valuing of families as a necessary and vital part of the teaching/learning process.

FAMILIES AS PARTNERS

Figure 5.1 All Children

All Children

- are unique
- come with knowledge
- come with experiences
- come with interests
- need to feel special
- need to be valued

Communication in the Family and Between Home and School is Essential.

- Home is the child's first school.
- People in the family are the child's first teachers.

Our years as educators and learners and our professional reading have convinced us that gaining family understanding and support for our teaching programs, our teaching practices, and what we value about education is essential for creating a successful teaching/learning environment. One of the great challenges for all of us as educators is to find the time and the means to communicate regularly and often with families. We need to find ways to show families the "what" and "how" of teaching and learning. Once they understand the "what" and "how," families will support us in our efforts at school and they will help to reinforce the learning at home.

In the two workshops outlined in this chapter, we use the 3 R's of retelling, relating and reflecting as a framework for clearly demonstrating and illustrating "how we talk and listen," and "how we learn and teach." In the first workshop, we suggest a framework you can use for working with families to encourage them to talk with and to listen to their children in meaningful ways. In the second workshop, we suggest a process for demonstrating to families in a concrete way how learners learn, and how we teach.

In both workshops, teachers and families participate together in meaningful and concrete learning experiences. Workshop leaders model and demonstrate the teaching/learning process and involve participants in small group cooperative activities. New knowledge, skills and attitudes are modelled, demonstrated and shared, and families and teachers gain understandings together. The second workshop in particular summarizes many of the ideas and practices we have discussed throughout *Retelling, Relating and Reflecting: Beyond the 3 R's.*

While we urge you to try these workshops with families, we have also used both workshops successfully with many groups including parents, grandparents, other interested community members, children, and our colleagues. We have organized the second workshop — "The Apple Workshop" — as a workshop for professional development for teachers. We present it as a university course session. This workshop provides participants with an opportunity to highlight and practise their own techniques of observing and recording as a way of evaluating what they value, and allows them to reflect on the value of workshops and one's own learning. With children, "The Apple Workshop" can initiate an exciting unit of study incorporating real experiences, literature, research and meaningful integration into many different curriculum areas. (See Figure 5.12, page 181.)

We invite you to try both workshops. The observations, interpretations and modifications will depend on the audience and on the time frame allowed.

We recommend a time frame of approximately sixty to ninety minutes. Ideally, a half-day is effective because it provides more time for participants to talk, ask questions and share with small groups and the whole group. A half-day also provides more time for the presenter to add the final touches — connections to theory and research. It allows for flexibility and makes it easier to modify and adjust the time frame to meet the needs of a particular group or situation.

Both workshops are most effective with groups no larger than forty to fifty people.

We hope you find your experiences using these workshops as fascinating and enjoyable as we have.

Good Luck!

USING THE 3 R'S FRAMEWORK TO LISTEN AND TO TALK EFFECTIVELY

This workshop outlines a suggested procedure for working with families to encourage them to use the 3 R's of retelling, relating and reflecting as a framework for talking with and listening to their children in meaningful ways.

Our goals for participants in this workshop experience are
- to demonstrate the importance of listening and talking with children
- to understand and use the 3 R's framework for talking and listening
- to illustrate **relating** — remembering, making connections to past experiences or events, sharing experiences
- to demonstrate some literature connections — in particular, using read-alouds and the 3 R's framework to encourage talking and listening (See Chapter 2, "Practising the 3 R's in Read-Aloud," pages 51-57.)
- to highlight the roles and responsibilities of learners, teachers and families

Beginning

- Display books and other print resources around the room.
- Place your materials in order as set out in the workshop.
- Organize tables and chairs in groups of four and six.
- Read aloud the book *Take Time to Relax* by Nancy Carlson (the members of a busy family are snowed in and, for the first time in a long time, enjoy one another's company, strengths and abilities) to acknowledge and value the fact that families are busy.
- Discuss the importance of taking time to talk with children.
- Use Figures 5.2 and 5.3 as overheads and also as a summary. (These figures are reproduced as Draft Planning Sheets 21 and 22, "Studies Have Shown..." and "Read-Aloud Experiences...")

Figure 5.2   Read-Alouds and Sharing Stories

> Studies have shown that when children are read to at home and when children and families share stories together, the children do better in school!

Figure 5.3   Read-Aloud Experiences Encourage. . .

> Read-aloud experiences encourage families to listen and talk with their children when stories are read and discussed.
>
> In fact, the **listening and talking** that are shared during these experiences are equally as important as the sharing of the literature.
>
> When families engage in storytelling, when they tell their own stories, when they really talk and listen to their children, they show their interest and love, and they help their children succeed in school and in life.

- Consider also showing Figure 5.1, "All Children" (see Draft Planning Sheet 20, "All Children").
- Invite the participants to turn to the person beside them and talk about WHEN and HOW they listen and talk with their children.
- Invite them also to discuss some of the challenges they experience in finding the time to talk with their children.
- Invite them to share possible solutions for finding this time.
- Invite participants to share their responses with everyone.
- Use Figure 5.4 (Draft Planning Sheet 23, "Families") as an overhead to highlight the points made in the figure.

Figure 5.4 Families

Families:

- make time for talking with children.
- find time for each child.
- are encouraging and positive.
- listen and accept without judging.
- use body language that models effective listening skills for their children.
- talk about their interests, hobbies, experiences, work—their lives.
-

During the workshop

- Share the 3 R's framework to help participants become better at listening and talking. (Consider using Draft Planning Sheets 3, 4, 5, and 6, "The 3 R's Framework: Retelling, Relating and Reflecting," "Retell," "Relate," and "Reflect," as overheads or give copies to each participant.)
- Read aloud the book *Wilfrid Gordon McDonald Partridge* by Mem Fox.
- Model the 3 R's framework:

"This book is about a little boy who brings back the memory of an elderly friend. When he presents her with a number of objects that are special to him, she begins to remember" **(retell)**.

   "This reminds me of my father-in-law who is also quite old. I remember one day I showed him a photograph of himself in a uniform and he started to talk about his time in the army" **(relate)**.

      "I wonder what this story makes you think about" **(reflect)**?

- Invite the participants to talk with the person next to them.
- Listen for the shared memories (relate) and the questions (reflect).
- Invite participants to discuss and identify their retell, relate and reflect statements.
- Invite everybody to take an object or photograph that holds a memory for them from their pockets, wallets, or purses.
- Invite them to share this memory with a person beside them.
- Ask if there are any individuals who wish to share their stories with the whole group.
- Again, invite participants to discuss and identify their retell, relate and reflect statements.

Continuing

- Give the participants an 8-page book as a reference. (See Draft Planning Sheet 7, "The 3 R's Framework in an 8-Page Book Format.")
- Explain how the booklet can be used when they read aloud with their children.

Note: Visit your public library or talk with your teacher-librarian or other staff members for suggestions for alternative titles to use for this workshop. For example, *Five Secrets in a Box* by Catherine Brighton is a story about a box belonging to Galileo which holds strange and fascinating objects that tell about the scientist's life and work.

HOW WE LEARN: "THE APPLE WORKSHOP"

In this workshop, we outline a process for demonstrating, in a concrete way, *how learners learn*. The workshop is based on a similar workshop that is presented by the High Scope Foundation in Ypsilanti, Michigan. We have modified, extended, personalized, and presented this workshop to many different audiences. We call our workshop "The Apple Workshop" because it is integrated with an apple unit of study.

We believe presenting "The Apple Workshop" increases teachers' confidence both in working with families and in their teaching practice. This workshop values the importance of teacher-family-learner partnerships and teamwork. It becomes a shared experience of "how we learn" and builds common understandings of "how we teach." The overall experience illustrates the value and importance of using real objects and related concrete materials, by inviting learners to manipulate, explore, and use language. Participants gain better understandings of:

- the philosophy of active/interactive experience-based learning (See Chapter 1, "Active/Interactive Learning," pages 6-9.)
- the value of talk and interaction
- the importance of acquiring baseline information for assessment and evaluation (See Chapter 3, "Beginning With the Learners" and "Getting To Know You," pages 105-106 and 117-143 respectively.)
- the methods used for planning curriculum
- the shared roles of all partners in the learning/teaching process (See Chapter 4: Negotiating Curriculum, pages 144-160.)

In this active/interactive workshop, we integrate the beliefs, theories and practice from the previous chapters and present them in a clear and meaningful way. Throughout, we model, demonstrate and use the 3 R's framework to encourage talk and thinking.

We invite you to present this workshop or different variations of this model by adding your individual styles and stories.

Our goals for participants in this workshop experience are
- to participate in an active/interactive learning experience
- to demonstrate the importance of using authentic objects and real experiences
- to communicate knowledge, ideas and questions to others
- to understand the value and importance of talking and doing
- to internalize the learning/teaching process
- to understand and use the 3 R's framework
- to demonstrate assessment and evaluation practices
- to understand how appropriate program planning and instruction emerge and evolve

- to highlight literature connections
- to illustrate how curriculum is integrated
- to illustrate the roles and responsibilities of all partners — learners, teachers and family members

Getting Ready

- Collect the materials. You will need the following for each group:
  - table knives (sturdy plastic or real)
  - paper towel or napkins
  - sets of 5 markers of different colours
  - paper (chart paper or large white paper)
  - tables and chairs
  - different kinds/colours of real apples (one per group)
  - plastic apples (one per group)
  - magazine pictures or photographs of apples (one per group)
  - large outlines (blackline masters — dittos) of an apple (one per group; see Draft Planning Sheet 25)
  - the word "apple" on a large flashcard for the presenter
- Collect books and other print resources about apples — fiction, non-fiction, poetry, posters, advertisements,... (See Figure 5.13, page 183.)
- Organize:
  - an overhead projector and screen
  - assorted quotes and statements on acetate referred to in this chapter (See Figures 5.1, 5.2, 5.3, 5.4, 5.10, 5.11, and 5.12; Draft Planning Sheets 20, 21, 22, 23, 1, 2, and 26.)
  - the handouts for the workshop
- Select an apple book to read aloud from the apple bibliography (Figure 5.13 on page 183; Draft Planning Sheet 27, "Bibliography").

Beginning

- Display books and other print resources around the room.
- Place your materials in order as set out in the workshop.
- Organize tables and chairs into groups of four or six.
- Before the workshop begins, invite a few participants to act as observers and recorders.
- Explain to these volunteers how to observe, listen, and record. (See Figure 5.5, next page; Draft Planning Sheet 24, "Observation Guide").
- Invite each participant to jot down quickly what they already know about apples. (**Note:** Some participants may write what they know about apples in a language other than English. Accept all types of recordings. This information becomes each person's baseline knowledge. See Figure 5.6 on page 171.)

During the experience

- Tell each group to select a recorder and choose one marker for jotting down information.

Figure 5.5   Observation Guide

OBSERVATION GUIDE

The Group Dynamics
- When do the participants get started?
- How do they begin?
- Who chooses the materials?
- How are decisions made?
-

The Recording
- Who records for the group?
- How is the recorder chosen?
- How is the paper used?
- What tools are used for writing?
- What type of script is used—upper/lower case, cursive or print style...?
- Does the recorder stand or sit to write, draw, sketch—body position?
-

The Language
- Who initiates the talk?
- Who directs?
- Who follows directions?
- Who follows others?
-

What Kind of Language Is Used?
Retell
- Who retells the directions? what to do?
- Who tells what they know?
- Who describes?
- Who retells using mathematical/scientific concepts?
- Who summarizes?
- Who...

Relate
- Who relates personal experiences, stories, memories?
- Who relates to mathematical/scientific concepts?
- Who...

Reflect
- Who asks questions?
- What kinds of questions are asked?
- How many questions are asked?
- Who reflects on mathematical/scientific concepts?
- Who shares insights, an "aha"—shows understandings?
- Who...

Figure 5.6 "Apple Workshop": What I Know About Apples, Written in Estonian

Task 1

- Invite each group to:
  - Choose **a real apple**.
  - Examine and explore the apple, using the materials provided (the knife and napkins).
  - Generate language about anything that is noticed about the apple, using all the senses (seeing, touching, hearing, tasting, smelling).
  - The group's recorder lists these words or phrases. See Figure 5.7 (next page).

Note: The volunteer observers and/or the workshop leader move(s) among the groups, recording exactly what they see (body language) and what they hear (dialogue). The workshop leader moves around to each group and intervenes by asking each group the same one or two questions — *"How many seeds are there in your apple? How did you decide how to make the first cut and why?"* The workshop leader

Figure 5.7   Apple Workshop: Group Notes

round, rolls
smells good
juicy
smells sweet
eight seeds in core
stem is off
Delicious is its name
fresh
crunchy
crispy
spots
shiny
white inside
red outside
brown seeds
stem at top
"an apple a day keeps the doctor away"
hard to cut, can be peeled
disappointing taste
    —sour, tart, tangy
hear crunching sound as chewed
hairy bottom, flower part has hairs
inside turns brown after a while
smells like a fall day in October
smells like spring trees budding

Tony
Saul
Chantelle
Sian

Oct. 20

models and demonstrates how to respond by practising the 3 R's framework of retelling, relating and reflecting during the workshop process.

"I noticed you cut your apple in half from side to side (retell)."

"I cut it this way when I bake apples and I put brown sugar and a sprinkle of cinnamon in the centre on each half (relate)."

"How did you decide to cut it this way (reflect)?"

• Invite everybody to:
    - read and review their lists of information (Figure 5.7).
    - talk about and discuss how learning is affected when they use all their senses
    - clarify any questionable information — e.g., Is it true that all apples have eight seeds?
    - share their recorded information
    - record the date and sign their names in corner

Task 2

- Invite each group to:
  - choose **a plastic apple**
  - examine and explore the plastic apple
  - reread and review the group's original list of observations (Figure 5.7)
  - use a different coloured marker and cross off any points that no longer apply and/or cannot be proven! (see Figure 5.8)

Figure 5.8   Apple Workshop: Reviewing Group Notes

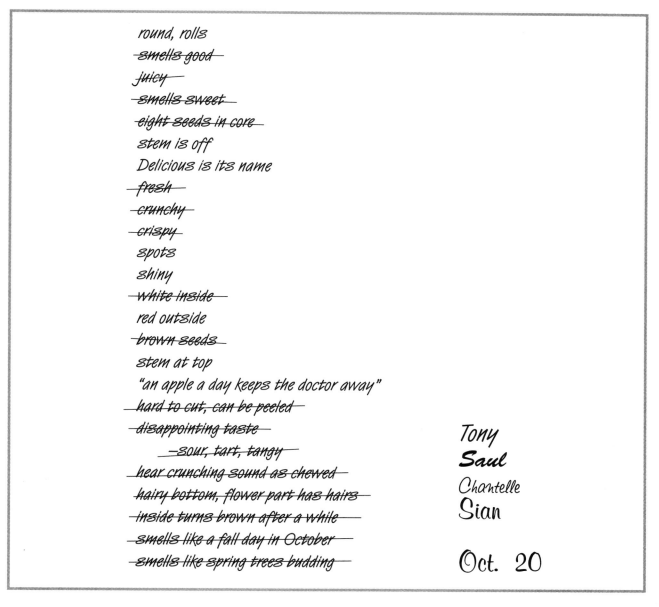

round, rolls
~~smells good~~
~~juicy~~
~~smells sweet~~
~~eight seeds in core~~
stem is off
Delicious is its name
~~fresh~~
~~crunchy~~
~~crispy~~
spots
shiny
~~white inside~~
red outside
~~brown seeds~~
stem at top
"an apple a day keeps the doctor away"
~~hard to cut, can be peeled~~
~~disappointing taste~~
~~sour, tart, tangy~~
~~hear crunching sound as chewed~~
~~hairy bottom, flower part has hairs~~
~~inside turns brown after a while~~
~~smells like a fall day in October~~
~~smells like spring trees budding~~

Tony
Saul
Chantelle
Sian

Oct. 20

- Encourage each group to:
  - talk about and discuss the process
  - share reviewed lists and ask for clarification about any questionable information
- Remind observers to continue to watch, listen and record.

Task 3

- Invite each group to:
    - examine and explore a **picture/photo of an apple**
    - reread and review the group's original list of observations (Figure 5.7)
    - use a different coloured marker and cross off any points that no longer apply and/or cannot be proven
- Encourage each group to:
    - talk about and discuss the process
    - share reviewed lists and ask for clarification about any questionable information
- Remind observers to continue to watch, listen and record.

Task 4

- Invite each group to:
    - examine and explore a ditto with **an outline of an apple** (Draft Planning Sheet 25, "'The Apple Workshop': Apple Outline")
    - reread and review the group's original list of observations (Figure 5.7)
    - use a different coloured marker and cross off any points that no longer apply and/or cannot be proven
- Encourage each group to:
    - talk about and discuss the process
    - share reviewed lists and ask for clarification about any questionable information
- Remind observers to continue to watch, listen and record.

Note: We realize that it is difficult to examine and explore a picture/photo and ditto/blackline master. However, for the purpose of this workshop, it is important to give the same instructions for each material. It is the difference in information gathered that makes the impact and communicates "how we learn." Through this process, we illustrate what effective learning and teaching environments look and sound like.

- Ask the participants to think about these questions:
    - How would people unfamiliar with apples (perhaps from a different country or culture) learn from only pictures or dittos?
    - What does this picture or ditto teach about size, shape, and colour of an apple?
    - Does this picture or ditto and the learning experiences associated with each provide accurate information? Why or why not?

Task 5

- Hold up **a flashcard with the word "apple"** printed on the card.
- Invite the participants to talk in their groups about these questions:
    - How might people unfamiliar with the word "apple" react if this is their first time seeing the word?
    - What feelings might they have as learners?
- Invite the participants to:
    - review the remaining point(s) on their lists
    - discuss and reflect back to their original lists and their learning experience with the real apple

> - in small groups and/or with the large group, discuss the implications of this workshop for learning and teaching. For example, participants discuss using real objects, taking field trips, talking to experts...

Continuing

- Invite volunteer <u>observers</u> to share what they have recorded. A sample observation page might look like Figure 5.9.

Note: It is interesting to encourage discussion about the talk on-task and the talk off-task and to invite the participants to consider how this talk affects the learning experience.

- Invite the observers to share their perceptions about their role with the whole group.
- Provide time for the participants to talk (retell, relate and reflect) about this workshop experience.
- As workshop leader, make connections between the task of the observer in this workshop and the teacher's role in observation in an active learning classroom.
- Highlight the role of the teacher as learner-watcher, learner-listener, and accurate recorder. **Note:** This is how observations and data are collected in the classroom. When learners are involved in discovery learning and working together, teachers observe and find out about the learners and how they learn. This data helps teachers choose teaching methods and plan appropriate programs.
- Invite the participants to review their notes indicating what they knew about apples before they started (**their baseline knowledge**) and what they have learned during this experience.
- Discuss the importance of establishing baseline information by emphasizing how baseline information and recorded observations are used for **assessing, evaluating and deciding on appropriate programs.**
- Outline how this baseline framework is used before and after different units of study.

Figure 5.9 Sample Filled-In Observation Guide

OBSERVATION GUIDE

The Group Dynamics

- When do the participants get started?
    - *Some started immediately.*
    - *Some talked first and then began.*
    -
- How do they begin?
    - *Some cut the apple right away.*
    - *Some felt and smelled the apple before and after cutting.*
    -
- Who chooses the materials?
    - *Some groups asked who wanted to choose.*

Figure 5.9   continued

- Some failed to hear the instructions and waited for the materials to be brought to them.

-

- How are decisions made?
  - Some made decisions by consensus.
  - In some groups, one person decided and everyone listened.
  -

The Recording

- Who records for the group?
  - Bill
  - Joan
  -

- How is the recorder chosen?
  - Some people volunteered.
  - Some discussed the decision as a group.
  -

- How is the paper used?
  - Some used the paper vertically; some horizontally.
  - Some cut out apple shapes.
  - Some used the lined side; some the blank side.
  -

- What tools are used for writing?
  - Some used the markers and followed directions with the colours.
  - Some used their own pens.
  - Some used pencils.
  -

- What type of script is used—upper/lower case, cursive or print style...?
  - Some used cursive writing.
  - Some used block letters.
  - Some used a combination of upper and lower case.
  -

- Does the recorder stand or sit to write, draw, sketch — body position?
  - Some recorders stood the entire time.
  - Some sat.
  - Some bent over writing.
  -

The Language

- Who initiates the talk?
  - the recorder
  -
  -

- Who directs?
  - the person cutting the apple
  -

Figure 5.9 continued

- Who follows directions?
  - *everyone else in the group*
  -
- Who follows others?

What Kind of Language Is Used?
Retell

- Who retells the directions? what to do?
  - *the recorder: "Well, here's what we need to do..."*
  -
  -

- Who tells what they know?
  - *Terry: "There are a variety of apples. Some are yellow, some are green and many are different colours of red. Some apples are good for cooking as well as eating; others are good for eating, but not for cooking."*
  -

- Who describes?
  - *Yasmin: "This apple comes from New Zealand. This apple is smooth and shiny. The skin of the apple has a different taste than the inside of the apple."*
  -

- Who retells using mathematical/scientific concepts?
  - *Tony: "We have ten seeds. How many did you count?"*

- Who summarizes?
  - *Bill: "Let's see what we have so far — this apple is shiny, smooth, red, has ten seeds..."*
  -

Relate

- Who relates personal experiences, stories, memories?
  - *Shannon: "My grandfather had an apple orchard and I used to spend my summers there."*
  -

- Who relates mathematical/scientific concepts?
  - *Marnie: "I remember doing an experiment in school to see how long it took different kinds of apples to turn brown."*
  -

Reflect

- Who asks questions?
  - *Sometimes one person asked all the questions.*
  - *Sometimes the group members took turns.*
  -

Figure 5.9 continued

- What kinds of questions are asked?
  - *Some yes/no questions.*
  - *Some "I wonder...", "What if...", "Why don't we try...", "What do you think will happen when...?"*
  - *Some made predictions, then checked their guesses.*
  - *The workshop leader asked: "How many seeds in an apple?" "How did you decide to make the first cut and why?"*
  -

- How many questions are asked?
  - *Some asked a lot of questions.*
  - *Some didn't ask questions — only made statements.*
  -

- Who reflects on mathematical/scientific concepts?
  - *Michael: "Do all apples float? Do they all sink after a while? If so, do they sink at the same rate?"*
  -

- Who shares insights, an "aha!" — shows understandings?
  - *Rena: "I thought all apples had the same number of seeds, but all of our apples had different numbers — anywhere from 6 to 14."*
  -

How We Learn

In this part of the workshop, you will present Figures 5.10., 5.11, and 5.12 (Draft Planning Sheets 1, 2, and 26, "How We Learn," "A Way of Looking at Learning," and "An Integrated Planning Web") as overhead acetates or charts.

The hope in this part of the workshop is for the participants to understand some of the theory about how children learn (indeed, how all people learn) based on the work and ideas of several renowned educators/researchers. It is important to emphasize and invite participants to realize the breadth of international research supporting the ideas we are presenting and that they are experiencing first-hand about "how we learn."

- Show Figure 5.10.
- Invite the participants to relate their experiences in the workshop to Figure 5.10 by reflecting and talking briefly about how they used their time, gained information, made decisions, and responded to one another during their explorations of the various examples of apples.

Fig. 5.10   How We Learn

HOW WE LEARN

Based on the knowledge of developmental patterns typical of learners, we see true learning as being initiated by the learner rather than being "handed down" or transmitted by the teacher. For these learning situations to occur, the following key components must be part of the learning environment:

Materials...

A variety of interesting materials are readily available and accessible to the learners.

Manipulation...

Learners are free to handle, explore, examine, study and work with the materials.

Choice...

Learners have opportunities to set their own goals, select materials, pose questions, and choose activities to seek out information and answers.

Language From the Learners...

Learners need to talk about what they already know, what they want to learn about, what they are doing and what they have done — and how.

Support From Others...

Support can be from peers, families, friends, experts, teachers... These " supporters" encourage the learners' efforts and help them extend what they are doing by joining in the learning, by helping them solve problems that arise, and by celebrating the learning together.

> - Based on the work by Dr. David Weikart and others in the High/Scope Curriculum as outlined in *The Teacher's Idea Book* by Michelle Graves (High/Scope Press, A Division of the High/Scope, High/Scope Educational Research Foundation, Michigan, 1989, page 4)

- Share an outline of Brian Cambourne's conditions of learning (Figure 5.11, next page; Draft Planning Sheet 2, "A Way of Looking at Learning").
- Relate each condition to the shared learning experiences of the workshop and invite participants to reflect on the workshop experience by thinking and talking about the following questions:
    - How were we immersed in the learning process?
    - What demonstrations were provided by the presenter and/or by the participants?
    - What were the expectations for our participation in this workshop?
    - How were we provided with opportunities to practise and accept responsibility for our learning?
    - How were we involved in approximating?
    - How did the presenter invite us to practise?

Figure 5.11   A Way of Looking at Learning

A WAY OF LOOKING AT LEARNING

This way of thinking about how we learn is based on the research and studies of Dr. Brian Cambourne, head of the Centre for Studies in Literacy at Wollongong University in Australia and author of numerous professional books and articles.
He calls the elements necessary for learning to take place "The Conditions of Learning."

Immersion...

a wide variety and number of resources, books, experiences...

Demonstrations...

teaching by showing concrete examples, modelling, demonstrating...

Expectations...

providing clear, appropriate messages...

Responsibility...

making choices, sharing ownership...

Approximations...

learning from and through mistakes, trying over and over — changing and trying again, guessing, risk taking...

Practice...

using, practising, having time...

Feedback...

responding—retelling, relating, reflecting...

Engagement with the learner and with learning occurs when there are frequent and continuous realistic and appropriate demonstrations of the "Conditions of Learning"

(*The Whole Story* by Brian Cambourne, Ashton Scholastic, 1988).

- Why is feedback so important and how can it be provided?

For example, say: *"We become **immersed** in the topic and experience using real apples, reproductions of apples, and print materials about apples; we see **demonstrations** of teaching, talking and responding, and we gain information and research from the presenter; we receive clear **expectations** that we are to participate and contribute, and the instructions are clearly stated; we take **ownership** and **responsibility** for our learning as each of us assumes a role in the group and chooses how and what we will do; we make **approximations** when we try various strategies examining the apples and making predictions; we are **engaged** in the learning process when we practise communicating, decision making, recording, and problem solving; we give and receive **feedback** when we exchange what we know and want to find out about apples by **retelling, relating and reflecting.**"*

- Discuss with the participants the implications of Cambourne's Conditions of Learning for teaching.
- Share with participants how you used the 3 R's during the workshop. Refer to Draft Planning Sheet 3, "The 3 R's Framework: Retelling, Relating and Reflecting."

Integrated Learning

- Read aloud a selection about apples, e.g., *My Apple* by Kay Davies and Wendy Oldfield.
- Discuss integrated learning and how experiences can stem from a book (fiction or non-fiction), poem, song or from a topic or theme. Show Figure 5.12 (Draft Planning Sheet 26, "An Integrated Planning Web") on an overhead.
- Discuss how adding print and text to learning experiences encourages research.

Fgure 5.12   An Integrated Planning Web

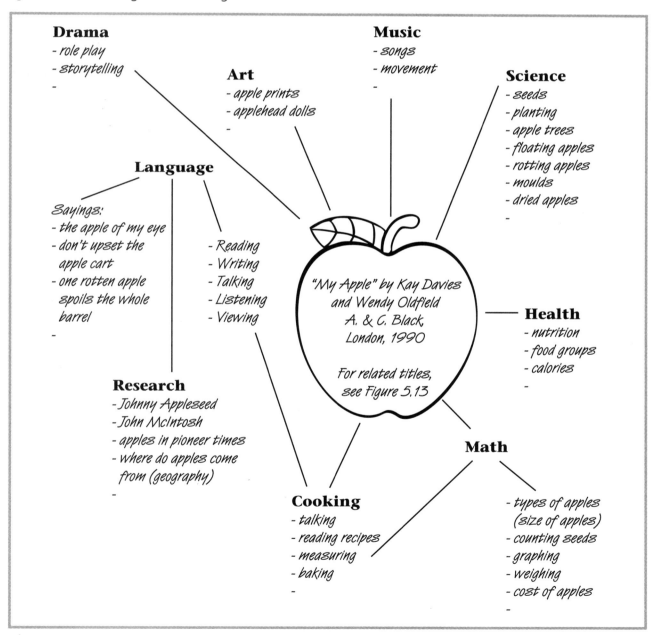

- Have available for participants a bibliography listing apple books and related literature. See Figure 5.13 (Draft Planning Sheet 27, "Bibliography"). Direct participants' attention to the books and other print materials you have displayed in the room.
- Have available for participants the story in Figure 5.14, page 184 (Draft Planning Sheet 28, "The Apple Workshop: 'The Little Red House With No Doors'") to read for pleasure and interest.
- Brainstorm with the whole group the implications of their experiences in the workshop for learning and teaching.
- Discuss possible variations and ways to use this workshop:
    - Use a different fruit for each group instead of each group using the same fruit.
    - Use other foods besides apples — carrots, potatoes, avocado...
    - Use other items besides food — old clocks, telephones, something that can be taken apart.
    - Plan a field trip as an extension activity (e.g., to an apple orchard).
    - Interview a grocery storekeeper or an owner of an orchard to find answers to questions.
    - Encourage participants to try some of the workshop activities at home with their own children.
    - Consider inviting families and their children to work together — a "family learning" evening.

Conclusion

- One way to end the workshop is by sharing Figure 5.1 on page 164 (Draft Planning Sheet 20, "All Children") as an overhead or chart, or as a handout.
- Have available copies of the professional article "How Do Children Learn by Handling Objects" by Connie K. Williams and Constance Kamii (*Young Children* magazine; contact the National Association for the Education of Young Children for copies of this article and for other articles about education.) This article highlights many of the ideas in the workshop by referring to Jean Piaget's theories about **"what children learn and how children learn by manipulating objects."**
- Have available as handouts copies of some of the information presented on the overhead transparencies (Draft Planning Sheets 20, 21, 22, 23, 1, 2, and 26).

Figure 5.13 Bibliography: Books About Apples and Other Related Books

BIBLIOGRAPHY: BOOKS ABOUT APPLES AND OTHER RELATED BOOKS

This list includes fiction and non-fiction.

Fiction

- *Albert's Field Trip*, by Leslie Tryon (New York, NY: Macmillan Children's Group, 1993).
- *Applebet: An ABC*, by Clyde Watson (New York, NY: Farrar, Straus, & Giroux Inc., 1987).
- *How To Make Apple Pie and See the World*, by Marjorie Priceman (New York, NY: Knopf, 1994).
- *Johnny Appleseed, A Tall Tale*, Retold and illustrated by Steven Kellogg (New York, NY: Morrow Junior Books, 1988).
- *Johnny Appleseed*, by Eva Moore (New York, NY: Scholastic Inc., 1964).
- *Apple Tree Christmas*, by Trinka Hakes Noble (New York, NY: Dial Books for Young Readers, 1988).
- *Mr. Brown's Magnificent Apple Tree*, by Yvonne Winer, Illustrated by Maya Winters (Richmond Hill, ON: Scholastic Canada, 1985).
- *My Apple Tree*, by Harriet Ziefert (New York, NY: HarperCollins Publishers, 1991).
- *One Watermelon Seed*, by Celia Lottridge, Illustrated by Karen Patkau (Toronto, ON: Oxford University Press, 1990).
- *The Seasons of Arnold's Apple Tree*, by Gail Gibbons (New York, NY: Harcourt Brace Jovanovich Inc., 1984).
-

Non-Fiction

- *The Amazing Apple Book*, by Paulette Bourgeois (Toronto, ON: Kids Can, 1987).
- *The Amazing Potato Book*, by Paulette Bourgeois (Toronto, ON: Kids Can, 1991).
- *An Apple a Day: Over 20 Apple Projects for Kids*, by Jennifer Storey Gillis (Vancouver, BC: Whitecap Books Ltd., 1993).
- *An Apple Tree Through the Year*, by Claudia Schnieper (Minneapolis, MN: Carolrhoda Books Inc., 1987).
- *Fruit*, Created by Pascale de Bourgoing and Gallimard Jeunesse, Illustrated by P. M. Valat (New York, NY: Scholastic, 1991).
- *The Life and Times of the Apple*, by Charles Micucci (New York, NY: Orchard Books, 1992).
- *My Apple*, by Kay Davies and Wendy Oldfield (London, Eng: A & C Black (Publishers) Ltd., 1990).
-

Figure 5.14 The Little Red House With No Doors

The Little Red House With No Doors

Once upon a time there was a little boy who grew tired of all his toys and games. He asked his mother, "What shall I do?" "You shall go on a journey and find a little red house with no windows or doors and a star inside. Come back as soon as you can." So the boy started out on his journey and he found a beautiful little girl and he asked her, "Do you know where I can find a little red house with no windows and doors and a star inside?" "Ask my father, the farmer, he may know." So the little boy found the farmer and asked him, "Do you know where I can find a little red house with no windows and no doors and a star inside?" The farmer laughed and said, "I've lived many years but I've never seen anything like it. Go ask Granny. She knows everything." So the little boy asked Granny, "Please Granny, where can I find a house with no windows and doors and a star inside?" "I'd like to find that house myself. It would be warm in the winter and the starlight would be beautiful. Go ask the wind. Maybe the wind knows." The wind whistled by the little boy and the boy said, "Oh wind, can you help me find a little red house with no windows and doors and a star inside?" The wind could not speak any words but it went on singing ahead of the little boy until it came to an apple tree and it shook the branches. Down came a beautiful red apple. The little boy picked it up and looked at it. It was a little red house that had no windows or doors. "I wonder?" said the boy. He took a jackknife from his pocket and cut the apple in half. "How wonderful!" There in the centre of the apple was a star holding little brown seeds. He ran home and showed his mother. "Look, I found it!" (Author Unknown)

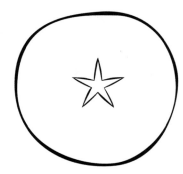

6

Final Reflections

"When we retell, relate and reflect, we experience the principles of how we learn, and we continuously make literacy and learning connections."
(page 186)

"We invite you to continue to make connections, and share your interpretations, your retellings, relatings and reflections — letting your mind wander through your memories, making connections, journeying through the windows of learning, from the past, to the present, and into the future."
(page 187)

As you read *Retelling, Relating, Reflecting: Beyond the 3 R's*, we hope you will make connections with what you know, what you remember, and your questionings, wonderings and insights. Literacy and learning connections come from within, when we think and talk. When we retell, relate and reflect, we experience the principles of how we learn, and we continuously make literacy and learning connections.

Personal Retellings: *Susan and Maxine*

We learned the challenges of collaborative writing. We believe time is critical for everyone to become writers, readers and lifelong learners. We discovered that leaving our draft manuscript for a period of time was an important part of our learning. This enriched our text. We learned that the content continuously changes when we practise the ideas in this book. Our learning and writing style evolved into large blocks of time spent together immersed in the pages and chapters. During this time, the writing was talk-driven — and our literacy connections emerged. Even though Retelling, Relating, Reflecting: Beyond the 3 R's was a collaborative venture, one partner tended to set the expectations. This person also demonstrated and modelled how to write and publish a book, based on previous experiences. However, the vision remained clear for both of us. Using the computer facilitated our writing and learning processes. As we sat at one computer, our text emerged from continuously talking together. Comments from reviewers, colleagues and friends helped us to revise, reorganize and complete this book. Our celebration will be having Retelling, Relating, Reflecting: Beyond the 3 R's help to foster and value life-long literacy connections.

Personal Relatings

We will always remember the experience of writing a book together — a three-year period of memories. These memories will remain a part of us as we continue to grow and change and look back on our experiences. Each time we read other personal and professional materials, we find ourselves referring to pieces and sections of this book. The ideas, messages, and experiences are with us always, everywhere...

Personal Reflections

We still wonder about how to truly make literacy connections with the child's first teachers — family members. We wonder about the impact of the computer and technology on literacy development. We wonder how to encourage learners, families and teachers to know and love literature as an integral part of learning. We believe that all learners, teachers and families have stories, and we wonder how to capitalize and use personal story as an effective strategy for professional development.

We look forward to meeting and having conversations with many of you about our personal and professional interpretations. It is our vision that this book will reach out to educators, families and learners, and invite lifelong learning and literacy connections. After reading *Retelling, Relating, Reflecting: Beyond the 3 R's*, talk to a friend about what you have learned, what you remember, and what you still wonder about. Each time we, as authors, revisit the images and the chapters in this book, we discover new meanings.

We invite you to continue to make connections, and share your interpretations, your retellings, relatings and reflections — letting your mind wander through your memories, making connections, journeying through the windows of learning, from the past, to the present, and into the future.

Appendices

LITERATURE BIBLIOGRAPHY: CHILDREN'S LITERATURE

Aardema, Verna. *Why Mosquitoes Buzz in People's Ears.* New York, NY: Puffin Books, 1993.

Ahlberg, Janet and Allan. *Each Peach Pear Plum.* New York, NY: Puffin Books, 1986.

Ahlberg, Janet and Allan. *The Jolly Postman or Other People's Letters.* London, UK: William Heinemann Ltd., 1986.

Aliki. *The Medieval Feast.* A Harper Trophy Book. New York, NY: HarperCollins Publishers, 1986.

Anno, Mitsumasa. *Anno's Counting Book.* New York, NY: HarperCollins Children's Books, 1977.

Arnold, Tedd. *The Signmaker's Assistant.* New York, NY: Dial Books for Young Readers, 1992.

Arnosky, Jim. *Crinkleroot's Guide to Walking in Wild Places.* New York, NY: Macmillan Children's Book Group, 1993.

Aubin, Michel. *The Secret Code.* Toronto, ON: James Lorimer & Co. Ltd., 1987.

Baker, Jeannie. *Where the Forest Meets the Sea.* New York, NY: Greenwillow Books, 1988.

Bang, Molly. *Dawn.* New York, NY: William Morrow & Co., Inc., 1983.

Baum, Frank L. *The Wizard of Oz.* New York, NY: Henry Holt & Co. Inc., 1982.

Bayer, Jane. *My Name Is Alice.* New York, NY: Dial Books for Young Readers, 1987.

Baylor, Byrd. *Everybody Needs a Rock.* New York, NY: Macmillan Children's Book Group, 1987.

Baylor, Byrd. *My Favourite Person.* New York, NY: Macmillan Children's Book Group, 1992.

Baylor, Byrd. *The Desert Is Theirs.* New York, NY: Aladdin Books, 1987.

Bedard, Michael. *Emily*. New York, NY: Bantam Doubleday Dell, 1992.

Bemelmans, Ludwig. *Madeline*. New York, NY: Puffin Books, 1993.

Berger, Barbara. *Grandfather Twilight*. New York, NY: Putnam Publishing Group, 1990.

Bjork, Christina, and Lena Anderson. *Linnea in Monet's Garden*. New York, NY: Farrar, Straus & Giroux, 1987.

Bjork, Christina, and Lena Anderson. *Linnea's Windowsill Garden*. New York, NY: Farrar, Straus & Giroux, 1988.

Blades, Ann. *Mary of Mile 18*. Montreal, PQ: Tundra Books Inc., 1988.

Booth, David. (Ed.). *Till All the Stars Have Fallen: Canadian Poems for Children*. Toronto, ON: Kids Can Press, 1989.

Booth, David. (Ed.). *Voices on the Wind*. New York, NY: Morrow Junior Books, 1990.

Bourgeois, Paulette. *The Amazing Apple Book*. Toronto, ON: Kids Can Press, 1987.

Bourgeois, Paulette. *The Amazing Dirt Book*. Toronto, ON: Kids Can Press, 1990.

Bourgeois, Paulette. *The Amazing Potato Book*. Toronto, ON: Kids Can Press, 1991.

Branley, F. M. *Gravity Is a Mystery*. New York, NY: HarperCollins Publishers, 1986.

Brett, Jan. *The First Dog*. New York, NY: Harcourt Brace Jovanovich Inc., 1992.

Briggs, Raymond. *The Snowman*. New York, NY: Random House Books for Young Readers, 1990.

Brighton, Catherine. *Five Secrets in a Box*. Markham, ON: Fitzhenry & Whiteside Limited, 1987.

Brighton, Catherine. *Dearest Grandmama*. New York, NY: Bantam Doubleday Dell, 1991.

Brighton, Catherine. *Hope's Gift*. New York, NY: Bantam Doubleday Dell, 1988.

Brighton, Catherine. *Mozart: Scenes from the Childhood of the Great Composer*. New York, NY: Bantam Doubleday Dell, 1990.

Brown, Marcia. *Stone Soup*. New York, NY: Macmillan Children's Book Group, 1988.

Brown, Margaret Wise. *Goodnight Moon*. New York, NY: HarperCollins Publishers, 1991.

Brown, Ruth. *The World That Jack Built*. New York, NY: Dutton Children's Books, 1991.

Browne, Anthony. *I Like Books.* North Pomfret, UK: Julia MacRae Books, 1988.

Browne, Eileen. *No Problem.* Cambridge, MA: Candlewick Press, 1993.

Bunting, Eve. *The Wall.* Boston, MA: Houghton Mifflin Co., 1990.

Bunting, Eve. *The Wednesday Surprise.* Boston, MA: Houghton Mifflin Co., 1990.

Burnett, Frances H. *The Secret Garden.* New York, NY: Puffin Books, 1987.

Burningham, John. *Mr. Gumpy's Outing.* North Pomfret, UK: Julia MacRae Books, 1992.

Burton, Virginia Lee. *Katy and the Big Snow.* Boston, MA: Houghton Mifflin Co., 1974.

Burton, Virginia Lee. *Mike Mulligan and His Steam Shovel.* Boston, MA: Houghton Mifflin Co., 1977.

Butterworth, Nick, and Mick Inkpen. *Jasper's Beanstalk.* London, England: Hodder & Stoughton, 1992.

Cameron, Ann. *The Most Beautiful Place in the World.* New York, NY: Knopf Young Readers, 1993.

Carle, Eric. *Papa, Please Get the Moon for Me.* Saxonville, MA: Picture Book Studio, 1991.

Carle, Eric. *The Secret Birthday Message.* New York, NY: HarperCollins Publishers, 1986.

Carlson, Nancy. *Take Time To Relax.* New York, NY: Puffin Books, 1991.

Caseley, Judith. *Dear Annie.* New York, NY: Greenwillow Books, 1991.

Cazet, Denys. *Are There Any Questions?* New York, NY: Orchard Books, l992.

Cazet, Denys. *Frosted Glass.* New York, NY: Macmillan Children's Book Group, 1987.

Ciardi, John. *You Read to Me and I'll Read to You.* New York, NY: HarperCollins Publishers, 1987.

Cleary, Beverly. *Dear Mr. Henshaw.* New York, NY: Bantam Doubleday Dell, 1992.

Cohen, Miriam. *No Good in Art.* New York, NY: Bantam Doubleday Dell, 1986.

Cole, Joanna. *The Magic School Bus Inside the Earth.* New York, NY: Scholastic Inc., 1989.

Cooney, Barbara. *Island Boy.* New York, NY: Puffin Books, 1991.

Cooney, Barbara. *Miss Rumphius.* New York, NY: Puffin Books, 1985.

Crews, Donald. *We Read: A to Z.* New York, NY: Greenwillow Books, 1984.

Crowley, Kate. *For the Love of Loons.* Toronto, ON: Key Porter Books, 1987.

Dahl, Roald. *James and the Giant Peach.* New York, NY: Bantam Doubleday Dell, 1984.

Davies, Kay, and Wendy Oldfield. *My Apple.* London, UK: A & C Black, 1990.

Dee, Ruby. *Two Ways to Count to Ten.* New York, NY: Henry Holt & Co., Inc., 1990.

Demi. *The Empty Pot.* New York, NY: Henry Holt & Co., Inc., 1990.

Demi. *Liang and the Magic Paintbrush.* New York, NY: Henry Holt & Co., Inc., 1988.

de Paola, Tomie. *The Art Lesson.* New York: Putnam Publishing Group, 1989.

de Paola, Tomie. *Tom.* New York, NY: Putnam Publishing Group, 1993.

Dorras, Arthur. *Ant Cities.* Let's-Read-&-Find-Out Book. New York, NY: HarperCollins Publishers, 1988.

Duvoisin, Roger. *The Camel Who Took a Walk.* New York, NY: Dutton Children's Books, 1951.

Edens, Cooper. *Santa Cows.* New York, NY: Simon & Schuster, 1991.

Esbensen, Barbara Juster. *The Great Northern Diver: The Loon.* Toronto, ON: Little, Brown & Co., 1990.

Feelings, Muriel, and Tom Feelings. *Jambo Means Hello: A Swahili Alphabet Book.* New York, NY: Dial Books for Young Readers, 1985.

Feelings, Muriel. *Moja Means One: A Swahili Counting Book.* New York, NY: Dial Books for Young Readers, 1987.

Fleischman, Paul. *Joyful Noise: Poems for Two Voices.* New York, NY: HarperCollins Publishers, 1992.

Fleischman, Paul. *Rondo in C.* New York, NY: HarperCollins Children's Books, 1988.

Foreman, Michael. *One World.* New York, NY: Arcade Publishing, 1991.

Fox, Mem. *Koala Lou.* New York, NY: Harcourt Brace Jovanovich Inc., 1989.

Fox, Mem. *Wilfrid Gordon McDonald Partridge.* New York, NY: Kane-Miller Books, 1989.

Fradon, Dana. *Harold the Herald: A Book About Heraldry.* New York, NY: Dutton Children's Books, 1990.

French, Fiona. *Snow White in New York.* New York, NY: Oxford University Press, 1990.

Galbraith, Kathryn O. *Laura Charlotte.* New York, NY: Putnam Publishing Group, 1993.

Galdone, Paul. *What's in Fox's Sack?* Boston, MA: Houghton Mifflin Co., 1987.

Gibbons, Gail. *The Seasons of Arnold's Apple Tree.* New York, NY: Harcourt Brace Jovanovich Inc., 1988.

Gibbons, Gail. *Sun Up, Sun Down.* New York, NY: Harcourt Brace Jovanovich Inc., 1987.

Gillis, Jennifer Storey. *An Apple a Day: Over 20 Apple Projects for Kids.* Vancouver, BC: Whitecap Books, 1993.

Godkin, Celia. *Wolf Island.* Markham, ON: Fitzhenry & Whiteside, 1989.

Goffstein, M. B. *Our Snowman.* New York, NY: HarperCollins Publishers, 1986.

Granfield, Linda. *Extra! Extra! The Who, What, Where, When, and Why of Newspapers.* Toronto, ON: Kids Can Press, 1993.

Hamley, Dennis. *Hare's Choice.* New York, NY: Bantam Doubleday Dell, 1992.

Handford, Martin. *Where's Waldo?* Boston, MA: Little, Brown & Co., 1987.

Hasler, Eveline. *Winter Magic.* New York, NY: Morrow Junior Books, 1985.

Heckman, Philip. *The Moon Is Following Me.* New York, NY: Macmillan Children's Book Group, 1991.

Heidbreder, Robert, and Karen Patkau. *Don't Eat Spiders.* Toronto, ON: Oxford University Press, 1985.

Heide, Florence Parry. *The Day of Ahmed's Secret.* New York, NY: Lothrop, Lee & Shepard Books, 1990.

Henkes, Kevin. *Chrysanthemum.* New York, NY: Greenwillow Books, 1991.

Hoban, Tana. *I Read Signs.* New York, NY: William Morrow & Co., Inc., 1987.

Hoban, Tana. *I Read Symbols.* New York, NY: Greenwillow Books, 1983.

Hooks, William H., Joanne Oppenheim and Barbara Brenner. *How Do You Make a Bubble?* New York, NY: Bantam Books, 1992.

Hutchins, Pat. *Don't Forget the Bacon.* New York, NY: William Morrow & Co., Inc., 1989.

Hutchins, Pat. *The Doorbell Rang.* New York, NY: William Morrow & Co., Inc., 1989.

Inkpen, Mick. *The Blue Balloon.* Boston, MA: Little, Brown & Co., 1990.

James, Simon. *Dear Greenpeace.* London, UK: Walker Books, 1991.

Jonas, Ann. *Reflections.* New York, NY: Greenwillow Books, 1987.

Jonas, Ann. *Round Trip.* New York, NY: William Morrow & Co., Inc., 1990.

Karlstrom, Nancy. *The Moon Came Too.* New York, NY: Macmillan Children's Book Group, 1987.

Keats, Ezra Jack. *The Snowy Day.* New York, NY: Puffin Books, 1976.

Kellogg, Steven. *Johnny Appleseed.* New York, NY: Morrow Junior Books, 1988.

Kessler, Leonard. *Mr. Pine's Mixed-Up Signs.* New York, NY: Scholastic, 1972.

Khalsa, Dayal Kaur. *Tales of a Gambling Grandma.* Montreal, PQ: Tundra Books Inc., 1986.

Kleinbaum, N. H. *Dead Poets Society.* New York, NY: Bantam Doubleday Dell, 1989.

Knight, Margie Burns. *Talking Walls.* New York, NY: Prentice Hall, 1993.

Kovalski, Maryann. *Brenda and Edward.* Toronto, ON: Kids Can Press, 1984.

Lasky, Kathryn. *Sea Swan.* New York, NY: Macmillan Children's Book Group, 1988.

Leaf, Margaret. *Eyes of the Dragon.* New York, NY: Lothrop, Lee & Shepard Books, 1987.

Leedy, Loreen. *The Furry News: How To Make a Newspaper.* New York, NY: Holiday House, 1990.

Leedy, Loreen. *Messages in the Mailbox: How To Write a Letter.* New York, NY: Holiday House, 1991.

Little, Jean. *Hey World, Here I Am!* Toronto, ON: Kids Can Press, 1986.

Little, Jean. *Little By Little.* Markham, ON: Penguin Books, 1987.

Lobel, Anita. *Alison's Zinnea.* New York, NY: Greenwillow Books, 1990.

Locker, Thomas. *The Young Artist.* New York, NY: Dial Books for Young Readers, 1989.

Lottridge, Celia, and Ian Wallace. *The Name of the Tree*. Toronto, ON: Groundwood Books/Douglas & McIntyre, 1989.

Lottridge, Celia. *One Watermelon Seed*. Toronto, ON: Oxford University Press, 1990.

MacLachlan, Patricia. *Sarah, Plain and Tall*. New York, NY: HarperCollins Children's Books, 1985.

Mayer, Mercer. *Me Too*. Racine, WI: Western Publishing, 1985.

McLerran, Alice. *Roxaboxen*. New York, NY: Puffin Books, 1992.

Micucci, Charles. *The Life and Times of the Apple*. New York, NY: Orchard Books, 1992.

Milstein, Linda. *Grandma's Jewelry Box*. New York, NY: Random House, 1992.

Moore, Eva. *Johnny Appleseed*. New York, NY: Scholastic Inc., 1964.

Moore, Inga. *Six-Dinner Sid*. New York, NY: Simon & Schuster Books, 1991.

Most, Bernard. *There's an Ant in Anthony*. New York, NY: Morrow Junior Books, 1992.

Mozart, Wolfgang Amadeus. *The Magic Flute*. New York, NY: Dover Publications, 1985.

Nichol, Barbara. *Beethoven Lives Upstairs*. Toronto, ON: Lester Publishing, 1993.

Noble, Trinka Hakes. *Apple Tree Christmas*. New York, NY: Dial Books for Young Readers, 1988.

Omerod, Jan. *Moonlight*. New York, NY: Lothrop, Lee & Shepard Books, 1982.

Oxenbury, Helen. *Helen Oxenbury's Numbers of Things*. New York, NY: Delacorte Press, 1983.

Polacco, Patricia. *The Bee Tree*. New York, NY: Philomel Books, 1993.

Pelham, David. *Sam's Surprise*. New York, NY: Dutton Children's Books, 1992.

Pieńkowski, Jan. *ABC*. New York, NY: Simon & Schuster, 1989.

Pieńkowski, Jan. *Shapes*. New York, NY: Simon & Schuster, 1989.

Prater, John. *The Gift*. New York, NY: Viking Children's Books, 1986.

Prelutsky, Jack. *The New Kid on the Block*. New York, NY: Greenwillow Books, 1984.

Prelutsky, Jack. (Ed.). *Random House Book of Poetry*. New York, NY: Random House Books for Young Readers, 1983.

Priceman, Marjorie. *How To Make an Apple Pie and See the World*. New York, NY: Knopf, 1994.

Prokofiev. *Peter and the Wolf*. Russian Folktale Publishers, 1987.

Raffi. *One Light One Sun*. New York, NY: Crown Books for Young Readers, 1990.

Rockwell, Thomas. *How To Eat Fried Worms*. New York, NY: Bantam Doubleday Dell, 1992.

Russo, Marisabina. *The Line-Up Book*. New York, NY: Puffin Books, 1992.

Rylant, Cynthia. *All I See*. New York, NY: Orchard Books, 1988.

Rylant, Cynthia. *Miss Maggie*. New York, NY: Dutton Children's Books, 1993.

San Souci, Daniel. *North Country Night*. New York, NY: Bantam Doubleday Dell, 1990.

Scheer, Julian, *Rain Makes Applesauce*. New York, NY: Holiday House, 1964.

Schnieper, Claudia. *An Apple Tree Through the Year*. Minneapolis, MN: Carolrhoda Books Inc., 1987.

Schoop, Janice. *Boys Don't Knit*. Trenton, NJ: Africa World, 1988.

Scieszka, Jon. *The True Story of the Three Pigs*. New York, NY: Viking Penguin Press, 1989.

Selway, Martina. *Don't Forget To Write*. Nashville, TN: Ideals Children's Books, 1992.

Seuss, Dr. *Dr. Seuss's ABC*. New York, NY: Random House Books for Young Readers, 1963.

Seuss, Dr. *One Fish Two Fish Red Fish Blue Fish*. New York, NY: Random House Books for Young Readers, 1960.

Shelby, Anne. *Potluck*. New York, NY: Orchard Books, 1991.

Shepard, Aaron. *The Legend of Slappy Hooper*. New York, NY: Charles Scribners' Sons, 1993.

Silverstein, Shel. *A Light in the Attic*. New York, NY: HarperCollins Publishers, 1981.

Silverstein, Shel. *Where the Sidewalk Ends*. New York, NY: HarperCollins Publishers, 1981.

Sloat, Teri. *From One to One Hundred*. New York, NY: Dutton Children's Books, 1991.

Smith, Robert Kimmel. *Mostly Michael*. New York, NY: Delacorte Press, 1987.

Stapleton, John T. *The Littlest Mermaid.* New York, NY: McClanahan Books, 1992.

Steig, William. *Sylvester and the Magic Pebble.* New York, NY: Gulliver Books, 1988.

Steptoe, John. *Mufara's Beautiful Daughters.* New York, NY: Lothrop, Lee & Shepard Books, 1987.

Stevenson, Robert Louis. *Block City.* New York, NY: Puffin Books, 1992.

Stickland, Paul. *Machines as Tall as Giants.* New York, NY: Random House Books for Young Readers, 1989.

Stow, Jenny. *The House That Jack Built.* New York, NY: Dial Books for Young Readers, 1992.

Tejima, Keizaburo. *The Fox's Dream.* New York, NY: The Putnam Publishing Group, 1990.

Thompson, Richard. *Sky Full of Babies.* Toronto, ON: Firefly Books, 1987.

Thornhill, Jan. *The Wildlife A·B·C·* Toronto, ON: Greey de Pencier, 1988.

Thurber, James. *Many Moons.* New York, NY: Harcourt Brace Jovanovich Inc., 1990.

Tompert, Ann. *Grandfather Tang's Story.* New York, NY: Crown Publishing, 1990.

Toye, William. *The Loon's Necklace.* Toronto, ON: Oxford University Press, 1977.

Tryon, Leslie. *Albert's Alphabet.* New York, NY: Macmillan Children's Book Group, 1991.

Tyron, Leslie. *Albert's Field Trip.* New York, NY: Macmillan Children's Book Group, 1993.

Turner, Ann. *Through Moon and Stars and Night Skies.* New York, NY: HarperCollins Publishers, 1990.

Ungerer, Tomi. *Moon Man.* New York, NY: Delacorte Press, 1991.

Van Allsburg, Chris. *Two Bad Ants.* Boston, MA: Houghton Mifflin Co., 1988.

Varley, Susan. *Badger's Parting Gifts.* New York, NY: William Morrow & Co. Inc., 1992.

Viorst, Judith. *Rosie and Michael.* New York, NY: Macmillan Children's Book Group, 1988.

Viorst, Judith. *The Tenth Good Thing About Barney.* New York, NY: Macmillan Children's Book Group, 1987.

Waddell, Martin. *Once There Were Giants*. New York, NY: Delacorte Press, 1989.

Wallace, Ian. *Chin Chiang and the Dragon's Dance*. Toronto, ON: Groundwood Books/Douglas & McIntyre, 1984.

Wallace, Ian. *The Sparrow's Song*. Markham, ON: Viking Kestrel, 1986.

Watson, Clyde. *Applebet: An ABC*. New York, NY: Farrar, Straus, and Giroux, 1987.

Wells, Rosemary. *Shy Charles*. New York, NY: Puffin Books, 1992.

White, E. B. *Charlotte's Web*. Cutchogue, NY: Buccaneer Books, 1990.

Wild, Margaret. *The Very Best of Friends*. Toronto, ON: Kids Can Press, 1990.

Wildsmith, Brian. *A B C*. Oxford, Oxfordshire, UK: Oxford University Press, 1981.

Willard, Nancy. *The High Rise Glorious Skittle Skat Roarious Sky Pie Angel Food Cake*. New York, NY: Harcourt Brace Jovanovich Inc., 1990.

Williams, Karen Lynn. *Galimoto*. Clearwater, FL: Reading Adventures, 1993.

Williams, Margery. *The Velveteen Rabbit*. New York, NY: Bantam Doubleday Dell, 1991.

Winer, Yvonne. *Mr. Brown's Magnificent Apple Tree*. Richmond Hill, ON: Scholastic Canada, 1985.

Wood, Audrey. *Heckedy Peg*. New York, NY: Harcourt Brace Jovanovich Inc., 1987.

Wood, Audrey. *Moonflute*. New York, NY: Harcourt Brace Jovanovich Inc., 1986.

Wynne-Jones, Tim. *Architect of the Moon*. Toronto, ON: Groundwood Books/Douglas & McIntyre, 1991.

Yolen, Jane. *Owl Moon*. New York, NY: Harcourt Brace Jovanovich Inc., 1984.

Zagwyn, Deborah Turney. *The Pumpkin Blanket*. Berkeley, CA: Celestial Arts, 1991.

Ziefert, Harriet. *My Apple Tree*. New York, NY: HarperCollins Publishers, 1991.

Zolotow, Charlotte. *The Storm*. New York, NY: HarperCollins Publishers, 1989.

Zolotow, Charlotte. *William's Doll*. New York, NY: HarperCollins Publishers, 1985.

198   RETELLING, RELATING, REFLECTING: BEYOND THE 3 R'S

KEEPING IN TOUCH PROFESSIONALLY

To help you match your needs and comfort levels, we have organized these resources into two sections: *Getting Started* and *Moving Forward*.

The resources in *Getting Started*:
- provide an overview of teaching and learning theories,
- provide information and guidelines about specific programming strategies,
- outline many practical ideas for classroom use,
- are reader friendly — easy to read and comprehend,
- are some suggestions for a first read.

The resources in *Moving Forward*:
- complement the titles in the first section,
- outline more information about how to integrate practical ideas and theory,
- provide further reading to extend and deepen knowledge about teaching and learning,
- are titles that model and illustrate "teacher as researcher."

The Irwin Book Club (IBC)

Irwin Publishing carries many of the most important and up-to-date professional resources available in Canada. Through membership in the Irwin Book Club (1800 Steeles Avenue West, Concord, ON L4K 2P3) you can keep in touch professionally.

When you join the Book Club (IBC), you will receive *Journal*, IBC's newsletter for educators. The newsletter contains articles by and for educators on a variety of topical subjects. If you purchase books during one year, you will continue to receive *Journal*. If you do not wish to purchase books or if you order through your board or your school, you can subscribe to *Journal*.

As a member of the Irwin Book Club, you will also receive four catalogues a year that list and describe recently published professional books.

 ## Getting Started

Atwell, Nancie. *In the Middle: Writing, Reading, and Learning with Adolescents*. Portsmouth, NH: Boynton/Cook Publishers, 1987.

An inspiring, sensitive look at how the reading and writing process works with adolescent learners. This book will become a handbook for teachers who work with this age group. You can modify and adapt this information to use with learners of any age and grade level including adult learners, especially teacher-education candidates.

Barrett, F. L. *A Teacher's Guide to Shared Reading*. Richmond Hill, ON: Scholastic Canada, 1988.

A quick one-sitting read that provides practical guidelines for using shared reading strategy. This small resource is about 40 pages long... a first read to begin including shared reading effectively.

Barton, Bob. *Tell Me Another.* Markham, ON: Pembroke Publishers, 1986.

    This book on storytelling provides many strategies with authentic examples to help you become comfortable and confident with storytelling as part of your program. Barton talks about selecting a story, making a story your own, reading stories to children and using storytelling effectively in a classroom.

Baskwill, Jane. *Parents and Teachers: Partners in Learning.* Richmond Hill, ON: Scholastic Canada, 1989.

    An honest account from all perspectives — teacher, parent, administrator — about how to share information with families. Specific ways of working together with families are explained. Many ideas, based on actual examples, are presented on how to improve home-school communications.

Butler, Andrea, and Jan Turbill. *Towards a Reading-Writing Classroom.* Orwell, New South Wales, Australia: Primary English Teaching Association/Irwin Publishing, 1986.

    An introductory book outlining "The Conditions of Learning" by Brian Cambourne. It matches the conditions with reading and writing experiences in the classroom. The book includes organizational and management tips and ideas for beginning daily writing and reading and setting up routines.

Calkins, Lucy McCormick. *Lessons from a Child.* Portsmouth, NH: Heinemann Educational Books, 1983.

    An account of a teacher and researcher's shared journey of observing and studying writing in a grade 3 classroom, especially with Susie, a young writer. This book reads like a novel and, at the same time, provides insights into and ideas about how children learn to write. A great first read for those interested in beginning the writing process.

Calkins, Lucy McCormick. *The Art of Teaching Writing, New Edition.* Portsmouth, NH: Heinemann Educational Books, 1994.

    A thorough account of the aspects of the writing process. This book is a "must have" because it deals with a wide range of writing topics, ideas, examples, strategies, questions and possibilities for all age and grade levels. You can read it selectively by beginning with those sections that most address your needs and interests. It is one of those "I-want-to-keep-it-by-my-desk" professional resource books. It is a BIG read.

Clay, Marie M. *An Observation Survey of Early Literacy Achievement.* Portsmouth, NH: Heinemann Educational Books, 1993.

    This book provides for the systematic observation of children's responses to classroom reading and writing in the first years of school. You will find it helpful when monitoring children's progress in any beginning literacy program. It is also a useful tool for administrators, resource teachers, researchers and teachers-in-training. Specific strategies and tasks are explained, including how to keep detailed observation records. This resource provides one way of determining which learners require more time, support and one-on-one teaching.

Clay, Marie M. *Reading Recovery: A Guidebook for Teachers in Training*. Portsmouth, NH: Heinemann Educational Books, 1993.

A companion volume to *An Observation Survey* (Clay, 1993). This guidebook is for training teachers to deliver the one-on-one supplementary program. This resource supplies specific components that shape the reading program for individual children. Sixteen teaching procedures are listed and described. The research behind *Reading Recovery* is provided for interested readers.

Cochrane, Orin, et al. *Reading, Writing and Caring*. Winnipeg, MB: Whole Language Consultants Ltd., 1984.

A book that will ensure the valuing of self-esteem and development of readers and writers. Many practical strategies to identify and support developmental stages of growth in reading and writing are provided. The book presents a well-organized description of language and literacy processes and how to set up a classroom.

Forester, Anne D., and Margaret Reinhard. *The Learner's Way*. Winnipeg, MB: Peguis Publishers, 1989.

An information source about what kindergarten, grade 1 and grade 2 programs look like, what their necessary components are and why these are essential. It begins with the theoretical framework and then provides many practical applications. Many highlighted reference charts invite both a quick and in-depth reading.

Forester, Anne D., and Margaret Reinhard. *On the Move: Teaching the Learner's Way in Grades 4-6*. Winnipeg, MB: Peguis Publishers, 1991.

A book that shows how the information provided in *The Learner's Way* (Forester, Reinhard, 1989) applies to grades 4 through 6. This resource gives a thorough account of the what's, how's and why's you can use when teaching junior language programs.

Gentry, J. Richard. *Spel...Is a Four-Letter Word*. Richmond Hill, ON: Scholastic Canada, 1987.

A reader-friendly account of the research related to spelling and how spelling develops. It helps you understand and see the spelling process as developmental. This book is a one-sitting read. Families and educators will find it a great resource for learning about and understanding spelling based on current research.

Goodman, Ken, Yetta Goodman, and Wendy J. Hood. (Eds.). *The Whole Language Evaluation Book*. Toronto, ON: Irwin Publishing, 1988.

This book is a collection from classroom teachers across the United States and Canada, a powerful resource that encourages teachers to value their learners and find ways to help them — focusing on what they can do rather than what they cannot do. The documentation of learning growth is stressed. There are many evaluation strategies for learners from kindergarten to adult education, including second-language. Record-keeping ideas, samples and suggestions are shared. A valuable resource to have on hand.

Graves, Donald. *Experiment With Fiction*. Toronto, ON: Irwin Publishing, 1989.

An account that shows how fiction is a natural genre for learners since almost everyone likes to tell stories. Graves suggests experimenting with personal stories and using them effectively in a reading and writing program.

Graves, Donald. *Explore Poetry*. Toronto, ON: Irwin Publishing, 1993.

This book involves you in both the reading and writing of poetry, for yourself and your students. Experiment with reading poetry aloud, "found" poems, writing poetry from prose, and acquiring poems through choral speaking. The "Actions" encourage a sense of play in the composing of poetry. Graves provides techniques and strategies for including poetry in your program. He also encourages you to be reflective and to examine your own practices about teaching poetry.

Graves, Donald. *Investigate Nonfiction*. Toronto, ON: Irwin Publishing, 1989.

Graves explores the nonfiction genre as a vehicle for inviting learners to write in this mode. He shows how nonfiction is different from fiction and how teachers can capitalize on what learners know and want to find out about through reading and writing. This book encourages teachers to examine different models and apply those models when recording their knowledge about the world.

Hagerty, Patricia. *Reader's Workshop — Real Reading.* Richmond Hill, ON: Scholastic Canada, 1992.

A one-sitting read that describes the readers' workshop and provides practical suggestions and mini-lessons that will help readers set up their own workshop and assess its effectiveness.

Hart-Hewins, Linda, and Jan Wells. *Real Books for Reading.* Markham, ON: Pembroke Publishers, 1990.

A reader-friendly resource that looks at using "real" books as the basic resource for a reading program. The authors suggest many children's books, organizing their bibliography around ten levels of children's reading development.

Hart-Hewins, Linda, and Jan Wells. *Read It in the Classroom!: Organizing an Interactive Language Arts Program Grades 4-9*. Markham, ON: Pembroke Publishers, 1992.

Another reader-friendly resource that shows how to organize an interactive language arts program. This companion book to *Real Books for Reading* (Hart-Hewins and Wells, 1990) uses similar practices with older learners. Many examples are provided to demonstrate practical applications.

Hart-Hewins, Linda, and Jan Wells. *Phonics, Too!* Markham, ON: Pembroke Publishers, 1994.

A book that discusses a much talked-about topic. It provides teachers with insights into the learning needs at different stages of reading and writing and describes innovative ways to teach skills and use literature for language instruction. You will find the many tips are useful in day-to-day teaching.

Jackson, Norma R. *The Reading-Writing Workshop: Getting Started.* Richmond Hill, ON: Scholastic Canada, 1992.

An easy-to-read guide that walks you through every step in the reading-writing process. It is full of flow charts, reproducibles, checklists and classroom-tested ideas. This resource has many options for those new to the workshop process and for those who are experienced with workshops. There is something for everyone.

Massam, Joanne, and Anne Kulik. *And What Else?* New Zealand: Shortland Publishing, 1986.

Many colour visuals, accompanied with text, provide information and instruction for creating a literate environment filled with print and artwork. This handy guide is great to have for easy, quick reference. The photos tell everything at-a-glance.

Meyers, Mary. *Teaching to Diversity*. Toronto, ON: Irwin Publishing, 1992.

This comprehensive, practical text provides readers with a valuable resource for classroom and ESL programs. It addresses the theory, the ideas and the challenges teachers face on a daily basis when working with second-language learners.

Peterson, Ralph, and Maryann Eedds. *Grand Conversations: Literature Groups in Action*. Richmond Hill, ON: Scholastic Canada, 1990.

This book suggests ways to organize and begin literature circles. Ideas are provided for inviting learners to talk about their reading, learning and thinking. Organization and evaluation suggestions, designed by teachers, are shared. This is a very practical guide and a quick read that you will find valuable to own.

Phenix, Jo. *Teaching Writing*. Markham, ON: Pembroke Publishers, 1990.

An outline of the writing process and what it looks like in the classroom and why. This book gives a wealth of practical, purposeful guidelines for implementing and enriching the writing process. Actual classroom examples paint a detailed picture of daily writing in progress.

Phenix, Jo, and Doreen Scott-Dunne. *Spelling for Parents*. Markham, ON: Pembroke Publishers, 1994.

This quick read is a helpful resource for everyone involved in education. It provides a clear overview of the changing world of spelling instruction. Teachers should read and know about it. Schools should have copies available to share with families. There are general tips for families.

Phenix, Jo, and Doreen Scott-Dunne. *Spelling Instruction That Makes Sense*. Markham, ON: Pembroke Publishers, 1991.

You are invited to explore the patterns of spelling development in this overview of spelling and how it fits into programs. Specific strategies and categories illustrate teaching tips and give you an understanding of how spelling works and can be taught effectively.

Picciotto, Linda Pierce. *Evaluation: A Team Effort*. Richmond Hill, ON: Scholastic Canada, 1992.

This book provides techniques that will help you evaluate learners in all curriculum areas. It is useful for new teachers, teachers changing their methods and teachers who are always looking for ways to increase evaluation efficiency and effectiveness. This book shows how families, learners and teachers can work together in the evaluation process.

Routman, Regie. *Transitions: From Literature to Literacy*. Portsmouth, NH: Heinemann Educational Books, 1988.

A resource that helps you begin the process of change from basals and worksheets to more meaningful, focused and authentic learning and teaching experiences. Routman describes how to use literature as the basis of your language program. *Transitions* includes a comprehensive "Resources For Teachers" section. This book is a BIG read. However, you can pick and choose those chapters that fit your needs and interests.

Schwartz, Susan. *All Write! A Teacher's Guide to Writing, Grades K-6*. Toronto, ON: OISE Press, 1987.

A practical guide that suggests one way to begin the writing process. It offers practical step-by-step procedures on implementing the writing process by following the stages of pre-writing, drafting, conferencing, editing and publishing. Sample activities are illustrated and described. You can photocopy sample checklists for classroom use.

Schwartz, Susan, and Mindy Pollishuke. *Creating the Child-Centred Classroom*. Toronto, ON: Irwin Publishing, 1990.

A practical book that illustrates ways to create a child-centred environment and program. The many visuals and examples will enable you to implement the suggestions immediately. All the examples appear as blackline masters at the end of the book. Lots of ready-to-use ideas for teachers.

Swartz, Larry. *Dramathemes*. Markham, ON: Pembroke Publishers, 1988.

A practical handbook with many suggestions and clear outlines on how to use children's literature to invite teachers and learners into the world of drama. The step-by-step framework makes it easy to follow and to implement. The suggestions work every time with everyone in every situation.

Trelease, Jim. *The Read-Aloud Handbook, Revised Edition*. New York, NY: Viking/Penguin, 1985.

Trelease talks about the need to read aloud to children and gives valuable suggestions on how, when and why to read aloud at home and at school. "Treasury of Read Alouds" is an extensive annotated bibliography. This excellent resource suggests books to buy, borrow, read and enjoy. A practical guide to own.

Moving Forward

Anthony, Robert, Terry Johnson, Norma Mickelson, Alison Preece. *Evaluating Literacy: A Perspective for Change*. Portsmouth, NH: Heinemann Educational Books, 1991.

This book presents a thorough, detailed look at evaluation based on a coherent philosophy of evaluation compatible with current views of literacy acquisition and student-centred instruction. The authors share many ways of looking at authentic evaluation which have been used and refined by classroom teachers. The differences between assessment and evaluation are outlined and incorporated. There is much food for thought in this practical book.

Atwell, Nancie (Ed.). *Coming To Know: Writing To Learn in the Intermediate Grades.* Portsmouth, NH: Heinemann Educational Books, 1989.

A book about writing to learn in grades 3 to 6. This collection is written by classroom teachers who are working with writing across the curriculum. One subject is report writing and ways to help children produce content-area writing that is as personal as their own stories. Students learn to take notes, conduct interviews, record observations, and design simple research projects for science, social studies, and reading classes. A variety of references is available in the appendices. You will find the appendix of prompts that teachers have assigned as learning log entries particularly useful.

Atwell, Nancie. *In the Middle: Writing, Reading, and Learning With Adolescents.* Portsmouth, NH: Boynton/Cook Publishers, 1987.

An inspiring, sensitive look at how the reading and writing process works with adolescent learners. This book will become a handbook for teachers who work with this age group. You can modify it to use with learners of any age and grade level, including adult learners and especially teacher-education candidates. You will return to this book again and again and each time you will learn more. (That is why we included it in both *Getting Started* and *Moving Forward*.) *In the Middle* won the 1987 Mina P. Shaughnessy Prize for outstanding research in the teaching of English and the NCTE's David H. Russell Award, 1990.

Atwell, Nancie. *Side by Side: Essays on Teaching To Learn.* Portsmouth, NH: Heinemann Educational Books, 1991.

In this sequel to *In the Middle*, Atwell explores the conditions that make it possible for children — and their teachers — to become writers and readers. In two key chapters, she reconsiders *In the Middle* in light of the experiences of other teachers and their correspondence with her. She proposes some intriguing revisions of the workshop model.

Atwell, Nancie. (Ed.) *Workshop 1 by and for Teachers: Writing and Literature.* Portsmouth, NH: Heinemann Educational Books, 1989.

A collection of teachers' stories about writing and using literature in the classroom. This resource examines what is possible when teachers and learners draw on what they know about writing, reading and literature. You will learn exciting new approaches.

Atwell, Nancie. (Ed.) *Workshop 2 by and for Teachers: Beyond the Basals.* Portsmouth, NH: Heinemann Educational Books, 1990.

A collection of teachers' stories about reading in the classroom. This resource explores a range of ways in which teachers use literature and responses as the heart of the language arts program. These stories describe classroom practices that extend the reading-writing workshop approach.

Barton, Bob, and David Booth. *Stories in the Classroom.* Markham, ON: Pembroke Publishers, 1990.

This collaborative resource describes the authors' storytelling experiences in classrooms. The power of storytelling is explained and described in an invitational manner.

Bialostok, Steven. *Raising Readers: Helping Your Child to Literacy*. Winnipeg, MB: Peguis, 1992.

A must-have resource for educators and families about helping children to literacy. This book is easy to read and deals with why we read, the role of phonics, some dos and don'ts, predictable materials, book choice, rhyme, rhythm, and repetition and many other topics. Issues are raised and ideas are offered for further discussion and investigation. A resource for schools to have available on a loan basis and one that families may wish to own.

Booth, David, and Charles Lundy. *Improvisation: Learning Through Drama*. Toronto, ON: Harcourt Brace and Company, 1985.

This book describes the basic elements of drama and provides a thorough exploration of how to use drama in the classroom.

Brown, Hazel, and Brian Cambourne. *Read and Retell: A Strategy for the Whole Language/Natural Learning Classroom*. Portsmouth, NH: Heinemann Educational Books, 1989.

This resource describes the "retelling procedure" which is an excellent holistic way to help learners gain control of various genres they are reading. This powerful technique will help you assess children's comprehension of texts and evaluate their control of language. There are many practical classroom examples that show the potential that this strategy provides for teachers and learners.

Calkins, Lucy McCormick with Shelley Harwayne. *Living Between the Lines*. Toronto, ON: Irwin Publishing, 1991.

A BIG read that goes beyond *The Art of Teaching Writing* and examines the power of notebooks in the writing workshop. It provides a new look at the qualities of good writing and how to help writers grow. It offers an introduction to literature that will enrich your classroom. The authors extend an invitation to develop new ideas about conferring, record keeping, mini-lessons and the organizational structures for the workshop.

Cambourne, Brian. *The Whole Story*. Richmond Hill, ON: Scholastic Canada, 1988.

This text offers a detailed description of language learning theory. The conditions of learning are thoroughly explained and examples give practical application. These learning conditions provide food for thought that you can apply to many, if not all, curriculum areas. The section on evaluating literacy development is both useful and practical.

Clay, Marie M. *Becoming Literate: The Construction of Inner Control*. Portsmouth, NH: Heinemann Educational Books, 1991.

A thorough, very detailed description of the interconnections that children build as they acquire control over the reading and writing in their first years of formal literacy instruction. Clay's book is a serious read and especially appealing to teachers who wish to examine the reading process in depth. It is the theory behind her *Reading Recovery* and *An Observation Survey*.

Cochrane, Orin, and Donna Cochrane. *Whole Language Evaluation for Classrooms.* Winnipeg, MB: Whole Language Consultants, 1992.

This resource will help you construct an evaluation system to meet your classroom needs. It provides evaluation strategies that you may pick and choose from to create a personal set of evaluation strategies. The format lends itself to immediate use. The authors invite educators to use these strategies, create new ones and to share them all with others.

Crafton, Linda K. *Whole Language: Getting Started... Moving Forward.* Katonah, NY: Richard C. Owen Publishers, 1991.

A book designed for two audiences: those already started and ready to move on and those wishing to start. It emphasizes the individual choices that teachers are making all the time. You can begin with this book and go back to it year after year. It is reader-friendly and includes case studies of several learners of different ages at different stages. There are many practical strategies just waiting for you to use.

Cullinan, Bernice E. (Ed.). *Children's Literature in the Reading Program.* (1989) and *Invitation to Read: More Children's Literature in the Reading Program.* (1992). Newark, DE: International Reading Association.

A set of two inspiring books about building or strengthening an effective literature-based reading program. Teachers will find practical, creative teaching strategies, recommendations of high-quality books and ideas about organizing and implementing reading programs. Great resources invite teachers and learners into the world of literature.

Cullinan, Bernice E. *Read to Me: Raising Kids Who Love To Read.* New York, NY: Scholastic Inc., 1992.

A one-sitting read, written in plain language, that provides a clear view of learners at different ages and stages. This great resource should be available in every school to share with families. A practical but powerful resource to own.

Fulwiler, Toby (Ed.). *The Journal Book.* Portsmouth, NH: Boynton/Cook Publishers, 1987.

A collection of articles in which everyone discusses journal keeping. The book talks about how learners of all ages learn to write, and write to learn, in ways that demand thinking. The writers view journal usage from every angle and in every situation. Although the book is long, you have the option of a long, detailed read or reading separate, short selections. A one-of-a-kind professional resource.

Gentry, J. Richard, and Jean Wallace Gillet. *Teaching Kids To Spell.* Portsmouth, NH: Heinemann Educational Books, 1992.

This companion to *Spel...Is a Four-Letter Word* (Gentry, 1987) includes more explanations and more strategies for readers to use in a spelling program. This book explains how to integrate spelling into a language program. The authors provide a much-needed bridge between traditional spelling instruction and whole-language approaches. Their book provides an effective word list to use to collect baseline data about what learners can already do in spelling and at what stage they are. It also offers guidelines for implementing a school-wide spelling program, word lists, tips for teaching predictable patterns and a variety of individual activities. It is a worthwhile resource to own and have on your desk.

Graves, Donald H. *Build a Literate Classroom*. Toronto, ON: Irwin Publishing, 1991.

This companion resource to *Discover Your Own Literacy* (Graves, 1989) describes the components of a literate classroom and invites teachers to assess their situations. This is a valuable resource for looking at one's own growth and development over time. Specific ways to begin, adapt and change are provided. These suggestions are based on a deep understanding of literacy development.

Graves, Donald H. *Discover Your Own Literacy*. Toronto, ON: Irwin Publishing, 1989.

Graves invites readers to examine their own literacy in order to better understand the literacy development of others. He presents a variety of ways to explore personal literacy growth and development. The premise of this exploration is that the understanding gained will have practical classroom application and value.

Graves, Donald H., and Bonnie S. Sunstein (Eds.). *Portfolio Portraits*. Portsmouth, NH: Heinemann Educational Books, 1992.

This thought-provoking exploration about using portfolios values the roles of all partners, especially the portfolio's owner, in developing guidelines for portfolio use. Teachers are invited to first create their own portfolios. Practical and authentic examples are shared.

Hansen, Jane. *When Writers Read*. Toronto, ON: Irwin Publishing, 1987.

A comprehensive resource that deals with reading and writing together and provides alternatives to the basal approach. Many ways are suggested for supporting teachers in the classroom.

Harp, Bill (Ed.) *Assessment and Evaluation in Whole Language Programs, Revised Edition*. Norwood, MA: Christopher-Gordon Publishers, 1991.

A thorough review that includes specific information about strategies that match current and innovative programs. Every chapter provides a wealth of information and ideas. This book is practical and thoughtful.

Harste, Jerome, Kathy G. Short, and Carolyn Burke. *Creating Classrooms for Authors: The Reading-Writing Connection*. Portsmouth, NH: Heinemann Educational Books, 1988.

An in-depth resource for those familiar with using reading and writing daily. One part reviews the theoretical parameters; the other part describes the practical application of several effective teaching-learning strategies and corresponding curricular activities. The authoring circle is the basic model for all these experiences. A valuable resource to read and re-read.

Harwayne, Shelley. *Lasting Impressions: Weaving Literature into the Writing Workshop*. Portsmouth, NH: Heinemann Educational Books, 1992.

A practical book filled with stories of learners and teachers. You are invited to explore the diverse roles literature plays in writing workshops. Harwayne re-examines the writing workshop and presents ways to weave literature into the workshop. The book follows the chronology of a school year and has a wide variety of samples to put into practice.

Heald-Taylor, Gail. *The Administrator's Guide to Whole Language*. Ketonah, NY: Richard C. Owen Publishers, 1989.

Give this practical resource to any administrator who wants more information about whole language. This book outlines what learners and teachers do in an effective learning environment. There are specific chapters on implementation, communication with families and assessment. References and suggestions appear throughout the text. An informative resource.

MacKenzie, Terry (Ed.). *Readers' Workshop: Bridging Literature and Literacy*. Toronto, ON: Irwin Publishing, 1992.

A collection by twenty-four educators who share similar understandings and practices. Classroom environments that invite and enable learners of all ages and abilities are described. You get the sense of belonging to a club. This book, which includes principles, practical ideas, ways to work with special groups, mini-lessons, how to's for responding to literature, is a valuable resource.

Routman, Regie. *Invitations: Changing as Teachers and Learners K-12*. Toronto, ON: Irwin Publishing, 1991.

A BIG read that follows her earlier book, *Transitions* (Routman, 1988). It encourages and supports by providing specifics for putting theory into practice. Routman invites all educators to reflect upon their teaching and learning. There is in-depth information, specific strategies and demonstration lessons for numerous topics. Once again, a comprehensive "Resource For Teachers" is included. You will return to this book again and again.

Scott, Ruth. *Spelling: Sharing the Secrets*. Agincourt, ON: Gage Publishing, 1993.

Scott talks about learners in the spelling system, ways to support spelling growth, and spelling strategies, and suggests resources to foster spelling growth. This book is reader-friendly, providing information and ideas in text, diagrams, charts, and photos. A very comprehensive resource for teaching and understanding spelling.

Short, Kathy O., and Kathryn Mitchell Pierce (Eds.). *Talking About Books: Creating Literate Communities*. Toronto, ON: Irwin Publishing, 1990.

A thoughtful book for teachers who are already confident and comfortable working collaboratively with learners. The contributors' common goal is creating classrooms in which students become members of a literate community using reading as a way to learn. The book gives examples of working with children's literature in specific curriculum areas and offers ideas on integrating literature into all curriculum areas. A book that deals with the power of literature.

Smith, Frank. *Insult to Intelligence: The Bureaucratic Invasion of Our Classrooms*. Portsmouth, NH: Heinemann Educational Books, 1988.

Smith gives readers information and support for making decisions and educational change. This book discusses many areas of education in a thought-provoking manner. Smith explains how learners progress and succeed when they are invited into the "learning club." This resource reflects his earlier writing and provides a springboard for his later works: *Joining the Literacy Club* (1988) and *To Think* (1990).

Strickland, Dorothy, and Lesley Mandel Morrow (Eds.). *Emerging Literacy: Young Children Learn To Read and Write.* Newark, DE: International Reading Association, 1989.

This book includes a collection of articles that highlight the language development of young children. It is particularly useful when developing literacy programs for learners ages 4 to 8 years. There is a wealth of information to ensure a broad understanding of early literacy principles and numerous practical ideas for promoting language and literacy growth. A good resource to have at one's fingertips.

Swartz, Larry. *Classroom Events Through Poetry.* Markham, ON: Pembroke Publishers, 1993.

Based on the author's own experiences bringing poetry into the hearts and minds of his students, this book features valuable information on students' responses to poetry, the role of the teacher in poetry exploration, the value of questioning, and many practical and classroom-tested strategies for introducing and presenting poetry. A must resource to have to help instill enthusiasm for poetry.

Watson, Dorothy. *Ideas and Insights: Language Arts in the Elementary School.* Urbana, IL: National Council of Teachers of English, 1987.

This resource contains a wealth of strategies integrated into authentic classroom experiences. Ideas and insights across a broad spectrum beginning with the world around us, writing, language across the curriculum, family involvement, assessment and evaluation are provided. You will find yourself using this resource often, in many different situations and for a variety of purposes. A handy book to own.

Wells, Gordon. *The Meaning Makers: Children Learning Language and Using Language To Learn.* Portsmouth, NH: Heinemann Educational Books, 1986.

Based on the Bristol Study, "Language at Home and at School," which the author directed, this book follows the development of a representative sample of children from their first words to the end of their elementary education. It contains many examples of their spoken and written language experiences and shows the active role that children play in their own learning. A cassette containing some of the longer extracts quoted in the book is also available.

Wilde, Sandra. *You Kan Red This!: Spelling and Punctuation for Whole Language Classrooms, K-6.* Portsmouth, NH: Heinemann Educational Books, 1991.

A readable book about spelling and punctuation from kindergarten through grade 6. It will help you understand how children learn about spelling and punctuation and the school's role in this process. It is a comprehensive handbook that addresses many ongoing questions. This book offers theory, research, discussions of writing samples and practical ideas. A good-to-have-on-hand school resource.

DRAFT PLANNING SHEETS

 These Draft Planning Sheets can be used as reference pages or as models. You can modify and adapt them to fit your particular needs and interests. We have included four categories: "Reference," "Sample Letters," "Learner Record Sheets," and "Teacher Record Sheets."

The Planning Sheets in the "Reference" category are useful when made into overhead transparencies and used with large groups. They can be photocopied to be used for individual reference or as handouts or can be enlarged to use as posters.

The Planning Sheets in the "Sample Letters" category are used to communicate with families and learners. The Planning Sheets in the "Learner Record Sheets" and the "Teacher Record Sheets" categories can be used as is or can be modified.

We hope you and your learners will find these Draft Planning Sheets useful and practical.

 ## Contents

Reference — to be used as overhead acetates, posters, and/or handouts

*NOTE: We have repeated the Introduction and Table of Contents for the Draft Planning Sheets so that they will remain readily at hand in the book.

Sample Letters

Learner Record Sheets

Teacher Record Sheets

DRAFT PLANNING SHEETS

 These Draft Planning Sheets can be used as reference pages or as models. You can modify and adapt them to fit your particular needs and interests. We have included four categories: "Reference," "Sample Letters," "Learner Record Sheets," and "Teacher Record Sheets."

The Planning Sheets in the "Reference" category are useful when made into overhead transparencies and used with large groups. They can be photocopied to be used for individual reference or as handouts or can be enlarged to use as posters.

The Planning Sheets in the "Sample Letters" category are used to communicate with families and learners. The Planning Sheets in the "Learner Record Sheets" and the "Teacher Record Sheets" categories can be used as is or can be modified.

We hope you and your learners will find these Draft Planning Sheets useful and practical.

 ## Contents

Reference — to be used as overhead acetates, posters, and/or handouts

*NOTE: We have repeated the Introduction and Table of Contents for the Draft Planning Sheets so that they will remain readily at hand in the book.

Sample Letters

Learner Record Sheets

Teacher Record Sheets

HOW WE LEARN

Based on current knowledge of developmental patterns typical of learners, we see true learning as being initiated by the learner rather than being "handed down" or transmitted by the teacher. For these learning situations to occur, the following key components must be part of the learning environment:

MATERIALS...

A variety of interesting materials are readily available and accessible to the learners.

MANIPULATION...

Learners are free to handle, explore, examine, study and work with the materials.

CHOICE...

Learners have opportunities to set their own goals, select materials, pose questions, and choose activities to seek out information and answers.

LANGUAGE FROM THE LEARNERS...

Learners talk about what they already know, what they want to learn about, what they are doing and what they have done — and how.

SUPPORT FROM OTHERS...

Support can come from peers, families, friends, experts, teachers... These "supporters" encourage the learners' efforts and help them extend what they are doing by joining in the learning, by helping them solve problems that arise, and by celebrating the learning together.

— Based on the work by Dr. David Weikart and others in the High/Scope Curriculum as outlined in *The Teacher's Idea Book* by Michelle Graves (High/Scope Press, A Division of the High/Scope Educational Research Foundation, Michigan, 1989, page 4)

A WAY OF LOOKING AT LEARNING

This way of thinking about how we learn is based on the research and studies of Dr. Brian Cambourne, head of the Centre for Studies in Literacy at Wollongong University in Australia and author of numerous professional books and articles. He calls the elements necessary for learning to take place "THE CONDITIONS OF LEARNING."

IMMERSION...

a wide variety and number of resources, books, experiences...

DEMONSTRATIONS...

teaching by showing concrete examples, modelling, demonstrating...

EXPECTATIONS...

providing clear, appropriate messages...

RESPONSIBILITY...

making choices, sharing ownership...

APPROXIMATION...

learning from and through mistakes, trying over and over — changing and trying again, guessing, risk taking...

PRACTICE...

using, practising, having time...

FEEDBACK...

responding — retelling, relating, reflecting...

ENGAGEMENT

with the learner and with learning occurs when there are frequent and continuous realistic and appropriate demonstrations of the "Conditions of Learning."
(*The Whole Story*, by Brian Cambourne, Ashton Scholastic, 1988)

The 3 R's Framework: Retelling, Relating and Reflecting

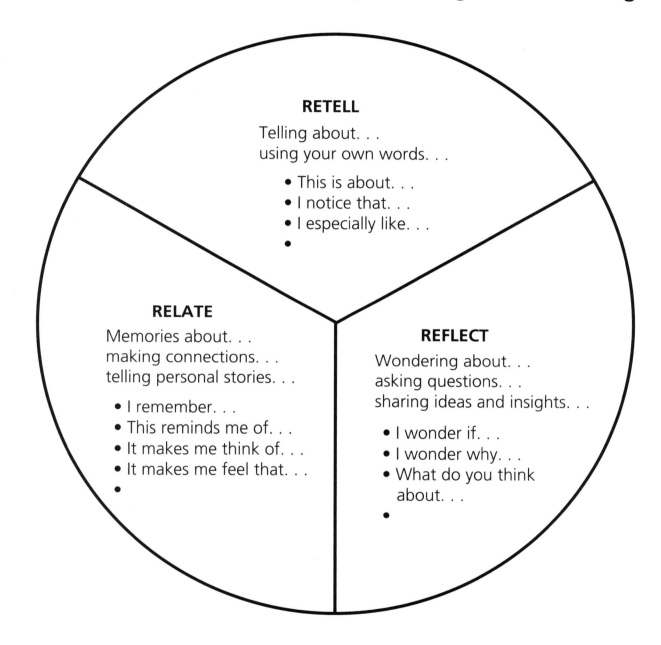

RETELL

Telling about. . .
using your own words. . .

- This is about. . .
- I notice that. . .
- I especially like. . .
-

RELATE

Memories about. . .
making connections. . .
telling personal stories. . .

- I remember. . .
- This reminds me of. . .
- It makes me think of. . .
- It makes me feel that. . .
-

REFLECT

Wondering about. . .
asking questions. . .
sharing ideas and insights. . .

- I wonder if. . .
- I wonder why. . .
- What do you think about. . .
-

RETELL

- tells back
- tells about one part
- describes
- explains
- lists
- identifies
- names
- recites
- illustrates
- summarizes
- paraphrases
-

- This is about...
- It happened...
- I noticed that...
- I like the part when...
- I especially like it when...
- In this piece...
- You mean to say that...
-

RELATE

- remembers
- makes connections to stories, characters, own experiences, feelings
- applies learning to new or similar situations
- compares
- contrasts
-

- This reminds me of...
- I remember when...
- It makes me think of...
- It makes me feel that...
- That happened to me, too, when...
- When I was young...
- That situation is just like...
- This is different from...
- This compares to...
- It sounds like...
-

REFLECT

- questions
- wonders
- predicts
- infers
- evaluates
- makes insights — "aha!"
- thinks about other possibilities or extensions
-

- I wonder how...
- I wonder if...
- I wonder why...
- I wonder when...
- The part about _____ really interests me. I think I will...
- This gives me an idea to...
- Why do you think...
- What do you think about...
- I think that...
- Now I understand that...
- I want to...
-

USING THE 3 R'S FRAMEWORK TO ASSESS AND EVALUATE

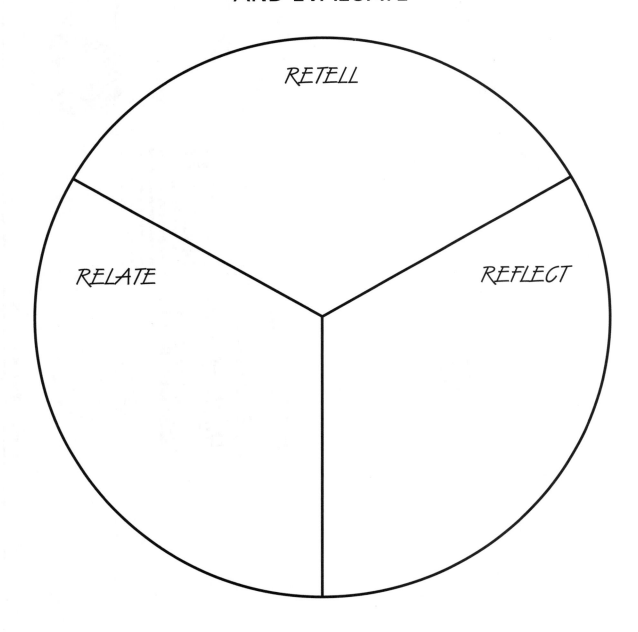

PAIRED READING GUIDE

Read for Enjoyment...Information...Meaning!
Don't correct if the meaning is retained!!

Before You Read...
- Talk about the title, characters, pictures...
- Predict what will happen in the story.
- Make connections... "This reminds me of another story, movie," etc.
- Ask questions... "I wonder why..."
-

Strategies To Use While Reading Together...
- Listen and make comments about the content of the reading.
- Point and follow along (for young children).
- When the learner cannot read a word, encourage the strategies of:
  - guessing
  - skipping
  - looking at the pictures or diagrams
  - thinking about what went before and what might happen next (context)
  - reading ahead to find out more
  - rereading
  - sounding out (using phonics)
  - looking at the root words or word parts
- When the learner is still unable to read the word, then **give the word.**
- If you have given the word a number of times, this material may be too difficult. Try:
  - reading together with the learner
  - reading and the learner reads the last word of each sentence
  - reading one line and the learner reads the next
  - reading the first paragraph, poem, or line, and the learner reads the same again
  -

During/After the Reading...

• Retell	• Relate	• Reflect
- This is about...	- I remember...	- I wonder if...
- I notice that...	- This reminds me of...	- I wonder why...
- I especially like...	- It makes me think of...	- What do you think
-	- It makes me feel that...	about...
	-	-

Note: Ask genuine questions to which you do not know the answers.

GROUP READ AND RESPOND

- In a group of four or five, choose a book or article to read together.

- Decide where you will read together.

- Decide who will read first.

- The first person reads a chunk.

- The others listen and then talk — taking turns **retelling, relating, reflecting.**

- The reader passes the book to the next person who reads a chunk while the rest listen and then take turns **retelling, relating, reflecting.**

- Continue to the end of the selection.

PAIRED READ AND RESPOND

- Divide into groups of two.

- Select the reading.

- Decide where you will read together.

- Decide who will read aloud first.

- That person reads aloud a chunk.

- The other listens and talks — **retells, relates, reflects.**

- Change roles.

- Continue to the end of the selection.

USING THE 3 R'S FRAMEWORK TO CHOOSE WRITING TOPICS

Listen to your teacher or another person share topic ideas.

RETELL

- the things/topics I know a lot about...
- what I am expert in...
-

RELATE

- the things/topics I care a lot about...
- what I feel strongly about...
-

REFLECT

- the things/topics I wonder about...
- what I want to find out more about (research)
-

Share with the person sitting closest to you topic ideas from these three areas.

Share what you plan to write about first.

Make your own list of topics to write about using the three headings above.

Add to your list and keep the list with your writing.

USING THE 3 R'S FRAMEWORK WHEN CONFERENCING ABOUT WRITING

RETELL

- Talk about the content of the writing, e.g., "I see you are writing about your trip to the airport."

RELATE

- Relate your personal experiences or feelings about the content, e.g., "That reminds me of the train station I was in last weekend."

REFLECT

- Ask questions to which you are genuinely interested in knowing answers, e.g., "I wonder why you look so sad in your picture?"

SOME PRE-WRITING STRATEGIES

- Use the 3 R's framework to help you choose writing topics:
  Think about:
  - the things you know a lot about, enjoy telling others about, and can talk about confidently **(retell)**;
  - the people, places and things you care about, like/love, and are passionate about **(relate)**;
  - the people, places and things you are interested in, want to find out about, have questions about, know a little about and want to learn more about **(reflect)**;
- Think about the books you have read, heard or discussed as possible ideas.
- Brainstorm possible writing ideas and record or list in chart form.
- Record lists of questions.
- Draw a picture and create a story in your mind.
- Talk your story through with a friend.
- Tell your story into an audiotape and listen to it play back.
- Reread books to examine specific patterns and techniques.
- Reread something you have previously read or written to think about it from a different point of view.
- Reread material and think about changing characters, settings, plots, formats...
- Brainstorm possible beginnings, endings, words, phrases.
- Create classroom reference lists from the brainstorming.
- Think about your audiences.

Note: Correcting spelling and checking grammar occur when writers reread, proofread and edit their work.

EXPECTATIONS FOR DRAFT WRITING

- Print your name or initial on each page.

- Date stamp every piece of writing. If you work on the same piece for three days, your writing should have three dates on it. Then everyone will know that this piece of writing is a three-day story/piece.

- Use a draft stamp on your writing so that anyone reading your writing will know this piece is "work-in-progress."

- If you are stuck, rehearse or tell your story to yourself or to a partner. Ask for suggestions.

- Write on every other line, so you can add words or phrases during revision.

- Work on one side of the paper, so that you can cut and paste, move parts around, take out or add words, phrases, sentences, paragraphs... during revision.

- Take one piece of paper at a time. Arrange and number the completed pages.

- Cross out words or letters as you write, rather than erasing. This keeps ideas flowing since using an eraser slows down the writing process.

- Do your best with spelling by writing the sounds you hear, see, and remember.

- Store your writing in your folder.

- Decide whether you want to publish; if you do, continue with revising and editing.

Note: Correcting spelling and checking grammar occur when writers reread, proofread and edit their work.

EXPECTATIONS FOR REVISING

- Read and reread what you have written to see if it makes sense and flows. Make initial revisions.

- Read your writing aloud to others for their questions, suggestions, and ideas.

- Think about what others have asked you or suggested.

- Make revisions:

    - Add or take out parts.

    - Rearrange words or ideas — cut and paste.

    - Change words or ideas to better ones.

    - Replace overused, unclear, and/or unnecessary words.

    - Use a variety of resources — other people, books, thesaurus — to find more interesting words.

    - Reread to another.

- Make final changes.

- Remember that correcting spelling and checking grammar occur when writers reread, proofread and edit their work.

Note: When you are responding to someone else's writing, remember to use the 3 R's framework — *retell* what the writer has written; *relate* — what does the writing make you think of?; *reflect* — what questions does the writing raise in your mind? Using the framework in this way will help you to help the writer make thoughts clearer and more meaningful.

EXPECTATIONS FOR PROOFREADING AND EDITING

This is when writers, peers, teachers, editors... correct spelling and/or check grammar by rereading, proofreading and editing.

- Read and reread your writing.

- Check the structure of your sentences, verb tenses, plurals, endings of words...

- Check capitalization, punctuation and grammar.

- Circle words you feel need to be checked for spelling. Use a dictionary, computer spell check, or other sources.

- Work with another to make shared editing changes.

- Consider rereading your piece aloud as a final "proofread."

- Put your work in the editing box.

- Final editing is completed by the teacher or volunteer.

EXPECTATIONS FOR SHARING/PUBLISHING

- Decide how you will publish — e.g., in book format, poster, mural, experiment, diorama, play...

- If you decide you want to publish a book, choose the format and cover — e.g., hard cover, spiral binding, accordion book, pop-up, book-in-a-box, character on a string, puppet book...

- Collect the materials you will need to put your book together.

- Choose the print size and font, and the number of pages.

- Make decisions about chapters, table of contents, index...

- Choose the materials and the styles you will use for illustrations.

- Put your story into final form — e.g., reprint the piece yourself, ask your teacher or a volunteer to input onto the computer, send to the in-school "publishing house"...

- Complete your illustrations, title page and cover. You may wish to cut and paste your original illustrations.

- Write the dedication page and an "About the Author" page. You may wish to include your photograph.

- Finalize your title.

- Share your published effort, and display for others to read.

Note: Remember, authors and illustrators have an editor do *their final edit*. Ask a teacher, a family member, or a volunteer to be your editor.

USING THE 3 R'S FRAMEWORK IN ASSESSMENT AND EVALUATION

INITIAL DIAGNOSTIC ASSESSMENT AND EVALUATION

Finding out what learners know:

- their knowledge — when they retell
- their experiences — when they remember, relate and make connections
- their reflections — their questions (what they wonder about and want to know) and their insights.

CONTINUOUS FORMATIVE ASSESSMENT AND EVALUATION

Watching, listening and recording when and how the learners retell, relate and reflect.

SUMMATIVE ASSESSMENT AND EVALUATION

Reflecting on what the learners can do and know, what they relate to and remember;

Using this information and the learners' wonderings, questions, and insights for program planning.

ALL CHILDREN

- are unique
- come with knowledge
- come with experiences
- come with interests
- need to feel special
- need to be valued

COMMUNICATION IN THE FAMILY AND BETWEEN HOME AND SCHOOL IS ESSENTIAL

- Home is the child's first school.
- People in the family are the child's first teachers.

Studies have shown that when children are read to at home and when children and families share stories together, the children do better in school!

Read-aloud experiences encourage families to listen and talk with their children when stories are read and discussed.

In fact, the **listening** and **talking** that are shared during these experiences are equally as important as the sharing of the literature.

When families engage in storytelling, when they tell their own stories, when they really talk and listen to their children, they show their interest and love, and they help their children succeed in school and in life.

FAMILIES

- make time for talking with children.

- find time for each child.

- are encouraging and positive.

- listen and accept without judging.

- use body language that models effective listening skills for their children.

- talk about their interests, hobbies, experiences, work — their lives.

-

OBSERVATION GUIDE

The Group Dynamics

- How do the participants get started?
- How do they begin?
- Who chooses the materials?
- How are decisions made?
- •

The Recording

- Who records for the group?
- How is the recorder chosen?
- How is the paper used?
- What tools are used for writing?
- What type of script is used — upper/lower case, cursive or print style...?
- Does the recorder stand or sit to write, draw, sketch — body position?
- •

The Language

- Who initiates the talk?
- Who directs?
- Who follows directions?
- Who follows others?
- •

What Kind of Language Is Used?

Retell

- Who retells the directions — what to do?
- Who tells what they know?
- Who describes?
- Who retells using mathematical/scientific concepts?
- Who summarizes?
- Who...

Relate

- Who relates personal experiences, stories, memories?
- Who relates to mathematical/ scientific concepts?
- Who...

Reflect

- Who asks questions?
- What kinds of questions are asked?
- How many questions are asked?
- Who reflects on mathematical/scientific concepts?
- Who shares insights, an "aha" — shows understandings?
- Who...

AN INTEGRATED PLANNING WEB

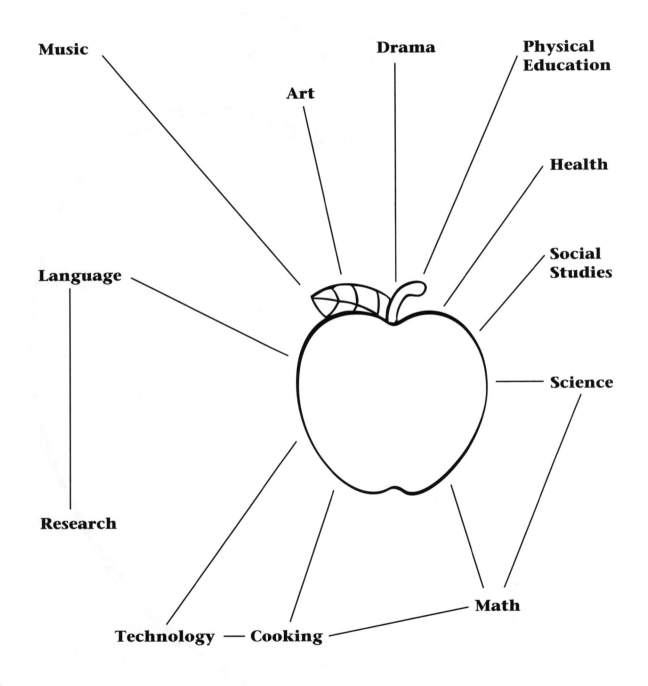

BIBLIOGRAPHY

This list includes fiction and non-fiction.

Fiction

- *Albert's Field Trip*, by Leslie Tryon (New York, NY: Macmillan Children's Group, 1993).

- *Applebet: An ABC*, by Clyde Watson (New York, NY: Farrar, Straus, & Giroux Inc., 1987).

- *How To Make an Apple Pie and See the World*, by Marjorie Priceman (New York, NY: Knopf, 1994).

- *Johnny Appleseed, A Tall Tale*, Retold and illustrated by Steven Kellogg (New York, NY: Morrow Junior Books, 1988).

- *Johnny Appleseed*, by Eva Moore (New York, NY: Scholastic Inc., 1964).

- *Apple Tree Christmas*, by Trinka Hakes Noble (New York, NY: Dial Books for Young Readers, 1988).

- *Mr. Brown's Magnificent Apple Tree*, by Yvonne Winer, Illustrated by Maya Winters (Richmond Hill, ON: Scholastic Canada, 1985).

- *My Apple Tree*, by Harriet Ziefert (New York, NY: HarperCollins Publishers, 1991).

- *One Watermelon Seed*, by Celia Lottridge, Illustrated by Karen Patkau (Toronto, ON: Oxford University Press, 1990).

- *The Seasons of Arnold's Apple Tree*, by Gail Gibbons (New York, NY: Harcourt Brace Jovanovich Inc., 1984).

-

Non-Fiction

- *The Amazing Apple Book*, by Paulette Bourgeois (Toronto, ON: Kids Can, 1987).

- *The Amazing Potato Book*, by Paulette Bourgeois (Toronto, ON: Kids Can, 1991).

- *An Apple a Day: Over 20 Apple Projects for Kids*, by Jennifer Storey Gillis (Vancouver, BC: Whitecap Books Ltd., 1993).

- *An Apple Tree Through the Year*, by Claudia Schnieper (Minneapolis, MN: Carolrhoda Books Inc., 1987).

- *Fruit*, Created by Pascale de Bourgoing, Illustrated by P. M. Valat (New York, NY: Scholastic, 1991).

- *The Life and Times of the Apple*, by Charles Micucci (New York, NY: Orchard Books, 1992).

- *My Apple*, by Kay Davies and Wendy Oldfield (London, Eng: A & C Black (Publishers) Ltd., 1990).

-

THE LITTLE RED HOUSE WITH NO DOORS

Once upon a time there was a little boy who grew tired of all his toys and games. He asked his mother, "What shall I do?" "You shall go on a journey and find a little red house with no windows or doors and a star inside. Come back as soon as you can." So the boy started out on his journey and he found a beautiful little girl and he asked her, "Do you know where I can find a little red house with no windows and doors and a star inside?" "Ask my father, the farmer, he may know." So the little boy found the farmer and asked him, "Do you know where I can find a little red house with no windows and no doors and a star inside?" The farmer laughed and said, "I've lived many years but I've never seen anything like it. Go ask Granny. She knows everything." So the little boy asked Granny, "Please Granny, where can I find a house with no windows and doors and a star inside?" "I'd like to find that house myself. It would be warm in the winter and the starlight would be beautiful. Go ask the wind. Maybe the wind knows." The wind whistled by the little boy and the boy said, "Oh wind, can you help me find a little red house with no windows and doors and a star inside?" The wind could not speak any words but it went on singing ahead of the little boy until it came to an apple tree and it shook the branches. Down came a beautiful red apple. The little boy picked it up and looked at it. It was a little red house that had no windows or doors. "I wonder?" said the boy. He took a jackknife from his pocket and cut the apple in half. "How wonderful!" There in the centre of the apple was a star holding little brown seeds. He ran home and showed his mother. "Look, I found it!"
(Author Unknown)

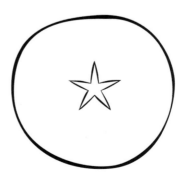

Dear Families,

Journals are used for children to express thoughts and feelings onto paper.

Children might write about books they have read or heard, about what they know or have learned, or about their experiences, memories, feelings, and how they connect these experiences and feeling with their lives. Children might record their questions and insights, draw pictures, make lists, write stories and poems, share feelings, design charts, sketch diagrams and/or explain experiments.

Please encourage independence and responsibility when children are writing. Journals are a place where children will "think in draft" — that is, they will write down thoughts and ideas quickly, sometimes in point form and sometimes by drawing. If children ask you for help, please help by discussing with them what they want to say, or by commenting on their ideas, order and flow of language. Please value their guesses about spelling and grammar. From their approximated spellings and grammar usage, I will see where to provide instruction and/or support. Therefore, in their journals, grammar and spelling will remain uncorrected. This journal is used as a vehicle to encourage understanding, thinking and reflecting.

It would be greatly appreciated if you would respond to your child's work by writing a letter in the journal. You might write about a part that you particularly liked, the connections or memories you have to similar experiences, and/or your questions, suggestions or insights gained from reading and sharing the journal. Remember to be supportive and encouraging.

Thank you for taking the time to show your continued interest and support.

Sincerely,

Dear Learners,

When you write a response to the books you are reading or have finished, or to something you have just experienced (a movie, a trip, a guest speaker, etc.), you may find the following suggestions helpful.

RETELL

- Tell about the story or experience: "This story (experience) is about...", "The first thing that happened was..."
- Retell your favourite part(s): "The part I like best is..."
- Make lists to emphasize something in the story or experience.
- Draw pictures to share a part of the story or experience.
- Make an audiotape.

RELATE

- Make connections to other stories, poems, experiences or things you know or have seen: "This reminds me of...", "This makes me think of..."
- Share your memories: "I remember when..."
- Share your feelings: "I feel..."

REFLECT

- Ask questions: "I wonder why...",
  "I wonder if...", "Why do you think...?"
- Share insights: "Now I understand why..."
- Make predictions: "I think that..."
- State plans: "Now, I want to..."

Have fun reading, writing and thinking!

Fondly,

HOMEWORK IN A BAG

What is Homework in a Bag?

- It is a bag of learning materials based on one topic or theme to be used at home and shared at school.

When does Homework in a Bag come to your home?

- It comes at least once a month.
- It arrives on a specific day of the week, e.g., Wednesday.
- It stays in your home for almost a week.
- It returns to school about 5 days later, e.g., Monday.
- It stays at school for one full day for reorganization.

Why is Homework in a Bag important?

- It provides a new and fun way to do homework.
- It is cooperative learning.
- It encourages making time for shared learning.
- It provides opportunities for making choices and decisions.
- It brings a variety of learning materials and topics into your home.
- It encourages talking, reading, writing, doing and thinking.
- It encourages literacy and lifelong learning.

How do you use Homework in a Bag?

- You and your child and/or other family members examine and use the materials in the bag to share and learn together by:

  - exploring
  - reading
  - talking
  - drawing
  - making
  - creating
  - writing
  -

Dear Families,

Please use this special journal to record your comments and reactions about the reading and activities you have done with your child during the Homework in a Bag learning experiences.

- You might write or print your comments or make drawings about:

  - what you already knew and what you have learned

  - what you remember from your own experiences

  - your questions or understandings

We invite both you and your child to use this journal. Please feel free to write in your first language.

Enjoy learning together.

Sincerely,

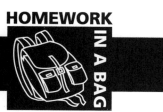

HOMEWORK
IN A BAG

THINGS TO DO TOGETHER

Read together.

Talk about the reading materials together.

- ### • Retell
    - Tell about the story or information: "This story is about...", "I learned that..."
    - Retell your favourite parts: "The part I liked best is..."

- ### • Relate
    - Make connections to other stories, poems, experiences or things you know about or have seen: "This reminds me of...", "I remember when..."
    - Share your feelings: "I feel..."

- ### • Reflect
    - Ask questions: "I wonder why...", "I wonder if...", "Why do you think..."
    - Share insights: "Now I understand why..."
    - Make predictions: "I think that..."

Try an activity you have read about in one of the books or magazines.

Dramatize the story.

- Act out a part of the story (with or without the use of props).
- Create a character — a paper-bag puppet, a finger puppet, a simple mask, a hat that a character wears, etc.

Illustrate your favourite scene.

- Use wax crayons, pencil crayons or coloured markers you may have at home.

Design, create and complete a new activity based on this same theme or topic — or create a bag of your own.

Dear Families,

To help us keep track of the materials in this bag, we have included a list of the items in the bag. Please check off the RETURNED column as you put materials back in the bag to be returned to school.

Thank you.

HOMEWORK IN A BAG CHECKLIST

_____

(Child's Name)

Check YES if the item has been returned.
Check NO if the item has not been returned.

ITEM	SENT OUT	RETURNED Yes	No
_____	_____	_____	_____
_____	_____	_____	_____
_____	_____	_____	_____

List the things you added to this bag.

_____

_____

Thank you for your participation!!

Dear Families,

This year, your child will be using and sharing **Homework in a Bag**. These bags of learning materials will be arriving in your home at least once a month for almost a week at a time — home on Wednesday and back to school the following Monday. Each bag will contain different learning materials based on a topic or theme.

With your child and other family members, examine and use the materials in the bag. Different reading materials have been included. Some of these books or magazines or newspaper articles may be appropriate for your child **to read to you**. Some you might **read together**, and some are included for you **to read to your child**. Research has shown that children who are read to regularly become confident readers. By reading to or with your children, you:

- help them see the importance that you place on reading and literacy.
- let them hear quality literature that they cannot yet read easily on their own.
- have an opportunity to share knowledge (retell), personal connections and feelings (relate), and wonder and ask questions (reflect).
- show your child by doing the activities together that you care about his/her learning.

A **Homework in a Bag journal** or **diary** is included in the bag for recording any comments, drawings, experiences, stories, questions and understandings. Please feel free to write in your first language.

Information with ideas for **things you and your child might do together** is included.

Please feel free to add to this bag.

These **Homework in a Bag** learning experiences will help you, as families, and me, as teacher, learn about your child. Enjoy learning together.

Sincerely,

Dear Families,

   Please complete the following and send the form to school with your child. Your feedback is very important and greatly appreciated.

1. How did the **Homework in a Bag** help you and your child learn and share together? Please give an example.

_____

_____

_____

2. How did brothers, sisters or other family relatives become involved in the **Homework in a Bag** experiences?

_____

_____

3. When would your family like to receive **Homework in a Bag**?

   ❑ every other week
   ❑ weekly
   ❑ other

4. How long does your family need to have the **Homework in a Bag** at home?

   ❑ one week
   ❑ two weeks
   ❑ less than one week
   ❑ more than two weeks

Please add any comments, suggestions, ideas, or questions about the **Homework in a Bag** experience.

Thank you for your time and participation.

                              Sincerely,

Dear Families,

This year, your child will be creating a personal portfolio. We are discussing portfolios as a way of celebrating each individual's interests, achievements and growth. We have invited a photographer, artist and writer to visit our class and share the contents of their portfolios. I, too, am creating a portfolio to model and demonstrate the process, and to tell the children about me. If you have a portfolio, either personal or professional, that you wish to share, please let me know and I will schedule a time for you to talk with the children.

I want the children to know how this process of gathering and collecting personal memories, souvenirs, photos, work samples, and cherished keepsakes enriches personal learning. We will be talking together about looking back, reflecting, and setting goals.

Please work together with your child to find treasures at home that show special experiences your child has had with people, places and things. Please use this search as an opportunity to add items to your child's portfolio that you think illustrate your child's interests and accomplishments. Some of these treasures might be:

- stuffed animals
- books
- photographs

- certificates
- trophies
-

The children will share their personal portfolios over the next few weeks and your child will have the opportunity to explain the importance of each selection. This process is one way to celebrate the special interests and talents of each child.

This experience with personal portfolios will be a first step towards developing a shared understanding of the purpose of portfolios. The next step will be for the children and me to work together to create an **academic and assessment and evaluation** portfolio that will illustrate individual and group efforts of growth and learning over the year. These collections will enable me to assess and evaluate the physical, intellectual, emotional and social growth of each child and will enable your child to see his or her personal growth. I will share this information with you throughout the year.

I appreciate your support and participation in the search to create this initial personal portfolio. If you have any questions or suggestions, please call.

Sincerely,

GROUP "LITERATURE CIRCLE" READING RECORD

Name of Teacher: _____

Name of Recorder: _____

Date Started: _____

Date Completed: _____

Signature of Group Members	Title of Selection (the same or different titles for each member)	Comments and/or Questions

READ, RESPOND AND CREATE

Name: _____

Teacher's Name: _____

Term: _____

Title of Selection	Responses (e.g., painting, Plasticene models, diorama, readers' theatre, block constructions, slide show, computer animation, video, etc.)	Date Started	Date Completed

Reflecting on My Process:

- What did I learn?
- What do I plan to try/learn next?
-

Teacher's Comments:

- What did I observe?
- What do I plan to teach next?
-

INDEPENDENT READING RECORD

Name: _____

Teacher's Name: _____

Term: _____

TITLE	Date Started	Date Completed	Check If Abandoned	Number of Pages

INDEPENDENT WRITING RECORD

Name: _____

Teacher's Name: _____

Term: _____

Title or Topic of WORK IN PROGRESS (DRAFT)	Date Started	Check If Abandoned and Filed	Record the Date Published and the Format

Note: You may decide not to finish certain pieces of your writing. You may decide not to publish certain completed writing. All your writing is important and should be filed in your writing folder. Your writing samples show how much you have learned and may give you ideas for future writing. You may decide to work on one of your filed stories and publish it at another time.

_____'S RÉSUMÉ

1. The best thing I did in school was

2. I can

3. I like

4. I don't like

5. My family

6. I would like to learn about

7. My 5 favourite books are:

    1.

    2.

    3.

    4.

    5.

Date: _____

Learner's Signature: _____

Teacher's Signature: _____

_____'S INTEREST SURVEY

1. The things I like to do after school are

2. The television programs I enjoy most are

3. My hobbies/interests/collections are

4. If I could take a trip, I would like to go to _____ because

5. If I could have a pet, I would like to have a _____ because

6. The sports I like best are

7. The school subjects I like best are

8. The kinds of stories I like to hear read to me are

9. The kinds of stories I like to read on my own are

10. Other things I'd like you to know about me are

Signature: _____

Interviewed by: _____

Date: _____

READING INVENTORY*

1. What do you think reading is?
   What do people do when they read something?

2. When you are reading and come to something you don't know, what do you do?

3. Who is a good reader you know?

4. What makes _____ a good reader?

5. Do you think _____ ever comes to something he/she doesn't
   know? Suppose _____ does come to something he/she doesn't
   know. What do you think _____ would do?

6. If you knew someone was having trouble reading, how would you help that person?

7. What would your teacher do to help that person?

8. How did you learn to read?

9. What would you like to do better as a reader?

10. Do you think you are a good reader? Why or why not?

Signature: _____

Interviewed by: _____

Date: _____

*Adapted from Carolyn Burke's "Reading Inventory" in *Reading Process and Practice* by Constance
Weaver, Heinemann, 1988, page 332.

THE DONUT MODEL

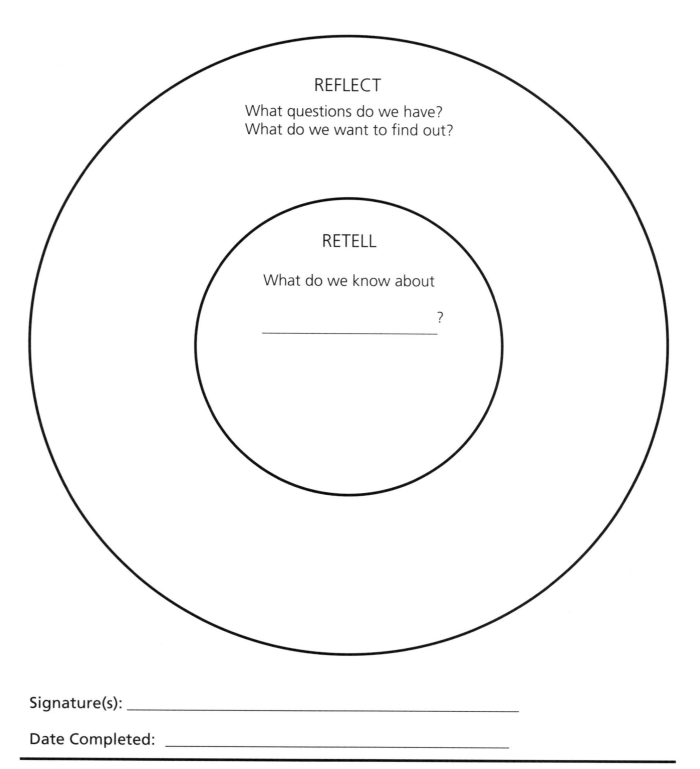

REFLECT

What questions do we have?
What do we want to find out?

RETELL

What do we know about

_____ ?

Signature(s): _____

Date Completed: _____

WE LEARN ABOUT ONE ANOTHER Date Completed: _____

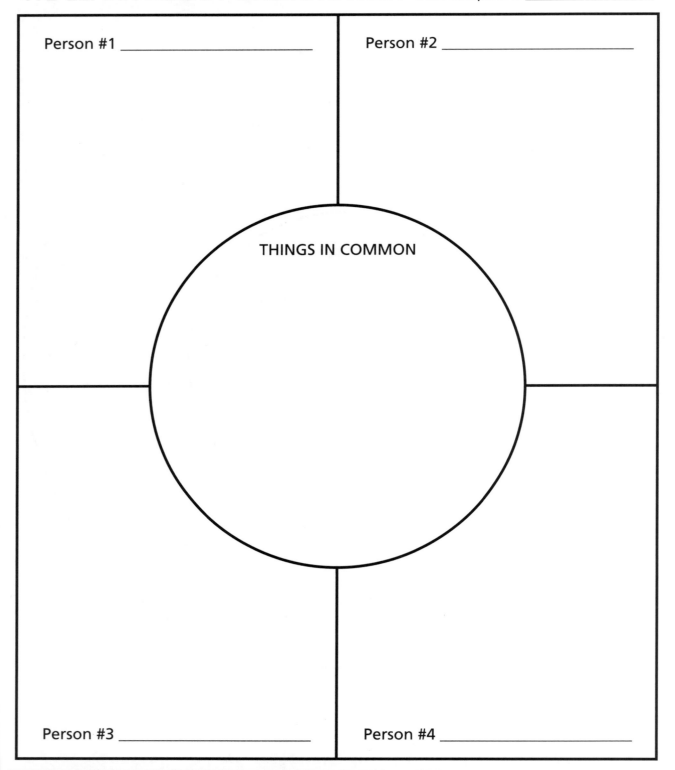

Person #1 _____

Person #2 _____

THINGS IN COMMON

Person #3 _____

Person #4 _____

THE 3 R'S FRAMEWORK AND NEGOTIATING THE CURRICULUM

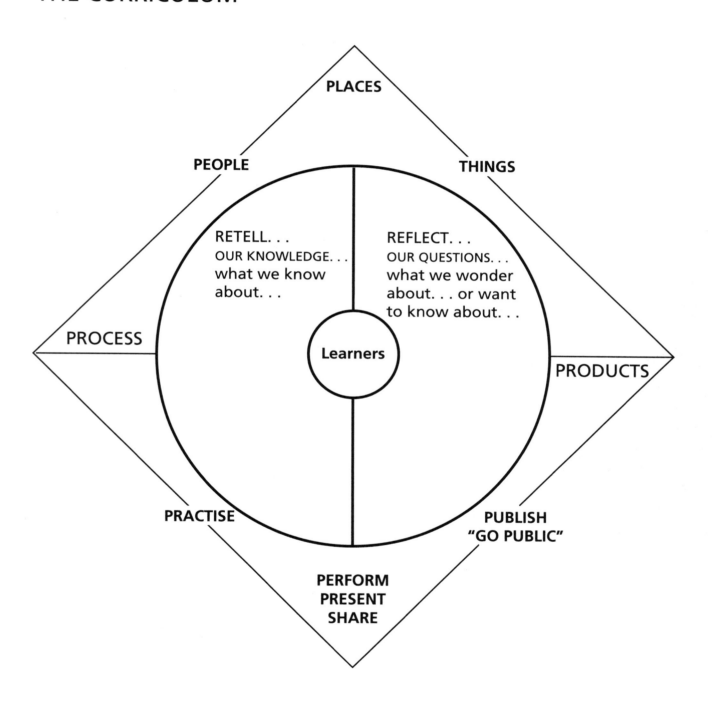

PLACES

PEOPLE

THINGS

RETELL. . .
OUR KNOWLEDGE. . .
what we know
about. . .

REFLECT. . .
OUR QUESTIONS. . .
what we wonder
about. . . or want
to know about. . .

PROCESS

Learners

PRODUCTS

PRACTISE

PUBLISH
"GO PUBLIC"

PERFORM
PRESENT
SHARE

PEOPLE	PLACES	THINGS
People we can invite, call, listen to, interview, ask opinions of, talk with. . . • • •	Places we can go to: • • •	Things we can explore: • • •

Signature(s): _____

Date Completed: _____

PRACTISE	PERFORM PRESENT SHARE	PUBLISH "GO PUBLIC"

Signature(s): _____

Date Completed: _____

BALANCING A LITERATURE-BASED PROGRAM: A YEAR-AT-A-GLANCE

	SOCIAL/EMOTIONAL		INTELLECTUAL		PHYSICAL	19 _____ to 19 _____
P.I.E.S.	**Self & Society** • Feeling • Sharing • Thinking • Reflecting • Succeeding • Celebrating	**Math, Science & Technology** • Problem Solving • Constructing • Predicting • Patterning • Investigating • Exploring	**Language** • Viewing • Dramatizing • Writing • Reading • Speaking • Listening		**The Arts** • Music • Drama • Movement • Visual Arts • Viewing • Creating	
September						First Term
October						
November						
December						
January						Second Term
February						
March						
April						Third Term
May						
June						

BALANCING A LITERATURE-BASED PROGRAM

Teacher's Name: _____

Grade: _____

Term: _____

TITLE OF SELECTION	TYPE OF LITERATURE (fiction, non-fiction, poetry, rhyme, folklore, concept, alphabet, fantasy, chapter book, picture book, wordless book, how-to...)	AREAS OF CURRICULUM FOCUS (Language, Math, Science and Technology, Self and Society, the Arts...)	AUTHOR/ ILLUSTRATOR (Canadian, American, International? Male/Female?)

SHARED READING RECORD

Teacher's Name: _____

Term: _____

TITLE	DATE INTRODUCED	DATE COMPLETED	COMMENTS

GUIDED READING RECORD

Title of Selection: _____

Date Introduced: _____

Date Completed: _____

Names of Learners	Comments

GUIDED READING RECORD

Title of Selection: _____

Date Introduced: _____

Date Completed: _____

Names of Learners	Comments

GUIDE FOR INVESTIGATING LITERATURE

Title of Book: _____

Author: _____

Illustrator: _____

Explore, think and talk about:

- **the book jacket/cover**
  - the title
  - the author
  - the illustrator
  - the publisher
  -
- **the title**
  - a statement, a question or a list of words
  - the number of words
  - the type of print
  - the punctuation used
  -
- **the title page**
  - the title
  - the author
  - the illustrator
  - the publisher
  -
- **the copyright page**
  - date of publication
  - how many reprints
  - copyright holder
  - original publisher
  - country (city) where published
  -
- **the end pages**
- **the dedication**
  - how it is worded
  - pictures...
- **information about the author and/or illustrator**
- **the illustrations**
  - initial impressions
  - colour
  - size
  - style
  - technique
  - background
  -
- **the format**
  - large and/or mini illustrations
  - where print is on the page
  -

- **the text**
  - size of print
  - type of print
  - amount on a page
  -
- **the language**
  - adverbs
  - adjectives
  - verbs
  - metaphors
  - unique words
  -
- **the language structures**
  - contractions
  - possessives
  - quotation marks
  -
- **the print**
  - style of print used
  - colour
  - size
  - shape
  -
- **the structure**
  - plot
  - sequence of events, key events
  - tension, conflict
  -
- **the characters**
  - how they emerge and develop
  - flat or full (highly developed)
  - what they say and do and when
  - interaction among characters
- **the setting** — place(s), period, time, predictions...
- **the time**
  - chronological
  - sequential, flashbacks, jumps forward, how is it noted
  -

- **the point of view** — author's position, first person, third person, how author's point of view is revealed...
- **the mood** — emotions, feelings, dialogue, attitude revealed by text, illustrations....
- **the symbols** — meaning through symbols...
- **the figures of speech** — metaphors, similes...
- **the style** — first impressions, the sound of the piece, how language, illustrations, characterization are used...
- **the beginning and the ending**
  - how does it begin, how does it end
  - what text, illustrations, print... are used, similarities and differences, connections...
- **the genre** — fairy tale, poetry, historical fiction, non-fiction...
- **the unique elements** — an unusual dedication, a book of letters...
- **the kind of book/format**
  - wordless
  - novel
  - picture book
  - paperback
  - how-to
  - pop-up
  - accordion
  -
- **curriculum connections**
- **other**

PLANNING SHEET FOR READING/WRITING WORKSHOP

Date: _____

- **Read-Aloud**

    Title: _____

    Author(s): _____

    Illustrator: _____

    Genre: _____

- **Mini-Lesson(s):**

    _____

    _____

    _____

- **Practising Reading/Writing and Conferencing:**

    Names of Individuals Who Meet With the Teacher:

    _____

    _____

    _____

    Names of Group Members Who Meet Together and/or With the Teacher:

    _____

    _____

    _____

Author's Chair/Reader's Chair:

    Names of Presenters:

    _____

    _____

    _____

    _____

Reflections/Notes:

PERSONAL ASSESSMENT: REFLECTIONS

- How comfortable am I using the framework of **retelling, relating and reflecting?**
- How do I model and demonstrate **retelling, relating and reflecting?**
- How do I invite learners to **practise retelling, relating and reflecting?**

- How do I find out what the learners already know and want to know **(baseline)?**
- What **assessment and evaluation** strategies do I use? Why?

- How do I **negotiate curriculum** and **integrate** what I believe the learners need to know?
- How do **I plan and provide "people, places, things" experiences?**
- How do I design and plan the components for **active/interactive** learning?

- How do I **organize and schedule my time** during the school day?
- How do I help the learners **organize and plan their time?**

- How do I **immerse** the learners in purposeful experiences?
- How do I plan and design appropriate **mini-lessons?**
- How do I select and present appropriate **demonstrations?**

- How do I make my **expectations** clear and explicit?
- How do I support and value **approximations?**

- How do I provide opportunities for learners to **practise** the skills and knowledge learned?

- How do I provide **choice** for learners?
- How do I provide opportunities for learners to be **responsible?**

- How do I **celebrate the learning?**
- How do I share **feedback** in authentic and purposeful ways?
- How do I **communicate with families?**

Signature: _____

Date: _____

POSSIBLE ITEMS FOR PORTFOLIOS

There are many possible items to include in portfolios to use for ongoing assessment and evaluation purposes. Some items will be chosen by you (teacher record sheets, samples of learner's work...), others will be provided by families (information, letters...), and still others will be chosen by the learners, often in consultation with you (work samples, self-evaluation...).

The list below is extensive, yet not exhaustive. We invite you to select the suggestions with which you feel most comfortable, keeping in mind a balance of curriculum areas and the needs of your particular learners. It is important that the experiences and records chosen be repeated at intervals to illustrate growth and development over time.

In these portfolios, you may wish to include:

- **Letters**
  - an introductory letter written by you explaining the use and purpose of portfolios (See Draft Planning Sheet 37.)
  - a letter written by the learner or by you introducing the portfolio owner
  - letters, questionnaires, surveys to and from families
  - information from other teachers of learners
- **A selection of work samples from the "Getting to Know You" experiences outlined in Chapter 3, pages 117-143**
  - The Donut Model
  - I Draw What I See
  - My Best Printing/Writing Sample
  - I Know My Numbers
  - Learning About Names
  - Learning About One Another
  - Personal Artifacts
  - My Book Collection
  - Coat of Arms and Related Book Titles
  - A Bookful of Bags
  - Line-Ups
  - Character Cubes
  - Written Conversation
  - Interview Bingo
- **Work Samples**
  - a self-portrait with a signature
  - a drawing of my home (and family)
  - a drawing of my friends
  - a drawing of my own choice
  - alphabet letters I can print
  - my name — first, middle, last
  - selections of different kinds of writing, e.g., personal (expressive), functional (informational), imaginative (poetic)
  - selections from writing folder collected over time and illustrating different stages of writing, e.g., draft, revised, edited and published writing
  - selections from personal journals, reading response journals, learning logs, notebooks, diaries, scrapbooks...
  - lists of words I can spell

- environmental print I can read
- names I can read
- my favourite book read and/or shared
- numbers I know and can record
- selected samples of number stories and problems I can solve
- science facts I know
- samples of completed research and evaluations
- record of experiments
- record of things I can do, make, design and create
- informal pre- and post-assessment, evaluation and/or tests/quizzes
- a video of independent work in large or small groups or by oneself
- **Teacher and/or Learner Record Sheets**
  - a learner's résumé (see Draft Planning Sheet 42)
  - an interest survey (see Draft Planning Sheet 43)
  - reading interview to find out attitudes and strategies learner uses when reading (see Draft Planning Sheet 44)
  - independent writing record (see Draft Planning Sheet 41)
  - curriculum checklists listing indicators of writing, reading, spelling, math, and/or art...highlighting development of skills and concepts over time
  - independent reading record (see Draft Planning Sheet 40)
  - shared reading record (see Draft Planning Sheet 52)
  - guided reading record (see Draft Planning Sheet 53)
  - group "literature circle" reading record (see Draft Planning Sheet 38)
  - investigating literature checklist (see Draft Planning Sheet 54)
  - audiocassette of a reading inventory conference
  - miscue analysis record
  - running record
  - retelling, relating, reflecting assessment and evaluation recording sheet (see Draft Planning Sheet 8)
- **Other...**

NOTES

NOTES

NOTES